I0720630

FOUR GREEN FIELDS

Copyright © 2018 by Greg McVicker, Mark Rickerby, and J.P. Sexton

First Edition – July 1, 2018

Cover photo by Jordan Whitt (Pixabay via Unsplash).
Cover design by two wee lads: Ryan Silo and Trevor Harper.
Creative content design and internal layout by Greg McVicker.

ISBN

978-1-989053-06-5 (Softcover)

978-1-989053-07-2 (eBook)

All rights reserved.

No part of this publication may be reproduced in any form, or by any means, electronic or mechanical, including photocopying, recording, or any information browsing, storage, or retrieval system, without permission in writing from the publishers.

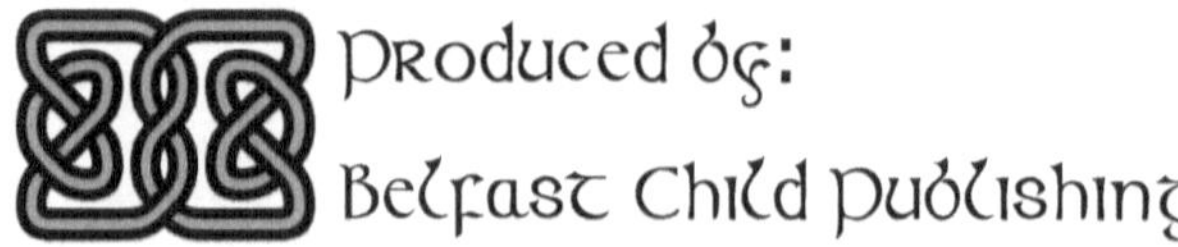

Produced by:
Belfast Child Publishing

Advance Testimonials:

"The read is an exhilarating seesaw of emotions that straddles both sides of the Atlantic covering immigration, family survival in a war zone and a playful indulgence in Irish culture lessons on perseverance. The 'voices' induce a knack for storytelling to a cooperative experience. The universal theme of cultural nourishment is central to the remembered stories and circumstances of growing up with the otherness of one's inherited bloodline.

There is a sagacity of self-analysis that becomes apparent with a reflective nod to the fourth voice as a muse. Apparently, all three voices echo individual tales, but the reflection morphs into a conventional attitude and universal sameness that becomes an important gift of friendship.

My experience in reading this was the acknowledgement of what was learned and what should never be forgotten. The collaboration brewed up a special blend of memoir that resonates in my mind and will continue to give me laughter and some tears, even as I write here."

Barbara H. O'Daly
Entertainment Properties Holding, Ltd.; Trustee
The Television Distribution Company;
C.E.O. and co-creator of "An Evening At The Improv"
Creative Writer M.F.A. Florida Atlantic University.

"There is a saying that there are only two types of people in the world, the Irish and those who wish they were. 'Four Green Fields' does indeed welcome the reader home to the Emerald Isle with vivid memories of the times known as The Troubles.

With prose and poetry, the authors lead us on a nostalgic and sometimes irreverent journey through their lives and those of their families.

'Four Green Fields' is an amazing collection of memories both touching and humorous, giving the reader a rare and fascinating glimpse into the lives and times of these Irish authors and their families. Highly recommended."

Frances Powell, Author of "A Ballysea Mystery" series.
"Lady of the Wye" and "The Bodyguard".

"What a wonderful read! These three authors take you on an adventure that never ends and leaves you wondering, what is going to happen next? You are welcomed into their worlds of joy, excitement and craic, as well as the pain, heart break and reflection of their similar yet different Irish upbringings.

If you ever wanted to join the "boys club" or just be in on the adventures and crazy stories of fun loving Irish lads, this is the book for you. They will leave you laughing, crying and waiting for the sequel. Let's hope there are more shenanigans to come."

Kristine Parkhurst Howser
Teacher, educator, world traveler and craic lover.
B.S., Northwest Missouri State University
M.A.T., Morningside College.

FOUR GREEN FIELDS

WILD IRISH BANTER & STORIES, SHENANIGANS & POETRY.

"We have always found the Irish a bit odd. They refuse to be English."
- **Winston Churchill.**

"If like Winston Churchill, you have found us to be a bit odd, then myself
and my fellow authors, Greg and Mark, have surely done our job. I don't
believe that it is possible to be a writer, at least one which people will find
entertaining, without being a bit on the quirky side. This of course is a
benefit to the reader. Being able to embrace our madness and that of our
families, is a trait not common to many. Unashamedly sharing it with the
rest of the world is even more rare. It could therefore be said that we are a
rare breed."

- **J.P. Sexton.**

"I once read a story about a non-Irish man who was invited to an Irish
wake. He saw everyone dancing and laughing and said, "They must be mad
carrying on like this after a funeral." His Irish host answered, "It's the
laughter that saves them from madness." That sums up the Irish race and
how it has survived so much misery through the centuries."

- **Mark Rickerby.**

"Just like the strands of Celtic knotwork intricately woven into one another
which produces a complicated yet beautiful creation, our aim with this
book is to do exactly that: sharing stories of our own survival, quite often
through times of much misery. In saying that, however, we are keeping
with the true Irish tradition by laughing at ourselves through storytelling, all
mixed with a pint of craic and a quart of shenanigans. After all, it is what
the Irish are known for!"

- **Greg McVicker.**

 Four Green Fields

Banter and Craic,
We'll bring it back.
California, Belfast, and Donegal,
We'll tell our stories and entertain them all!

Sláinte mhaith agus go n-éirí an bóthar libh,
(Good health and may the road be successful for you),

Mark Rickerby   **Greg McVicker**   **J.P. Sexton**

PS: If you're wondering about the placement of our names, it's to do with where we hail from. **Mark Rickerby** kicks with his right foot. **J.P. Sexton** with his left although to be completely honest, he is quite a head the ball.

As for **Greg McVicker**, here I am stuck in the middle with you!

It is with honour this book features contributions by and is lovingly dedicated to the cherished memory of a wonderful, fellow Belfast author, the late John Sidney Rickerby. Rest in Peace.

Four Green Fields

Table of Contents

Four Green Fields

ᴡhaᴛ's ᴛhe cʀaic?

"There are no strangers here; Only friends you haven't yet met."

- **William Butler Yeats.**

Céad Míle Fáilte! What about ye? And what's the craic?

First, and without further ado, we would like to take just a wee moment here and extend **One Hundred Thousand Welcomes** to every one of you who have chanced upon this book. But before we get too far into the banter, stories, shenanigans, and poetry as told by the three of us wee lads who hail from County Antrim, County Donegal, and sure, why not, County California by way of Belfast, Northern Ireland, let us introduce ourselves.

Before we do, though, I would like to point out the word **'craic'** is often mispronounced in several parts of our wee blue and green planet. I have heard people say *"cray-ick"*. To the ears of an Irish lad, this may as well be the sound of nails being slowly dragged down a chalkboard, or teeth being rubbed on sandpaper and then a block of cement. If you are cringing from what you just read, let me fix this for you. It is pronounced **"crack"**.

Now that we have that sorted, sit tight, as we all have the 'Gift of the Gab' and could end up talking the leg off a stool, so we could! But sure, isn't that what being Irish is all about? Stories and a bit of craic, all nicely wrapped up in shenanigans while enjoying a pint or a cup of tea and sitting amongst others, including our dearly departed, all the while having a wake in honour and celebration of their lives! Anything for a bit of a céilí! That might sound a wee bit morbid, so it might, but sure, if it didn't, it wouldn't be Irish, so it wouldn't!

This is the first of two or perhaps even three books which we are currently considering (I guess I should have maybe asked my two fellow authors about that before putting those words down on paper). Sorry, lads. It's out in the open now! The idea behind this project actually came about by way of a suggestion from one of our other authors, J.P., who you will get to know in just a wee minute – well, I guess that actually depends on how fast or slow you choose to read.

During a conversation after one of our joint book launches at the Dublin, Ohio Irish Festival, J.P. mentioned that we should give this a wee go. The more I thought about it, (well actually, that was only today when I sat down to start typing up this introduction), it made sense that we should do a book on Ireland by itself, and a second one that looks at cultural experiences and engagements with people from all demographics in other parts of the world as has been experienced by each one of us, rather than lump them into one book. The third book, well, that will be the B side of all the material that didn't make it into this book. I am sure it will include more crazy adventures of three Irish authors (remember, one by way of County California via Belfast) as we go forth in promoting this book and the shenanigans which will accompany it.

Believe me, and unless we suddenly become famous overnight and have a wee New York Times Bestseller on our hands or win the Man Booker International Prize since we are all international because we live in different parts of the world, we will pay a hell of a lot more money in making two or three different books than we will make from them. But, to have a sequel behind this makes us seem much more important (kind of like Star Wars, Harry Potter, or perhaps even Lord of the Rings, so it does. Well, it could also be very much said that occurrence is only within our own wee collective heads, so it is). Nevertheless, here we go…

As you will see here, these opening introductions are written like how we Irish speak: very much from the heart and soul. We are known as storytellers for a reason, in that how we write is how we speak. Engaging the audiences that afford us the chance of doing so, even if the recipient is giving us such an opportunity since they are more interested in the sounds of our accents rather than what we actually have to say! Here is a wee bit about each of us all, in no particular order, but you may require bog roll (toilet paper) to dry your eyes…

GREG MCVICKER

"Worse than the ordinary, miserable childhood is the miserable Irish childhood, and worse yet is the miserable Irish Catholic childhood."

- **Frank McCourt.**

To start, I am trying to be all Celtic like here but am not sure how some of you are going to be able to read that wild looking font up there with my name. The g's look like snakes. You will get a chance to read about snakes on page fifty-nine in a wee tale about our auld Patron, Saint Patrick. Some of you might already know of him. And, if you haven't already realized, the provinces of Ireland: Ulster, Munster, Leinster, and Connacht, are often referred to as the *Four Green Fields*, just as there are four authors sharing their stories here. Thus, the namesake of this book is fully reflective of that.

Anyways, and to help you out a wee bit, my name is **Greg McVicker**. I am a proud Irish author, poet, and storyteller who was born and raised in the city of Belfast, Northern Ireland. I am absolutely delighted to have this wonderful opportunity of sharing these pages with two of my most brilliant of fellow Irish authors, **J.P. Sexton** and **Mark Rickerby**. They'll introduce themselves in just a moment. I would, however, also like to take a minute to honour the memory and writing of a wonderful, fellow Belfast author who departed from this world not long ago. His name is **John Rickerby**. Part of John's storytelling will be included in this book through the eyes of his son, Mark.

Although I grew up just on the outskirts of this magnificent city, one which has the distinct honour of being known for Titanic's birthplace (before some auld lad decided to steer the damn thing into an iceberg and bring her maiden voyage to an untimely end), Newtownabbey was the area I knew as my community. Much happier memories from my childhood days growing up there are now featured in my humorous personal memoir,

The Adventures of Silly Billy: Sillogy, Volume 1! containing a collection of short stories (with a lot more to be told.) But sure, more about that later.

My mother, Catherine Devlin, and my father, Charles McVicker, were born and raised directly in Belfast within large Irish Roman Catholic families (as my granny would say, a wee birdie told me the Roman Catholic church was vehemently opposed against all forms of birth control in Ireland, and thus, why there are many families with hundreds of siblings running about within them). Obviously, my grandparents bought into that same ideology and followed suit. Either that, or there was nothing much to do during a World War era but produce offspring.

To be serious, my parents grew up in a district that was often attacked when times took a drastic turn within our beloved city. I will try to help give you an idea through my writings, although it doesn't come anywhere near close to describing what it was quite literally like to live in hell. My father could not get work in Belfast or anywhere in Northern Ireland due to the blackened, horrendous history which had darkened our doorsteps for thirty-five years and is locally known as '***The Troubles***'. Thus, my father left Belfast, joined the Merchant Navy, and spent twenty-nine years of his life working at sea so that he could provide for his wee family.

To give you a better understanding of his background during that period of living in hell, only a small minority of Catholics had been selected to work for Harland and Wolff (H&W) shipbuilders. Not only was this the biggest, single shipyard in Northern Ireland, but the world. As I mentioned here within the second paragraph of my introduction, this is where the largest ship of its time, the Titanic, was built along with the Olympic. In case you did not know, there is a conspiracy theory that the ship which sank is not the Titanic, but her sister ship, the Olympic. A debate to be held at another time. However, as was the case with several businesses and industrial firms including H&W, they wouldn't ask if you were a Catholic or a Protestant but asked what school you attended. Although they did not ask for religious affiliation, this determined who was offered employment and who was ignored thereafter.

In 1957, my da applied to Mackie's, an engineering firm which also was one of the largest employers in Northern Ireland. It too had a shady history of excluding Catholics from the workplace. His mother, my granny, Elizabeth McVicker, brought him down to fill out an application. They took all his information and said that they would get back to him. Of course, this was met with the same response most Catholics received: they never did get back to him.

Around 3:30 p.m. on the afternoon of Friday, June 28, 1957, his older brother, my Uncle Barney McVicker, spotted my da in the yard of the Brookfield Mill on the Crumlin Road, where he was employed, and asked if he wanted to go to sea. As the sea schools weren't producing enough junior staff fast enough, there was a mass number of vacancies which had to be filled. As such, my da jumped at this opportunity and asked to be released from his job. He went home to pack a few items but didn't have time to wash up before he left. As he was heading out the door, he was met by his mum who said, "Charlie. You're a disgrace. The dirt from the mill left a tide mark around your neck." But there was no time to waste. Along with three of their cousins, my Uncle Barney brought them to the shipping pool, a place where sea men would go for assignment to a ship. Although they weren't provided with their seaman's union or discharge books, they were all assigned to different ships. That night, my da, as did his cousins, sailed out of Belfast Lough for the first time. He was assigned to the Empire Cymric, an ex World War II tank landing craft used for cross Irish channel ferrying. The usual run of this ship was from Larne to Preston but made the occasional diversion to Belfast. Countless number of young Catholic lads were left with little to no options and did the same: they went to work at sea.

As a result, there was a mass exodus of Catholic youth from Northern Ireland, which also manipulated the power of the vote in favour of the Unionist Party. In hindsight, I guess this perhaps is part of the reason why I have composed several pieces, all of which are featured in this book and are appropriately titled, including: ***Belfast City Asylum, Stolen Identity, In the Name of Religion,*** and ***Everlasting Homesickness.***

I only recently learned life for my da was good out there at sea, a clean life as he described it. No smoking, no pollution, no political shite, and no hatred, just healthy fresh air to breathe. Providing that self-discipline was followed along with money being managed properly and not spent on 'the drink and fegs' or 'having a girl in every port', it was certainly achievable. This, however, and by way of its own measure, became the ruin of many a sailor. Thankfully, my da did not fall into those traps.

This very moment, as I write this, my da shared with me around 1957 and 1958, when he went down to the docks to join his ship, and, as his coaster departed by way of Belfast Lough out towards sea, he'd sail past the Canberra, a massive passenger ship. In 1982, throughout the era of the Falklands War, his group was deployed to South Georgia on the RFA Tidespring under the codename 'Operation Paraquat.' Even though this was roughly 3,000 miles to the east, South Georgia fell under the jurisdiction of the Falklands. The Canberra was referred to as the 'The Great White Whale', as she stood out like a sitting duck. This ship was commandeered by the British government who used it as a troop carrier.

Since my father sailed in and out of Belfast Harbour so often, however, he recalls that another ocean liner, in for a re-fit, had enormous, white graffiti painted onto its hull. Without fail, this captured his attention every time. The following statements, along with other extremely vicious slurs and prejudiced remarks which plagued the dock walls in and around the Belfast shipyards, were made front and centre for all to see and were not in their acronym form:

God Save the Queen.

Fuck The Pope.

No Taigs Here [a reference specifically for Catholics].

Kill All Taigs Dead.

My da often wondered why this was not addressed. Simply said, this was the greeting and farewell messages provided to passengers and crew from around the world, sailing into Belfast Harbour and our city only to be met with racist overtones and sectarianism. The message may as well have read:

"Welcome to our sanitarium. Now get the fuck out while you can!"

My da was a very proud, honest, and hard-working man. After joining his first ship, he began as a catering boy. In those days, his shift was seven days per week from 6 a.m. until 7 p.m. although the catering staff were granted an hour off each afternoon to have a nap. His pay was nine pence an hour, or three quarters of a shilling (there was twelve pence to a shilling, two hundred and forty pence to a pound). With pure determination, he worked his way up through the ranks.

Later, after he joined the Royal Fleet Auxiliary with his official title as a Ship's Cook, he could work up to 400 hours of overtime each month. Since there wasn't much else to do when out sailing the world's oceans for weeks on end at a time, he worked and made sure his pay packet came home to keep his family alive.

My father's feverish dedication to work continued every time he got a chance to come home on leave. He took up employment opportunities in Belfast and would go to work on building sites to assist with restoring communities that were devastated during the period of intense bombing campaigns. The life that accompanied this, however, was not as well-lived as what he experienced at sea. When rebuilding a Catholic district, if asked where he was working with his regular job, his response was always carefully calculated: "The Merchant Navy." It was viewed amongst some circles as a discredit to work for the Ministry of Defense within the British government. I daresay my comments are seriously lacking in that they are a tremendous understatement! But, I am quite mindful this is how my father found work, put food on the table, and kept a roof over the heads of his family. Since Northern Ireland was shrouded in spiteful turmoil, whenever

an opportunity became available, it had to be taken. But it came with
significant danger.

When entering Protestant communities and being asked where he
worked, he would always respond with, "The Royal Navy." It was a way of
survival; blending in alongside of the other blokes who took up the same
opportunity of having a job. Clearly, it was a clandestine approach, all the
while hopefully ensuring he went unnoticed and was nothing more than
another workman, putting new windows into homes which had theirs
blown to bits with each successful explosion. Unfortunately, and tragically,
every one of those bombs would claim more than just sticks, bricks, and
mortar depending on the selected target(s): human, infrastructure, or both.

To provide a brutal account of one his recollections during this period,
he told me there were workmen in the upstairs of a home cleaning up
splintered fragments of glass with brooms. British soldiers on foot patrol
saw this, mistook the broomsticks for rifles, and opened fire without
question, killing innocent civilians trying to make an honest day's pay.
There were countless times that my father had been in homes to fix
shattered dreams and broken glass, only to return the next day since a
second bomb had gone off during the night. Reflecting this very moment
as I put these words to paper, I realize that my da was taking his life into
his own hands. This leaves me shaking my head in disbelief. What kind of a
country did we grow up in? If I am to be completely honest with myself, it
was a fate worse than hell! There truly is no other way to describe it other
than it brings to light why I write about so much about our experiences. I
have been asked if this is therapeutic for me. I suppose in some ways it is,
but in others, I'm not so sure.

My da shared another instance. He had been working in the New Lodge
(a Catholic district) and was in the upstairs bedroom of a home in need of
repair. Again, the task he was assigned to do was to put glass into the
frames which were blasted to smithereens. At times, the window frames
were also badly damaged and had to be replaced as well. As he went about

his job, the lady of the home said there had been a riot in the area recently - an occurrence that was not uncommon in Belfast or nearby communities.

He recalled that a fellow who was out on the front porch of his home was shot by the British troops patrolling the area. The father went out to bring in the body of his son and was also shot. Frantic, and without giving a second thought to the trauma which was now unfolding, the sister went out to assist her father and brother. Subsequently, she too was shot. By every account of being sad, yet despicably sickening, all three were declared dead on the scene. While a mother lost her two children and a husband, my father said the hairs on his arms and the back of his neck were standing on edge. Anger and hatred placed a dark and ugly shroud over both sides of the community as tit-for-tat revenge was immediately sought and planned. It wasn't only the homes that took a direct hit with each blast as a result of **The Troubles**. The death toll steadily climbed as well. I guess one of the best forms of employment to be involved with during this time was to be that of an undertaker.

During this time and in not trying to minimize the painstaking events that immeasurable numbers of families tried to come to grips with, my mother gave her four kids a wonderful childhood experience. Well, it certainly wasn't an easy task. Her efforts were unending. She tried absolutely everything in her power to protect each one of us from the dreadful times in which we grew. I must admit though; I am being extremely polite here with my thoughts. Cultural identities, including ours, were being decimated by means of torture, shootings, bombings, and ethnic cleansing. There was only so much she could do, including giving us English names so we could blend into the larger and dominant society. As a result, we were denied our true Irish heritage and overall sense of being.

Our names were often replaced with 'Fenian' and 'Taig' when others learned of our imposed religious upbringing. We did not display this publicly; well, I guess other than on Ash Wednesday when we walked home from school with a thick blob of black shite smeared across our collective foreheads made by a Priest's oversized thumb. Although the Irish

Roman Catholic church was trying their very best to indoctrinate us with the sign of the cross, they may as well have instead drawn a friggin' X there. Simply put, there was no escaping the holy identifier we had been cursed with on that very day each year. Even if we weren't wearing our school uniforms which often gave us away by virtue of colour, tie, and the badge sown onto our blazers, this certainly did without question.

We did not fly the Irish tricolour outside of our home. We did not join the cause. We did not take sides. Yet, there were those who felt we deserved to be targeted daily because of the churches we attended, as well as our school uniforms that basically said:

"I'm a Roman Catholic but to you, I'm a Fenian bastard."

The freedoms of our childhoods soon took a drastic turn when the cancer that we had been so well protected from was brought directly to our doorsteps. This reality became our living abyss; an experience I have recurring nightmares about thirty-three years on and have yet to shake. I can't count how many times I have been chased, beaten, had to fight, or have been shot within my dreams.

There were numerous occurrences in which my mum received phone calls from the schools my older sister, Karen, and older brother, Joseph, attended in Belfast, asking she drive out to pick them up; or they were asked to seek shelter at my Uncle Jimmy's house near the Waterworks on the Antrim Road, since he was not far from where they went to school. Incidents such as this happened more frequently than I truly care to remember as I had accompanied her on many of those rescue trips. The issue here was much the same as was seen within the largest shipbuilder and engineering firm in Northern Ireland: employment opportunities were awarded to the Protestant majority whereas a minority of Catholics may have been called in for the same job. Kids of our religious denomination were left standing in the pouring rain since bus drivers could easily distinguish them by their uniforms and refused to stop. The mentality from that timeframe is beyond comprehension but was very much considered the norm although there was nothing normal about it.

One of the worst days that thousands of families including my own experienced was Tuesday, May 5, 1981. That day will forever be cemented into the hearts and minds of people from both sides of the community. This was due to the political tensions that had gripped Northern Ireland in fear and pure, voracious hatred. After sixty-six days of refusing food and water, the first of ten hunger strikers, who were protesting British rule and the treatment of Irish prisoners, died. The eerily familiar sound of bin lids calling for an immediate uprising began. Soon thereafter, riots erupted, Belfast was at war, vehicles were set on fire, and Catholic school kids were again left to be human targets and shields for anyone who rubbed their hands in preparation to take shots at them. My sister and brother were amongst those who were left stranded yet again. My mum was with her sister that day, my Aunt Maureen, who moved back home to Ireland after living in Nova Scotia for several years. Screaming at the top of her lungs and cursing like there was no tomorrow, my mum began scrambling to get her car into Belfast.

Getting to my sister and brother was an arduous task as our police force, the Royal Ulster Constabulary, had erected barricades and checkpoints. Before you ask and perhaps feel that there may have been an ounce of fairness, this force was also made up of a 95 percent majority of people from the Protestant community. As I have said before, none of us ever asked for this and although we were never part of the rubbish and sectarian hatred which raged so freely on all around us, without rhyme nor reason, it was simply part of the times in which we grew up in. As I already said, it was the norm although there was nothing normal about it.

We often had the chance to see the warzone on an extremely personal and intimate level when heading into Belfast to visit my mum and dad's families each week. As we played on the footpath outside my granny's house, we suddenly froze and stood silently while intently staring at the British soldiers who were stationed along the street, our childhood curiosity getting the better of us about how they held and pointed their rifles, along with their camouflaged clothing and protective vests capped by their black beret. During some of those visits I would notice that they too, had black shite smeared on their faces, although this wasn't done by the local priest nor did it look like a feeble attempt to make the sign of the cross. This was followed up by our ma quickly ushering us into the house in case bullets started flying, or one of the troops decided we were a threat, even though we were fully unarmed. I still have a hard time coming to terms with this. Memories from that part of my childhood have not left me, nor do I believe they will anytime soon even though people have said, "Move on."

In saying that, I'd like to challenge comments shared with me at a recent book signing by a fellow Irish author. He too, is extremely familiar with what we were all exposed to during *'The Troubles'*. He felt we were not affected because we lived on the outskirts of Belfast in Newtownabbey, and had never hurled a brick, stone, or a Molotov cocktail at a passing armoured British patrol. I am sure there are enough of you reading this and would agree with me: the unfathomable mentality we grew up surrounded by affected *all* families, whether they chose to become involved in the conflict or made every effort to completely avoid it. In my opinion, all that was ever proved by this was a bastard time within a bastard war. As one friend, Linda Donnelly (nee Stanley), who grew up around the corner from me on the Knockview Road, stated recently:

> *"We were very lucky to live where we did in such a terrible time in the history of Northern Ireland. We were known as the children of the troubles. Now we are the adults of peace."*

To this day, I still cannot comprehend what it was all about. Perhaps you will come to see this yourself through some of my writings as you move forward through this book. Much of them form the foundation of and bring to light my memories and questioning of why we were ever exposed to such violent and traumatic events in the first place. We had nothing to do with the political war raging around us. And even though I go home on a regular basis while in search of my identity and to try and find a sense of belonging, the scars from those years remain part of who I am. I guess that is my 'One Cross to Bear' in this life (and yes, a shameless plug to one of my other books). Ack sure, why not?

Anyways, although much of my writing takes a hard look at life from my own experiences, you will see I have included much of the happier banter and craic that we Irish are known for. Pieces such as, ***Chuckie Our Da, Murphy's Law: My Friend of Misery! Dublin Cream Bun*** along with another called ***Bless Me, Father*** are but just a few. I also included short wee stories from my childhood days which will hopefully bring about as much laughter as well as shock as to how much trouble we got into. The same applies to my fellow authors, **J.P., Mark** and **John,** whose writings beautifully grace the pages of this book. If we did not poke fun and have a laugh at ourselves along the way of this amazing journey as well as work through much of the madness we grew up in, we would be missing the point behind this book completely.

Before turning these pages over to my fellow authors, I would like to switch gears for just a moment and take this opportunity to reflect upon a life-changing event that hit extremely close to home. On April 6, 2018 near Armley, Saskatchewan, Canada, an unspeakable tragedy stuck when sixteen members of the **Humboldt Broncos**, who were an ice hockey team within the Saskatchewan Junior Hockey League (SJHL), were suddenly taken from us; thirteen more were seriously injured.

The news of this crash rippled throughout every corner of this world and brought a small hockey community made up of players, parents, coaches, managers, billets, family, and friends into each of our hearts and minds. Many of us who have become part of the hockey community have taken those same bus trips across this vast country without ever passing much thought of something like this happening. We place our faith in the hands of the women and men who transport us back and forth to arenas and hotels. We are always grateful for the work they do while we sit back and chat, read, and listen to our rambunctious kids at the back of the bus.

The outpouring of grief and support that followed this tragedy made me pause for several days while considering the precious gift of life. My now sixteen-year-old son, Ciarán, a goalie of ten years, is currently in pursuit of his own goals and dreams of playing in the next phase of his endeavours within the Manitoba Junior Hockey League (MJHL), which is also closely aligned to the SJHL.

Although only seven weeks on, we ourselves have followed the simple, yet beautiful idea of placing one of Ciarán's goalie sticks outside of our front door in our hopes of bringing every hockey player home safely after each practice, game, tournament, or championship.

Thus, I would like to say to everyone affected by this awful tragedy that you forever remain within our thoughts and prayers as you continue the difficult process associated of coming to terms with the painful events which changed the dreams and goals of so many in the blink of an eye. Familiar across the hockey community that intertwines so many of us, we are, and we remain, **#HumboldtStrong!**

With that, I would like to say cheers and thanks to my amazing parents, Catherine and Charles, for providing me an opportunity in being able to tell my own wee story here within the pages of this book! You will have a chance to learn more about them both as you follow my life adventures in the pages and stories ahead. In the meantime, however, the dearly beloved John Sidney Rickerby is up next, as is told by his son, Mark.

John Rickerby

"Here's to good Irish friends – never above you, never below you, always beside you."

- **Irish Proverb.**

I wish my father were here to write this himself. He would have loved to meet Greg and J.P. They are exactly the kind of people he loved to surround himself with. Not just because of their shared love of his hometown, Belfast, but because of their humor and passion for living. Their and my outlet is writing. My father's was singing. He loved nothing more than entertaining his friends at The Mayflower Club in North Hollywood, California, or on long bus trips to Laughlin, Nevada. I've been told he could stand at the helm of those buses and never run out of songs, stories and jokes for the entire six-hour trip. Though I took my parents on quite a few trips to Laughlin and Las Vegas, I never took one of those bus trips with him and his friends, one of my many regrets.

I cherish the memory of those long drives through the Mojave Desert to Vegas now. They gave me a chance to really talk to my dad. He was old school in the sense that he didn't talk openly about feelings. I am the complete opposite. Belfast and Southern California are two different worlds, especially the Belfast he knew. His youth there from his birth in 1933 until he moved to Canada in 1955 were rough times for even the meanest characters, let alone a child. He covered almost all of it in his book **The Other Belfast – An Irish Youth**. I say "almost" because just when I thought the book had all the good stuff – the stories I had heard growing up a hundred times – he would tell another one that it couldn't possibly do without. I would actually pull over in the desert during those long drives just to take notes. Other stories were excavated more sneakily, with a miniature tape recorder in my pocket while having a pint together at some pub or listening to him regale his friends with a tale of the auld country. This was when he was at his best, spinning stories without the impediment of typing or writing.

Even as a child, I was amazed by his ability to transfix a crowd, or just a few houseguests, with stories and songs. But, again, despite these God-given talents and the countless compliments he received on both of his passions, he never pursued a career in the arts. His father worked for the Great Northern Railroad for over forty years and rarely missed a day's work, and that work ethic was passed along to him. He got a job as an insurance claim adjuster in his twenties and remained one for his entire working life until he was dragged into retirement at the age of seventy-five.

Never one to ride someone else's coattails, he started his own company and it flourished for almost forty years. When he retired, he offered the company to me and hoped I would take it, but I couldn't. I told him I was proud of everything he had accomplished – leaving school at fourteen to support his parents and running a successful business for four decades despite having no formal education while dozens of similar businesses run by college graduates rose and fell around him, but I wanted to give writing a real chance, not half a chance. Any artist who has chosen between security and insecurity will know what I mean. Having "something to fall back on" feels too much like giving oneself a 50/50 chance of failure right from the start. So I had to say no when he offered me his business and a guaranteed six-figure a year income for life. It hurt him at first, but when he read my first few stories in the *Chicken Soup for the Soul* books, which now number twenty, or the foreword to his book *The Other Belfast*, he always came to me and said, "Son, you made the right decision." I always remember those as some of the greatest moments in my life. Boys always want to make their fathers proud, but this desire was magnified by my desire to justify that decision to not take over his business and prove that I was more than just a conceited dabbler at writing.

Despite that decision, his influences on me are many and powerful. I wanted and still want to be as successful at writing as he was at what he did

 Four Green Fields

for a living. I also want to be loved as much as he was, by everyone. All those years, I was watching. Nobody called his office without getting a joke, or without being asked how they were doing and knowing he really cared. He remembered the names of everyone's children, and the smallest problems they were dealing with. He gave jobs to people in dire situations even if they were not qualified for the work, then patiently trained them. He was never dishonest, though he could have been without detection and could have amassed much greater wealth doing so. In fact, he lost valuable accounts because he refused to lie when he was flat-out asked to. I always ribbed him that he was the last boy scout, but he knew I was proud of him. His success and longevity in business had as much to do with his charm as it did with his business acumen.

I had worked at the "family business" off and on for years but never really enjoyed it. People making insurance claims, I found, were hard to satisfy because of the simple facts that one can never have enough money, and greed corrupts. It was not good for the soul to be lied to on a daily basis, only to be regularly accused of not being fair to claimants when I did my best to get them everything they deserved, as my father had always done. It really was a "thankless job."

I was primed to dislike claims adjusting work by hearing my father complain at the dinner table every night during my youth about being lied to. I couldn't understand why he loved that job so much, especially when, even then, I knew if he went out and auditioned for a singing gig, he would get it. He was THAT good.

I knew he was that good because during many long, languid, California summers, I had the rare privilege and joy of hearing him sing in the shower as I lay in bed. The one I remember most was *Early One Morning*.

Early one morning, just as the sun was rising
I heard a maiden singing in the valley below
"Oh don't deceive me, Oh never leave me,
How could you use, a poor maiden so?"

I also recall *Goodbye Mrs. Durkin*, which could have been his song –

Goodbye Mrs. Durkin, I'm sick and tired of workin'
No more I'll dig your praties, no longer I'll be poor
As sure as my name is Barney, I'm off to Califarny
Instead of digging praties, I'll be digging lumps of gold.

He sure did dig up some gold in California. The first half-dozen years of my life were a bit lean but he bought his first house in Santa Monica when I was eight and would buy three others, each one bigger than the last, before settling in Glendale when I was fifteen.

On those deliciously irresponsible summer mornings, with no school to get ready for, lying in bed listening to my father singing, the house would fill up with the manly aroma of Old Spice cologne and I would plan my day – usually hanging around our pool (our last house was the only one that had one so it was a big deal) and listening to The Beach Boys with friends, back in the day when tanning was a big priority and I would never get old.

As I thought about the girls at school or how I was going to scrape together enough change to get some gasoline into my 1969 VW Bug to get to the beach, he would abruptly open my door and say, "Get out of that bed and do some work or I'll pull you out by your left knacker!" As an awkward teenager who had not yet found his voice – at least as it applies to the Belfast craic that requires – nay, demands - an immediate and equally caustic response, this was always disconcerting and an unpleasant way to be roused from slumber. It is my excuse for hating early mornings to this day.

Alternately, my father would mimic reveille, the bugle call that wakes up soldiers, in a purposely annoying, nasally tone and maximum volume. Some days, he would even add words sung to that tune –

It's time to get up!
It's time to get up!

It's time to get up in the morning!
It's time to get up!
It's time to get up!
It's time to get up in the morning!

Can anyone blame me for not being a big fan of early rising to this day?

But I digress. I joked with my father it was his fault that I turned down the family business. When he asked why, I told him, "Because I heard you sing every morning. I heard pride in your voice when you talked about your work, but I heard joy when you sang, and I saw it in the faces of everyone listening when you sang at the pub or at parties. I wanted to be able to make people feel that way."

I like to sing, and I've been told I'm pretty good, but I have no delusions about myself. The apple fell a fair distance from the tree in that regard. I'm okay, but my dad was great. Pitch perfect.

So helping him finish his book was a joy for me, and him, and gave us a chance to become even closer in what turned out to be his final decade on this earth.

He wrote *The Other Belfast – An Irish Youth* in bits and pieces over the course of forty years but never completed it. Seeing he was getting older and showing no signs of making that dream come true, I took it upon myself to organize the hand-written stories in tattered cardboard boxes in his garage. We published the book in 2010. He passed away in December of 2014 due to complications from Parkinson's Disease and Dementia. It was a hard ending for such a good man. But as the saying goes, it's not how he died that matters, it's how he lived.

He would never call himself such, but he was a peace activist in the 1970's, helplessly watching on TV as his beloved hometown was thrown into turmoil and bloodshed. He was interviewed on television and radio and contributed numerous articles to the Los Angeles Times, the Belfast Telegraph, and other publications about the Irish situation, the most well-known being "Who Killed Little Michelle?" He received death threats because of his efforts.

The finality of death allows few consolations, but I have a few, the main one being helping him finish *The Other Belfast.* I thought I knew him before working on that book with him, but I didn't know how much I didn't know. It was a true journey of discovery. I found myself wishing I would have written it decades earlier when I was a teenager and he and I were too often at odds with each other. Knowing more about what he had survived surely would have alleviated any resentment I felt toward him. People are a lot like jigsaw puzzles – without all the pieces, we can never see the full picture. Of course, I didn't have the inclination or ability to write well then. Just another way youth is wasted on the young.

Shortly after his book was published and I put a copy of it in his hands, he came to my house and said, "I never finished that book because deep down inside. I thought, "Who am I to write an autobiography? I never went to the moon or cured cancer or survived a POW camp. But after reading it, I realized that my life had been extraordinary in its own way. You made that possible."

It was one of the proudest moments of my life. My biggest regret, however, is that I didn't help him finish it earlier so he would have had more time to share it with friends and hear some of the great reviews he has received on it. It gives little consolation when friends say "we do things when we're ready to do them" or even when they tell me they know of no other son or daughter who helped their parents finish a memoir. He had so little life left by the time the book was finished, and Parkinson's Disease stole so much of his memory, he didn't even recognize the book as his own, or me as his son, for the last few years of his life. It was heartbreaking, and memories of those dark days still keep me up at night.

Something else I did in desperation as Parkinson's Disease was erasing him was to find all of his old karaoke recordings in yellowed and torn cardboard boxes in his garage and put together a CD of his recordings titled ***Get Rickerby Up for a Song!*** - something someone would inevitably shout out at a pub when they found out he was in the room.

His autobiography and that CD are treasures to me now that he is gone, and promoting his legacy with them eases the pain a little of losing him. Greg McVicker has helped me in this regard by generously sharing my father's book and a poem he wrote titled ***Ulster*** on the Facebook page for his book ***Through the Eyes of a Belfast Child***, which my father certainly would have enjoyed. You will get to know my father better in the following pages, but first, allow me to tell you a little bit about myself . . .

MARK RICKERBY

"Life isn't about finding yourself. Life is about creating yourself."

- **George Bernard Shaw.**

I was born in Santa Monica, California. My father moved to Ontario, Canada, and sent letters to my mother, who was still in Belfast, begging her to come there and marry him. She did so and they stayed together for over fifty years before his death. He used to joke, "Irish men may not be the most romantic, but they're dependable. They're always there every morning, drooling on the pillow."

My mother and every other woman I've ever known who married a Belfast man just rolled her eyes and shook her head good-naturedly at comments like these as if to say, "Ach, there he goes again, the eejit." It's a look that all Irish women have in common, an expression of acceptance and surrender to their incorrigible husbands, with a hint of love and amusement.

I will share excerpts from my father's memoir in these pages, as well as my own memories of the Belfast he knew. I only visited three times in my life but no matter how long one stays there, a year or a day, the people and energy of that remarkable city leave indelible, happy memories. My fellow authors are perfect examples of why my father was so devoted to his hometown and cherished the memories of his friendships there. There's just something special about Belfast people and the Irish in general, north or south, Catholic or Protestant. They are fully alive and awake, hot-blooded, filled with emotion that demands artistic expression in its various forms as surely as a pressure-cooker requires a steam vent.

As a child, I was swallowed up by the California lifestyle and culture. I loved baseball, skateboarding, surfing, shell collecting and comic books. My relatives in Ireland would send me the Beano and I enjoyed it but never quite as much as American comics. My dad tried to get me interested in soccer, his favorite sport as a child, but I remained steadfastly devoted to baseball, the all-American game. My friends and I would play in the street, using any object we could find for bases (usually swiped, unread newspapers) and tennis balls instead of baseballs to avoid breaking car windshields.

Out of desperation to bond with my father, however, I started playing soccer for the AYSO league. (American Youth Soccer Organization.) I enjoyed kicking the ball around at the park with him. He was in his essence then, and I was amazed at how far he could kick the ball, often yelling "Pick it out!" as he did so, something he and his friends in Belfast probably yelled and I never really understood. He also expanded my vocabulary with words like "pockle" – the Belfast word for klutz - when I kicked the ball badly.

My dad volunteered to coach my first soccer team, and hired one of his friends from Belfast, Jimmy McMechan, to be his assistant coach. I'm sure I would like Jimmy now but at the time, he scared the hell out of me. He wasn't a big man but he had a face like an old saddlebag, was missing several fingers from being tortured at a POW camp in Vietnam, and seemed to be righteously pissed off almost all the time. He would yell very unpleasant comments during our games such as "move your arses!" and "You play like my Aunt Minny!" Why he had an aunt who played soccer badly was another question entirely.

The main problem was I was not from Belfast. The emotional distance between the two is as great as the physical distance. My dad and Jimmy were taught very early in their youths there that one had to be tough to survive. They were also self-made men who left home early for other countries and worked their way up in whatever business they happened to land a job at. There were no lofty dreams supported by the safety net of a well-to-do family. It was sink-or-swim for them back then, and that kind of desperation – in addition to the psychic residue of growing up during the Great Depression - never leave a man, especially when their own kids came along and they were truly put to the test.

I had it a lot easier. So easy, in fact, that I didn't see the point of winning a soccer game. It just didn't matter that much to me. While the game raged around me, I would be studying the majesty of a cloud formation, or the intricacy of a tiny flower nestled in the grass at my feet, only to be awoken from my reveries by my father yelling, "Get your head out of your arse, ya bloody eejit!" Sometimes he would say something more subtle like, "You're missing a great game!"

Of course, the son of the coach got an extra ration of this kind of "help." During a game one Saturday afternoon, the whistle blew for halftime and my dad was storming along the sideline cursing me when I decided I'd had enough.

It was an unusually cold and bitter day for California. The first half of the game had been a real medieval skirmish. My shins were bloodied and I was covered with bits of grass and turf. The groundskeepers always seemed to mow the lawn right before the game and leave all the trimmings. The coach of the other team would later be disqualified for recruiting older boys and lying about their age. Suffice to say we were getting a good pasting and my dad was not one bit happy about it.

He had just finished telling me once again to remove my cranium from my posterior, and Jimmy had likened me to his Aunt Minny for the seven hundred and twelfth time when I finally started to lose my mind. Without thinking, I pelted the ball in my father's general direction. I was to learn that something magical happens when one kicks a ball with just the right amount of anger and a kind of zen-like thoughtlessness. I bent that baby like Beckham. It was beautiful to watch as it arced across the sky, but my horror mounted as I realized it was heading directly toward my father's anger-reddened bake. It careened off the side of his head, a direct hit, as the crowd gasped. I immediately jumped, turning in the air, and landed on my knees facing the opposite direction, pretending to closely inspect something on the ground.

"I know it was you, ya wee shitehawk! You're the only one out there!"

he yelled.

"Who, me?"

"You did that on purpose, didn't ya?" he screamed.

I looked over innocently and pretended I was too far away to hear him.

He stormed away and yelled, "Why don't you kick like that during the game, ya buck eejit?"

The answer to that question, of course, was motivation. The second half of that game was not pleasant, let me tell you. But as I wrote in *The Other Belfast*, in an addendum to his chapter devoted to soccer, I eventually realized that his frustration toward me as a player was not mean-spirited. It came from his desire to see me experience the same feeling of elation he felt all those decades ago when he first discovered the freedom and camaraderie of a team, and he ran along soccer fields with such grace and speed, he felt as if his feet weren't even touching the ground. That's a good thing to want for a child, regardless of methods.

But, alas, the inability to see through our parents' behavior to their deeper motivations is yet another way youth is wasted on the young. Understanding comes too late. Fortunately, I was able to thank my dad verbally and in writing when that lazy teenager became a man proud to be much like him.

At that awkward age, I rejected many things he cherished, including Irish music, opting instead for The Beach Boys or Jan and Dean, which he was equally indifferent to. I also groused when he dragged my brother Paul and I to the Scottish Highland Games every year. Of course, seeing men in dresses was always interesting, and to children, particularly California children, they were dresses no matter what they called them. I usually found myself enjoying the various spectacles at the games such as boulder-throwing and pole-tossing. For those who have never witnessed this IQ test, it involves large, pale, swarthy men throwing what looks like a telephone pole, the goal being to make it flip over. It's an amazing feat of strength, designed solely for the purpose of causing lifelong back problems and inguinal hernias.

One of dad's friends, who shall go nameless to prevent embarrassment, found a bunch of telephone poles lying on the ground next to the parking lot in preparation for the event and decided to give the pole toss a try. The problem was he was a wee man, completely untrained in such an event. My brother, friends and I watched in rapt wonder as he pulled one out of the pile, walked it up hand over hand, nestled it into the crook of his neck, wedged his fingers under it, and actually got it off the ground.

"See, boys! This isn't so heavy! This is easy, so it is!" he yelled.

Then the pole started to lean. He walked in that direction but overcompensated, causing it to lean the other way. He then ran that way, setting off a study in Sir Isaac Newton's Third Law – for every action, there is an equal and positive reaction. Soon he was running to the left for twenty feet or so, then to the right, then back to the left, growing dangerously close to the parked vehicles. Our gasps rose and fell with his efforts until his grip finally weakened and he dropped the pole. We watched in horror as it fell across and shattered four windshields, then rolled down the car hoods, leaving deep gouges in the paint. We all stood silently, mouths agape, wondering what to do - including him. After a few horrible moments, he yelled "Run!"

Because he was the adult, of course, we did so, the lesson for all us impressionable children being, "If you damage the property of others, run away and avoid all responsibility."

I didn't know it at the time but I was blessed to be raised by men such as these in this close-knit community of Belfast-raised Californians. Most of them were quite mad. They gave me plenty of reasons to laugh as a child and to write as an adult. They unknowingly provided a treasure trove of stories. They filled my knapsack until it could hold no more.

Of course, this inspiration was usually unintentional and even discouraged by some of them. For instance, when I was still in my twenties, the Scottish husband of one of my parents' friends asked, "What are ya go'n tay do with yar life, lad?"

At this point, I still wasn't sure and was only toying with the idea of being a writer. I hadn't built up the necessary confidence yet. The impending conversation wouldn't help.

I told him very matter-of-factly, as if it were the easiest career in the world to get into, "I'm going to be a writer."

I didn't know this man too well so I didn't really know what to expect and was thus unprepared for his response.

"A writer?" he said incredulously, "What are ye go'n tay write aboot? Yuv nevarr even been in a war, fer fox sake!"

I countered, "There's more to write about than getting your arse blown off."

He laughed unguardedly and brought up Hemingway's military service. I'm proud to report that I didn't allow this assault to go unchallenged. I said, "There's this thing called imagination. Ever hear of it?"

He got up and left the room, muttering expletives.

I was able to stand up for myself and my career choice because I had been well-schooled all my life in the peculiar habit some people from the auld country have of taking a good, long piss on anything that resembles ambition. I've heard the same criticism from Belfast natives numerous times so I know it's not just me.

Some cultures nurture and encourage each other, especially children. The Jewish culture is a good example. It's all about building the confidence of children so they can become responsible, successful adults. The tradition of Bar-mitzvah's and Bat-mitzvah's is a rite of passage in a world largely devoid of them, a clear separation between childhood and adulthood from which there is no going back. But even before these rituals, a fuss is made over the children for even the smallest accomplishments. Allow me to demonstrate.

Little Jerome, a Jewish child, and wee Jimmy, a Belfast child, both write a poem. In Jerome's house, his mother says, "Everyone gather around. Jerome is going to recite his poem. He's so brilliant, that boy." And all the adults listen in reverent silence as Jerome recites his poem, and applaud raucously afterward, even if it stinks to high heaven.

Meanwhile, in the Belfast house, wee Jimmy nervously tells his da he wrote a poem. His ma may say "Oh, that's wonderful, Jimmy!" hoping to launch a preemptive block to what she fears the father will say, but he is undeterred. He peers skeptically over his newspaper and says, "Oh, ya wrote a poem, didja? Excuse me, dear, but is that Billy Shakespeare I'm lookin' at? Maybe my specs need cleanin'."

Seeing wee Jimmy becoming discouraged, his da lightens up, but not entirely. "Ach, I'm only kiddin' ya. Away ya go! Let's hear your poem. I'm sure it's sheer genius. Off ya go."

Not missing the sarcasm, Jimmy says, "Ach, forget it. What was I thinkin' writin' a bloody poem anyway?"

Having successfully kicked the crap out of any sensitive, artistic impulse, thus preparing him for life in the real world, the father snaps his newspaper and goes back to reading the soccer scores.

Years later, wee Jerome is a lawyer and wee Jimmy is driving a forklift at the local hardware store, but somewhere in the back of his mind he knows he's an artist and the desire to create still nags at him, so he teaches himself how to play a guitar. He writes his first song and is eager to share it with his mates. He goes to the pub and finds them in their usual spot, surrounded by empty pint glasses.

They see him carrying a guitar and one says, "Hey, boys! Look! It's Van Morrison!"

    Four Green Fields

And thus the slaggin' begins.

"I wrote a song," wee Jimmy says meekly.

"Oh, didja now!" one of his mates says. "Hey, Billy, is that Bobby Dylan over there?"

Seeing that Jimmy is somewhat crestfallen, he lightens up and says, "Ach, I'm just pullin' your leg. Let's hear your wee song. Make us all misty and teary-eyed with your musical stylings. Right, away ya go."

By the time he's finished, every last wisp of air has been sucked out of wee Jimmy's sails. He says "forget it" and sits down. Then his mate says, "That's right. Sit down, have a pint like the rest of us, and stop trying to break out of your wee, insignificant world."

Okay, maybe he doesn't come right out and say that but that's the message.

I say this only half-jokingly. There's too much self-deprecation and keeping each other down in the Irish world, which makes it even more of a wonder that so many Irish men and women have contributed so much to mankind in every field imaginable. Then again, maybe these challenges are exactly what have made the Irish so strong and talented. As Homer wrote in *The Odyssey*, "Smooth seas don't make good sailors."

My father "took the mickey" out of me every day of my life. I didn't understand it at first, but it gave me a deep well of stories and made me seek the rarified world of artistic self-expression. If I had been perfectly happy, maybe I wouldn't have had so much to write about, or the ability to do so. Yes, I realize I'm contradicting myself. If everyone in Ireland stopped slagging each other, all artistic output would probably come to a screeching halt. So maybe we're all better off just adjusting to it as I eventually did.

It would also be comforting in a sad kind of way if this treatment had been done intentionally and scientifically, but I fear the origins are not so noble or healthy. It took me far too long to develop the sense of humor to stop taking slagging seriously, and the off-the-cuff wit to fire back with equal firepower. My father was taken aback by it at first but his shock quickly turned to pride, perhaps recognizing himself coming out in me finally. "That boy has a tongue that could clip a hedge," he once said, after being on the receiving end of his own brand of humor. I will tell that story shortly, which I have fondly titled ***Nosehead versus Chief Littlefoot***.

Before I go, I just realized I was supposed to talk about myself here. I've always been uncomfortable writing bio's but for the record, as Greg mentioned, I have stories in twenty ***Chicken Soup for the Soul*** titles to date, am the co-creator and head writer of an upcoming western TV series, am one of several screenwriters for Six Rivers Entertainment, and have been published in some magazines, such as *Black Belt* and *Inside Kung Fu.* (My dad tried to get me into boxing – a sport he excelled in as a child and loved almost as much as soccer - but after watching *Kung Fu Theater* every weekend as a child, I chose martial arts. I could never understand a sport with no flipping or chokeholds, and one that intentionally leaves out more than half of the human body's weapons – feet, knees, elbows and the forehead, used chiefly to deliver what they call in Northern Ireland "the Belfast kiss." Or what the Scottish call a "Glasgow Kiss.")

I'm sure it has become clear by this point that my father's perspective and mine in the same book will be a contrast between Northern Ireland and America. He was 100% Belfast, I'm 50/50, in just about every way – blood, interests and attitude. And I'm as proud of both as I was of my da. I miss him every day. Being able to share him and his love of Belfast with you is the best anesthesia I've found for the pain of losing him.

J.P. Sexton

"We are all born mad. Some remain so."

-   **Samuel Beckett.**

I am not sure whether or not we are all born mad, but I wholeheartedly agree with Mr. Beckett that some remain so. I happen to come from a long line of those who *remain so*.

For me, familial insanity is an interesting study. God knows, I have many subjects (myself included) on which to base my study.

Upon reflection, I came to realize that just about every person on my immediate paternal and maternal side were a "wee bit off" and many are/were much more than just a wee bit. The only exception to this was my grandmother, Katherine Houton. My grandmother was a quiet, unassuming, gentle lady who was married to Danny Houton - one of the craziest bastards in all of Donegal, if not all of Ireland. Their children must have taken after their father, as they all had his crazy streak and none more so than my mother – Sarah.

When I think of my mother and father, the one saying which springs to mind is; "there is somebody for everybody." I would be hard pressed to tell you which one of them was crazier than the other. They were both equally mad as hatters. When I was young, I didn't realize that I must have had a fair dose of madness running through my blood. Maybe I fought it, due to living with a pair of mad things and seeing first hand, on a daily basis how they just about managed to function (of course functioning as far as our family goes was more of a theory rather than a proven fact).

The more I think about it though, the more I lean towards agreeing with Mr. Beckett that we are in fact all born mad. Young children have no filter and therefore say and do the craziest things. As they get older, they are taught that they can't say certain things in public, so they learn self-censorship. As we get older, however, many of us care less about the opinions of others and live our lives in a manner that is more in keeping with our true nature.

I started writing creatively when I was around ten years of age and attending Primary school in Carndonagh. My short stories and poetry over the years were what I would call "tame." Although I had been brought up as a cross-border smuggler at that same time, apparently I was not yet ready to write about these escapades (which I did many decades later in my memoir, ***The Big Yank – Memoir of a Boy Growing Up Irish***).

I remember feeling depressed for quite a while when I turned thirty. The main reason for the depression was that I didn't yet have a book (s) published. When I later told some people what I was going through, they replied that I had plenty of years ahead of me to write, and having a book published would come about in its own good time. Some also suggested that I had experiences yet waiting to happen, which would have a huge impact on what I would write in the future.

Looking back, I now realize that the folks who shared these thoughts with me were more prophetic than they could have imagined. Over the past twenty-five years I have traveled fairly extensively around the world, finding myself in places and situations which were anything but ordinary. From spending two years in Riker's Island - one of the most dangerous jails in the United States to liaising with rebel forces in Mozambique and later dodging bombs in Bosnia during the Balkan wars, I experienced unique facets of life that most people could not begin to imagine.

I am currently writing about these experiences in a follow-up book of memoirs and at the same time planning future fictional stories which will have a good dose of mystery and International intrigue. I am also happy to share that I have begun to write more poetry, which I had been neglecting for far too long. My more modern-day poetry is somewhat hard-hitting and I suppose one could say darker than what I would have written years ago. I am sure that my years spent in war zones and places of great conflict have significantly influenced my current writing.

However one wishes to categorize my writing is fine by me. I don't feel the need to limit myself to a set genre. I would describe my writing as freestyle, which is in keeping with the way I have basically lived my life, for the most part. The idea of boxing myself in does not suit me. I like to keep myself guessing just as much as the readers as to what I will write next, or what my characters will come out with. I'll share this one tip; in the future, I expect to see a good deal of dialogue with the potential for some of it to raise an eyebrow or two!

Sláinte!

- J.P.

"The reasonable man adapts himself to the world; the unreasonable one persists in trying to adapt the world to himself."
-   **George Bernard Shaw.**

Our Fathers:
Hallowed Be Thy Names

Holy Communion, Holy Terror, Holy Frig!

"One of the very best rules of conversation is to never say anything which any of the company wish had been left unsaid."

- **Jonathan Swift.**

As mentioned previously, I've only been to Belfast three times, at the ages of five, fifteen and thirty-six, and only briefly on each trip, so my main connection to Belfast is my father. But man, what an introduction.

He was the embodiment of every stereotype about the Irish. He had a soft and a hard side. He was a poet, singer and storyteller but he could also be a bit pugnacious when someone got his dander up, and he had the boxing training to back it up. However, he always did his best to promote peace.

The only time I ever remember him actually hitting anyone was one night when he and my mother were dancing and someone neither of them knew "cut in" and asked her to dance. My father graciously stepped away and joined his friends at their table. A minute or so later, one of his friends motioned to him to look at my mother. The guy was whirling her around so fast, her feet were barely touching the ground. My father could tell she wasn't enjoying this treatment so he started walking quickly toward them. He was halfway there when the Patrick Swayze wannabe lost control and dropped my mother on the floor. My da saw red and "hit him a dig in the bake" as he would put it. The next thing old Twinkle Toes knew, he was sitting on the floor, feeling his jaw to make sure it was still attached. He skulked out the back door never to be seen again. All present agreed he deserved it.

However, my father's shocking and inappropriate sense of humor was more of a concern to me than his temper ever was. I'll share a few for instance's.

One of his grandest displays of inappropriateness occurred at the Glendale Adventist Hospital after having his entire stomach removed due to stomach cancer. I would find out decades later from a friend of his that my father told him he didn't expect to survive, yet there he was, lying in his hospital bed, flirting with the nurses. He was forty-five and I was fifteen at the time, but already well-acquainted with the joy he took in shocking people with jokes that ought not be uttered in mixed company. Anybody other than a Belfast native would have been too depressed to crack a smile after losing a major organ. His body wasn't intact but his sense of humor was, and he was about to outdo himself yet again.

He had already developed a reputation from saying "give us a kiss" to nurses when they would lean over to fix his sheets. They would be shocked at first but eventually realize he was harmless and only laugh and say something like, "Oh, Mr. Rickerby, you're incorrigible!" A nurse walked in he and I hadn't seen before. She looked about eighteen and took her job and herself very seriously. She had a clipboard and started asking my da a seemingly endless series of questions, many of which included abbreviations nobody but a hospital staff could have possibly been familiar with.

Every time she used another abbreviation, he looked at me, hoping I had a clue, but I would just shrug my shoulders. She asked, "Have you had an LBM today?" Again, my father asked her what that stood for. She became impatient and rather condescendingly replied, "Loose bowel movement."

My father said, "No, I haven't, but I would like to have an NSE."

The nurse searched through her abbreviation checklist for a minute but couldn't find that one. The tables turned, she asked my dad to tell her what it stood for. He smiled and said, "A nude sexual encounter."

Her face turned fire engine red and she stormed out of the room. I said, "Dad, you're gonna get thrown out of here!" but he just laughed and said the usual, "F*** 'em if they can't take a joke."

Fifteen minutes later, a hospital administrator came into the room and said, "Mr. Rickerby, I realize you're a bit of a kidder, but these girls are all seminary students and very sheltered. I had to let that nurse go home for the day. She may never come back. Please try to control your wit a little, at least with the younger nurses."

Honest to the end, he replied, "I can't make any promises."

All my father ever said to me about girls when I was in high school was "keep 'em guessing." When I was out of high school, noticing I was making quite a career of skirt-chasing, he said, "I'm pretty sure if I sawed the top of your head off and looked at your brain, there would be a vagina in there." (He used a different word.) Giving him the benefit of the doubt, I thought he was at least a little chagrined with me for not taking women seriously enough. After all, he married my mom in his mid-twenties, they were still together, and he never played around on the side as far as I knew. Then one day he took me aside and appeared to have something serious on his mind. I thought he was going to say something like, "Listen, son. Women are people, too, and they deserve respect and honesty. Do unto others and all that."

No.

He said, "If I was your age, I'd run off to Europe and screw myself stupid." Thus ended any and all of my da's advice on the opposite sex. And for better or worse, I took that advice. I once made love to a beautiful Italian girl against the stone wall of a church in Milan at midnight as she cried, "Si, Marco! Si! Bellissimo! Stupendo!" I eventually figured out that the playboy lifestyle, in the long run, leads to terrible emptiness, but I don't regret my youthful wanderlust, or just plain lust. As the saying goes, we're only young once. And if I have to answer for that little incident in Milan at the pearly gates, I doubt even then that I'll say it wasn't worth it.

My wife is a good Christian. Me, not so much. I struggle with the "big questions" a bit. But I go to church with her because she's happier when I do, and because I want to raise our two daughters with a church family. The point is I know most of the people at our church.

I brought my parents along one day and the pastor announced it was time for Communion. The ushers handed out the tiny plastic cups filled with punch and the equally tiny clam chowder crackers. Everyone was holding them, waiting for the pastor to finish his sermon, when my dad ate the cracker and drank the punch too soon. I noticed everyone looking and whispered, "Dad, you're supposed to wait until the pastor gives the okay."

He answered, "I couldn't help it. I'm f***in' hungry!" as if one cracker no bigger than his thumbnail and a quarter-ounce of punch would make a dent in his hunger. I thought his eating Jesus' flesh and drinking his blood without permission was bad enough, then he cussed in church, making no effort to whisper. I made some joke like "I can't take you anywhere." He said his usual, "F*** 'em if they can't take a joke," cursing yet again. A few more gasps, some whispering, and a chuckle or two resounded through the sanctuary. As usual in situations like this, I stopped talking to him to avoid further social mortification.

On another occasion, I had purchased tickets to see one of my favorite singers at a small theater in Hollywood. The venue only sat about two hundred. I brought my girlfriend (now wife), a friend, and my father. This artist is a folk singer, a genre of music that is a haven for singers who don't happen to possess classical singing voices. This one was quite nasally. Within a minute of his first song, my father said, "This guy needs some work on his adenoids." His staunch fans seated in the row in front of us turned around and fired indignant glares at him. I asked my dad to please be quiet, but he was not finished. Far from it.

Knowing he was getting on my nerves, and that this was my favorite singer, he leaned over and said, again loudly, "He looks like a gay blade."

This time everyone two rows ahead and two rows back looked at him in shock and horror. I covered my face with my hand.

Mind you, this was Hollywood, very close to West Hollywood, one of the epicenters of homosexuality, where anything resembling homophobia or intolerance is not taken lightly. Fortunately, this particular artist was straight so most of his fans were, too. Otherwise, there might have been an attempted lynching that night. If the artist heard, he didn't let on. As usual, I tried to make myself invisible but my friend, who also has parents from Belfast, laughed uproariously, understanding that this kind of humor is designed to shock the sensibilities but has no malice in it. It is the intention that matters, after all, and my father's only intention was always to get a laugh and stun people out of their imprisoning comfort zones.

He was advanced in age at this point and, as is often the case with the elderly, most people probably felt he had earned the right to be eccentric and offensive. He was part of a world that existed before the term "politically correct" was even coined, a lot like the father in the sitcom *Everybody Loves Raymond*. He had no internal editor. No group was safe, including his own.

I was surprised he used the term "gay blade" that night – something right out of a 1970's schlock crime drama – because he never used it before. He usually called gay people shirt tail lifters or puff merchants. The former wasn't hard for me to figure out, but I never could quite understand what a puff merchant was. A seller of puffs? Puffs of what? Anyway, the more offended people were, the more he seemed to enjoy it. It was as if he were telling them to stop taking themselves so seriously. And let's face it – the current generation is way out in the lead when it comes to hypersensitivity and the inability to laugh at oneself, so much so that they need "safe zones" filled with crayons and other childhood toys to comfort them when their feelings have been hurt. The Archie Bunker's of the world are not only not considered harmless buffoons anymore, they lose their jobs and receive death threats. I don't think this is a healthy development. The theme from an old TV show called Candid Camera said it well –

Aside from these larger events that stand out in my memory, there were smaller, daily comments I could always depend on. If we were sitting in a car and there was someone walking by in the crosswalk with an unusual physical characteristic, I would just wait for it. I was never disappointed. He seemed particularly fascinated by noses, or nebs as he often called them. He was also fond of "snitchpiece" - a term he apparently invented because a) I've never heard anyone else use it, and b) I Googled it and it doesn't exist. Occasionally, he would bust out the classic "honker", too. This was ironic because his own nose was not petite by any standard. I even suggested to him one day that the reason he was so fixated on big noses might be that he was always trying to find ones that made his own snitchpiece seem smaller. As expected, his response was the usual, "Shut your gub, ya cheeky, wee shite." Mind you, I was a grown man at this point who outweighed him by forty pounds, but no matter. The children of Irish fathers are both cheeky and wee no matter their age or the size disparity between them.

In fact, there is a fixation on size that pervades Ireland, as evidenced by the terms "wee" and "big" before just about every man's name. Allow me to explain.

Two Jimmy's are walking down the street. One is five-foot-seven, the other six feet tall. Their mates see them coming and one of them says, "There's Wee Jimmy comin'! And look, he's got Big Jimmy with him!" I don't know if a doctor or institute ever prepared a chart showing where the cut-off points for the wee and big labels are, but it seems that any man below, say, five-foot-eight is forever saddled with a "wee" before his name, and any man over five-foot-eleven or so is bestowed with the coveted "big" before his name. Since nobody knows what to call those who fall somewhere between five-eight and five-eleven, they are fortunately spared.

My da and I were sitting in a restaurant one day when an elderly man with an iron lung walked in. He was in bad shape, God bless him. Being a hippy-dippy, metaphysical, Leo Buscaglia self-help book reading Los Angeles type, my heart immediately started to bleed for him. My da not so much. He leaned in to me and said, "Look at the state of that. The wee man's transparent. One clean shirt'll do him." As usual, I was aghast, shocked and horrified, then laughed in spite of myself, then got mad at myself for laughing, then got annoyed with him but not really, then realized I had completely invalidated my disapproval by laughing at all, which of course he thoroughly enjoyed.

In his defense, my father's self-deprecating humor was equally merciless. He once told me he was at the mall and saw an old man gazing intently at him. He thought, "What's that old bastard staring at?" A few seconds later, he realized he was looking at himself in a mirror.

As he got older, he developed a rather pronounced curvature of the spine. When he was young, he was 5'10 (and thus spared either the "Wee John" or "Big John" titles) but the curvature brought him down to about 5'8. He joked, "I'm actually 6'6. I just need someone to put me into a mold of a guy with a straight back and slam the door shut on me."

My da often joked that large probosci ran in his family. He once showed me a photo of his parents, sister and himself standing in the sand at Donaghadee and said, "The raw material from all of our noses would be more than enough to construct a fifth person."

Writhing with embarrassment as my father disrupted live performances and even movies was nothing new to me. In fact, the audience making themselves part of the show somehow is a fine tradition in Belfast. In *The Other Belfast*, he told stories about the absolute pandemonium he would always walk into at the Park Picturehouse on Saturday nights. One night,

 Four Green Fields

he was making his way to an empty seat when he got hit across the side of the head by a stale loaf of bread. It exploded, sending crumbs flying everywhere. He looked around but since everybody in the theater was laughing, there was no way to determine who the culprit was. As he found his seat and rubbed the growing lump on his cranium, he wondered why anyone would throw an entire loaf of bread full-force in a crowded room, but also why they brought it to a movie theater to begin with.

Another time in Belfast, he was watching a theater troupe doing some Shakespearean play. It was an attempt to bring culture to the savages, a little like the scene in the movie Tombstone when the cowboys were cursing and firing their pistols at the actors. The actor was holding the body of his dead lover, crying and asking, very melodramatically, "Whatever shall I do?" or something to that effect, when someone in the audience yelled, "Get her knickers off!" The actor winced but bravely forged ahead, repeating, "Whatever shall I do?" Another ruffian yelled, "Buck her while she's still warm!"

That was it. The actor stormed off the stage and solemnly vowed never to perform in Belfast again.

When I was about sixteen, I got it into my head that I was going to be a professional bodybuilder. I struggled and strained with weight and pulleys but nothing grew. The Mr. America contest was being held in Santa Monica and my parents took me and a friend, dropped us off at the civic auditorium, then went to see my mom's cousin. She and her husband, Danny (what else?), were also from Belfast. When my friend and I were at the show, we ran into Lou Ferrigno, a 6'7, 260-pound brute best known for playing *The Incredible Hulk* in the 1970's. My father and Danny picked us up at the end of the day and we excitedly told him, "We met Lou Ferrigno!" Rather than being wowed like we were, my dad said, "Ferrigno, frig yes!" Danny answered, "Frig you, frig me!" They both laughed but my friend and I were annoyed at them for insulting our hero.

Lou was unfriendly, as the newly famous often are, and I can see why they made fun of a name that sounded like "frig no" but I was too young at this point to appreciate Belfast humor, and too star-struck to take part in the ribbing, so I fired back, "Why don't you go back and say that to his face? That ought'a be good." Danny glared at me with his big, red gub and my dad called me a cheeky, wee shite.

I could always depend on him to make at least one horrifying remark when we were in public together, so much so that I hijacked a catchphrase from the black community – "It's a black thing. You wouldn't understand." Of course, I changed the word "black" to "Belfast." Except for a blessed few, most Americans really don't understand.

Even his apparently merciless comments about the old timer with the iron lung was probably an attempt to accept his own impending senior status and mortality. Joking about something is a pretty good antidote for fearing it, and much healthier. After all, the alternative - becoming a neurotic insomniac and complaining endlessly to anyone who will listen - stinks.

One of my da's old friends and business associates, Joe Porazzo, stood up in the church where his memorial service was held to say a few words. It all started out ordinarily enough until, to everyone's horror, he repeated a dirty joke my dad had told him decades earlier. I won't repeat it for the sake of decency, only to say that it contained the word "balls." Laughs mingled with gasps throughout the sanctuary. The laughs came from the Irish in attendance who understand this special brand of humor that is strongest in the places and times where and when it most shouldn't be. The gasps came from those who just don't get it and usually never will. The minister, who was sitting in a chair against the wall to the right of the podium, put his face in his hands after hearing this joke and kept them there for at least five minutes. Nobody was sure if he was crying or hiding laughter. I finally decided it was the latter and immediately liked him immensely.

 Four Green Fields

Joe's joke came as a surprise to me, too, because he isn't even from Belfast. As you may have guessed from his last name, he's Italian! Either my dad's sense of humor rubbed off on him after all those years or he felt telling an inappropriate joke and shocking the too easily offended, as my da so loved to do, would be the best way to pay tribute to him. Then again, Italians aren't exactly overly serious, either. In fact, I've never met an Italian I didn't like. If my father's spirit was sitting in that church that day, I'm sure he laughed his arse off hearing that joke again. And to those who were offended, he would've said what he always did - "F*** 'em if they can't take a joke."

This is yet another way I feel my da's influence. I whisper inappropriate jokes to my poor, frustrated wife in church constantly. She laughs a little, then catches herself and tells me to have some respect. Of course, it's too late because she already laughed. If she only got mad and mad only, I might stop. No, not really. Like my da, it would just make me worse. There's just something about the air in a church, so silent and thick with solemnity, that seems to demand irreverence.

In the 1940's and 50's Belfast my dad knew, there was nothing to do on Sunday's because the church basically outlawed fun, even going so far as to tie up and lock the swings at the public parks in case anyone tried to enjoy themselves for a minute. There was an old joke about a reverent old lady who even went as far as to tie up the swing in her canary's cage. Having nothing else to do, my da and his mates would duck into a different kind of church every week. They felt this was very open-minded of them, except for the fact that they weren't seeking spiritual enrichment as much as they were hoping to meet girls.

One such Sunday, his best friend, Lionel Frost, got a case of gas so wretchedly awful he almost cleared out the entire church, which was packed when they sat down. Odor-induced recidivism. Since they sat in the back, the stench didn't make it to the priest (or preacher, or rabbi,

depending on what kind of church they chose that day) so he couldn't
figure out what he had said to make everyone mad enough to storm out.
My da's other friends were red with embarrassment from being stared at by
the disgusted, angry bakes of the regular church-goers, wondering who
these interlopers were, but Lionel sat there staring intently at the preacher
with a faint, enchanted smile as if he were enraptured by his sermon,
thereby avoiding all guilt. They were finally the only ones left of the
formerly full house, except for a few who had probably lost their sense of
smell due to some injury.

When they went outside, my dad's most sensitive and gentile friend,
Harry "Hutchy" Hutchison, said, "For God's sake, Frosty, somethin'
must've crawled up your hole and died. That was bloody awful."

As always, Lionel, who was a legendary farter, answered, "Jealousy will
get you nowhere, my good man."

If Harry persisted in his criticisms, Lionel would shame him further by
saying, "That's just envy talking. You see, those weren't your pale, imitation
farts; your bread and HP sauce farts like the kind you let. God knows what
your ma's feedin' ya. Those were good, old-fashioned meat and potato farts
with a little dash of turnip thrown in."

Sometimes Lionel would talk to his farts before releasing them, saying,
"Speak, oh toothless one!" or "Speak, oh chocolate lips that never told a
lie."

Hutchy still went church-hopping with them after that day, but to avoid
further social mortification, he always ducked out immediately at the first
detection of one of Lionel's signature emissions.

Though I often wished I could make it through one movie or show or
dinner without my father attracting the wrong kind of attention to us, I will
go to my grave believing that it's far healthier to be irreverent toward
others and oneself than to be deadly serious all the time. What kind of a
world is that to live in? My father smoked, drank and never exercised but

made it to eighty-one anyway. I daresay laughter and his ever-present outlet – singing with all his heart - were both his exercise and his medicine.

chuckie our da

"It's not that the Irish are cynical. It's rather that they have a wonderful lack of respect for everyone and everybody."

- **Brendan Behan.**

After reading about the antics of Mark's beloved father, John, as well as that of J.P.'s dad (which you will come to see in the two stories following this one), I was inspired to write an ode to my own father, Charles, and to his never-ending sense of Irish wit, while also paying my respects to the poor, defenseless buggers who have unwittingly come into contact with it.

Some of you might be wondering if I'm taking the mick and making fun of a famous Irish saying, especially amongst those of us who speak our traditional language of Gaeilge. (Others call it Gaelic.) The true version of this saying has been heard in movies about Irish rebels who were involved with part of the uprising:

Tiocfaidh ár lá.

For those of you that don't speak our language and are currently trying in vain to say Tiocfaidh and making it sound like complete and utter shite, it is actually very easy. In spoken English, it is a version of my da's first name: Chuckie, which is slang for Charles.

Now, if you are sitting comfortably, repeat after me for your very first lesson in the Irish language:

Chuckie are laah.

There you go. Wasn't that simple? I should perhaps provide a footnote here for you readers to not say that out loud if you are ever in Northern Ireland, visiting a pub, having a few jars, and have no idea who is in your company. There is a good chance that you might be met with a few, muscular men surrounding you before finding your wee arse firmly planted outside on the cold Belfast pavement and without a pint to drown your sorrows. Nobody wants to end up with piles on their holes, either.

In its proper translation, Tiocfaidh ár lá (chuckie are laah) is an Irish saying which means, "Our day will come." Back home, it is used by many in the hope and belief that the twenty-six counties which make up Southern Ireland (Eire) and the six counties that make up Northern Ireland (Norn Iron) will become one country. Whether or not that will ever happen in my lifetime and with the current movement underfoot regarding Brexit (the exit of Great Britain from the rest of the European Union) is yet to be seen.

By the way, did you know that when the Patron Saint of Ireland, St. Patrick, chased all the snakes and demons out during the fourth century, they crossed the Irish border into County Down, took up residency at the Parliament Buildings, Stormont, and went on to form the Northern Ireland Assembly. This is a little-known fact created by yours truly! The other story floating about is he brought Christianity to Ireland through this method although I personally think my version of events is much better, so I do!

Sitting with my da today, I learned an awful lot more about his childhood I never knew before. This provided me with a greater understanding as to why he loves to be such a menace to society, while managing to keep it all in legal and good-spirited fun. Part of the reason is that he was raised in a large Irish Roman Catholic family (twelve were born, but two died in infancy, one was killed as a toddler, knocked down by a lorry while playing outside of her home at 4 Leopold Street in Belfast.) Everyone competed for equal space and attention, whether positive or negative. The latter usually prevailed.

One day, as a child, my da was having a heated argument with his older sister, my Aunt Maureen, with whom he is very close. (All these years on, he still loves to wind her up. It seems he knows which buttons to push and she falls for it every time. In fact, my cousin, who also has my da's namesake, takes great pride and joy in following in my father's footsteps and winding his ma much the same way. The poor woman gets no mercy.) Anyway, the disagreement began when their mum, my granny, Elizabeth, went to church on the Crumlin Road in Belfast. Like many other Catholic families, she did this faithfully.

During their time, mass was not simply held once on Sunday's. It was a daily event, with up to ten mass times per day starting at 6 a.m., and four masses occurring in different areas of the one church every hour! The main altar, two side altars, and one at the rear always had a full congregation with every mass that was said.

At some point, my Aunt Maureen left the family home at 348 Crumlin Road and made her way up to the church. She entered and took no notice of what was going on all around her, focused in staking her claim, then began screaming out:

"Mummy, mummy. Charlie hit me with a broom."

My granny was completely mortified as her daughter didn't hold back. Even to this day, my da takes every opportunity to tease my Aunt Maureen and tells her that she is not a McVicker.

Back in the day, literacy was a huge problem. The person going door-to-door to conduct the census had tremendous issues with spelling. Many of the families were poor and uneducated and did not know how to spell their own names. They could only say them. Thus, the last name of each family was often entered inaccurately. This same issue occurred within hospitals. Both my da and my Aunt Maureen were born in the Jubilee hospital in Belfast, whereas their siblings were born in the McVicker family home.

For whatever reason, my granny's surname was registered on my Aunt Maureen's birth certificate as McHugh, effectively making this my aunt's surname. It was seven years before my granny went down to the registry offices to have this corrected. However, as my da said, they do not issue a new birth certificate but only add an amendment. Thus, he takes great pride in telling his sister that she is not his relative due to her name being listed as Maureen McHugh. This makes my aunt see red every time, and she always tells my da their mum corrected this. Each instance, my da offers one of his unfiltered responses to get another rise:

"My mummy is not your mummy."

My aunt goes off the deep end. Even in their later years of life as they are now, my da takes great pleasure in bringing this up time and time again. As my ma would say, "he's full of the badness."

It seems my da was very much a holy terror in his youth. In speaking to Mark about this, as well as reading about his beloved father within these pages, I began to wonder if John Sidney Rickerby was Charles Timothy McVicker and vice versa. Perhaps Mark and I are blood relatives. Stranger things have happened, especially coming out of the Emerald Isle.

My da has a younger brother, Tommy McVicker, and would fight the peace out with him as well. As a result, both Charlie and Tommy had to attend confession at the same time. There was a priest in the area who used to give children a half-crown (which was two shillings and sixpence, or thirty pence) if they would take his name for their confirmation. My father was one of them. So many kids took Fr. Timothy up on this offer to have a spot of money, he had to stop asking kids if they would like to be called after him since it was costing him a small fortune.

When Charlie and Tommy arrived, there were ten confessional boxes located on either side of the church. Like a hockey dressing room, the name of each priest was above the confessional box. Knowing what lay in store, Fr. Timothy would put Charlie in one side, Tommy in the other, and sit between the two of them. As the wee slider curtains were drawn at the same time, both young lads started in unison with the priest, making the sign of the cross and muttering the opening prayer, "Bless me father, for I have sinned." Charlie started by saying, "Father. Tommy kicked me out of bed" only to be met with my uncle retaliating by saying, "Father, I did not kick him out of bed, Charlie kicked me out of bed." Thus, World War III began in the confessional.

They had created such a reputation for themselves by fighting back and forth, people flocked to the church and took up position among the pews to hear the riot unfolding between Charlie and Tommy McVicker, while Fr. Timothy tried his best to mediate the situation. They were instructed to then say three Hail Mary's and an Our Father, before being told to never do this again, then unceremoniously chucked out of the confessional by the priest. Laughter would fill the hallows of the church by everyone else in attendance, who had gathered not only for their own confession, but to witness this ritual. However, according to my Granny Elizabeth, I do know my Uncle Tommy was no angel. McVicker bloodlines run deep and although they fight the peace out, they fought hard for each other, too!

Another time, Charlie and Tommy were at the ten o'clock mass, which was held specifically for the children. The pews within the church, front to back, were chockablock with kids. The church was divided into two sections. Down the middle isle, girls were separated on the left and boys on the right. All looked towards the altar. The priest conducting the mass would climb a small spiral staircase (which happened to be in front of the girl's section) and entered the pulpit to give the day's sermon crafted for those in attendance.

Up there, the priest had a bird's eye view of the entire congregation, including Charlie and Tommy, who were up to their usual antics of excessive McVicker mischief. Of course, this immediately caught the attention of the priest.

In a loud voice, as if booming like the Almighty Father speaking from the heavens above, the priest stopped the sermon and bellowed,

"CHARLIE AND TOMMY McVICKER. COME UP HERE!"

Four Green Fields

Sheepishly, and as if the hand of God had been placed upon their shoulders, my da and uncle excited the pew they were sitting in. With all eyes now on them instead of the priest, they made their way towards the front of the church, genuflecting excessively in front of the altar so they wouldn't get shot by the priest or struck by a bolt of lightning. They then made their way up to the pulpit.

Once up there, the priest put Charlie and Tommy on full public display to the entire church – Exhibit C and Exhibit T – to show that children who acted like buck eejits during mass were going to be chastised before being sent to their subsequent execution in the confessional box with Fr. Timothy after the sermon concluded.

The priest continued speaking to his faithful congregation, explaining what happens to naughty children who show disrespect in the house of God. As their punishment, he then instructed both Charlie and Tommy to go and sit amongst the girls. This backfired, as my da and uncle considered this to be quite the positive reward. The two of them totally relished in the celebrity-like status the priest had unwittingly bestowed upon them, as they were now known by their first names by all of the wee girls who lived in the district.

Even though confession was said and having now been granted absolution for the umpteenth time for their sins, it was like water of a duck's back for my da and his brother. Their mischievous ways continued with other authoritative figures from the district. But, they were careful to protect their friends more so than themselves.

On one occasion, the two of them snuck into private property which contained an apple orchard and proceeded to make a small feast for themselves. A peeler (Note: this is someone known as a police officer in Norn Iron, not someone who removes their clothes for a living) who lived in the house came out and grabbed a hold of my Uncle Tommy. The peeler began to fire questions at my uncle while nearly pulling his ear off. While wailing out loud, Tommy's response was both immediate and honest:

"Officer! Officer! There's no one here with me! There's only my brother, Charlie, and he's up the tree!"

You can imagine my da's not-so-loving thoughts upon hearing his hideout being given up by his wee brother. The officer took Charlie and Tommy home to their da, my granda, William McVicker, who proceeded to knock the shite out of the two of them for causing him more grief.

My granda was a well-known barber on the Crumlin Road, and took care of many of the lads in the area. But, like many fella's, he had a terrible fondness for the drink: Guinness and Irish whiskey. Funny enough, his barber shop, which also doubled as his house, was conveniently located beside the Wheatfield pub (which sadly, along with the house, was burnt to the ground during The Troubles). As he went about his trade, fulfilling each punter's request of "short back and sides" or a "bee bop", he had a habit of excusing himself mid-cut. He would slip out the back door of his house, go in to the Wheatfield pub, and proceeded to enjoy a pint of Guinness followed by a whiskey chaser. He then went to place a bet at the bookies before returning to his unsuspecting client who was left waiting fifteen to twenty minutes. Strangely enough, not once did he miss a cut or nick the skin of a punter sitting in the chair with his shears, even though he was probably half blootered.

He hated doing kids cuts because their mummies had to stay with them. He would place a board across the arms of the chair to get them up high enough, but they wouldn't sit still. My granda took issue with this and wanted to strangle a few in the process. And here I am, his grandson, working as a social worker in the field of Child and Family Services. How the hell did that occur? Even though a bunch of heathens, perhaps Divine Intervention is at play here. There is no other way to explain this other than perhaps the Creator is rubbing my granda's nose into the clouds.

 Four Green Fields

Would you happen to believe Chuckie Our Da fancies himself as being a bit of an actor? While in port at the Dublin Wharf, my da's second ship, the Ulster Herdsmen, was used for the filming of a 1959 movie called *Shake Hands with the Devil*. Because of her age, the ship had been turned into a cattle boat and had been used to transport livestock down to Walls End on the other side of the Mersey in Liverpool. She also sailed to Glasgow and County Cork with livestock. The ship, which had been renamed the "Lady Carlow" for the movie, was procured for the deadly shootout scene between the British and the Irish Republican Army. The scene was set in 1920. The Ulster Herdsmen and her full naval crew were hired for one week, which meant that my da was in the film production. He was paid £5.00 per day for standing around and doing nothing other than acting an eejit which, by all accounts, came much more naturally to him.

He was working on the deck of the ship, playing the part of a deckhand. Thus, his clothing was extremely tattered which made him look more like a scarecrow than playing the part of an actor.

Although special walls had been erected to segregate the lead actors – which included James Cagney, Don Murray, Dana Wynter, and Glynis John – from the throngs of adoring fans and well-wishers who had gathered around, my da found himself caught up in and amongst the action. Coming off his ship, as he came around a corner, girls started screaming and cheering, throwing themselves at him and asking for autographs. Not being one to disappoint, Chuckie Our Da started signing their books with the following verse which was often used as Valentines wishes during my day:

My heart is like a cabbage,
I cut it up in two.
The leaves I give to others,
My heart I give to you.

I think fame and fortune went to his head thereafter as many young ladies were going crazy over him, swooning because they thought they had met a real-life film star because they had seen him on set during the filming of the dock scenes. He must have believed his popularity preceded that of The Beatles as he went to several screenings thereafter. However, in my mind, I think the priest who put up with him and my Uncle Tommy may have gotten a hold of the film producers and shook hands in exchange for his own deal with them as his devil.

It later came to light that my da's scene never made it past the cutting room floor, subsequently ending his movie career along with his fifteen minutes of fame. This answers why he attended so many screenings: he was hoping to see if he could find himself.

Upon completion of filming which ended his celebrity status, the Ulster Herdsman sailed to Rosslare Harbour, County Wexford. When they arrived, my da and his crewmates took shore leave and went to a dance. Once the local heavies learned they were from the North of Ireland, stealing all the girls since they had quite a few punts from their movie stint, they said, "You black northern bastards." My da informed them he was a Catholic. It made no difference. He was still a black northern bastard. It left me wondering how many confessional boxes were filled the next day, both fella's and sailors begging for clemency.

It was actually my older sister, Karen, who coined the phrase Chuckie Our Da shortly after our father (who aren't in Heaven, Hallowed be Thy Name) was home on one of his leaves from sea. This term of endearment came long after she learned he was not a telephone as she had thought. Since he was away for such long periods at a time, he could only call home while his ship was docked in port. Our ma, Catherine, would hand Karen the receiver and say, "Here. Talk to your daddy."

At this very moment, my da just informed me that while in port Plymouth, Portsmouth, or Torquay, he went to the same phone box every time and without fail. The cost of each call was two shillings for three minutes. But this particular phone box was broken and would keep spitting

Four Green Fields

his money back out at him after he had inserted it to extend his time when the pips went to say more money was needed. As a result of this, he would stay on the phone for hours, or until my ma got tired listening to all of his mad shite.

By his own honest admission, he robbed the post office blind and asked that I not add this story to the book in case the post office comes after him and puts him in jail. I am contemplating whether I should let this chance for peace of mind go beggin' or not.

As you have learned and will hopefully come to appreciate, sons such as Mark, J.P., and myself were and are often left to recoil into our bodies like turtles seeking shelter when our da's opened their gubs at what we would consider to be the most inappropriate and inopportune of times. Quite often, this involves perfect strangers.

For instance, I was recently out with my da picking up a couple of buns and four tins of soup. For a man who spent his life at sea, one would not expect a Chief Petty Officer Chef to be now choosing to eat like a bird and the kind of somber-looking meals that were fed to prisoners back in his day. (Speaking of which, that brings another story to mind about Chuckie and jail, but I'll get to that in just a wee minute.) Since he is apparently happy with his meal choices now, I really have nothing to complain about. The complaint I do have, however, is when he decided to approach a lady who was standing a short distance from us and minding her own business. My father left my side and felt it was a good time to launch into one of his moments. As usual, I was left wondering, "Jesus Christ. What is he up too now?" It is always an unpredictable and cringe-worthy event.

With his thick Belfast accent, he walked up to his unsuspecting victim. As if in slow motion, I reeled in horror as the words freely flowed out of his gub and onto the ears of the lady and everyone else within hearing distance. As usual, there was no filter to his comment.

"My mummy always told me to be nice to old ladies."

The woman who had been pre-selected as the recipient of his unrelenting lack of flattery looked at him but said nothing. It took a split second, which felt more like an eternity, to see if she truly understood what it was he said. Her face was blank, which meant a second opportunity for him to pounce.

"My mummy always told me to be nice to old ladies."

As this time, I did not know whether to make a hard exit stage right, turn on my heels and walk straight back out of the doors that I had only seconds before walked through, or make a run for it. It was clearly and painfully obvious to my forty-something year-old eyes, which have no cataracts and are not adjusted by corrective lenses, that the lady was more than twenty years my father's junior. He's well into his late seventies. Who's calling who old here? And why is that even appropriate? I was surprised she did not take her handbag and beat him about the head with it for in this moment, it was wholly warranted and very much well-deserved.

Picking up his chosen items, we made our way towards the cash register to pay. In hindsight, I should have made the choice to take the lead and head to the self-checkout to avoid further embarrassment. Of course, with hindsight always being twenty/twenty, we instead found ourselves in an empty register line along with the next unsuspecting young lady who was standing behind the till.

After placing the goods on the belt and scrutinizing her name, which had been scrawled onto her shirt with a permanent marker, my da launched into one of his moments of being exasperated, asking where she received her name from as well as her country of origin by way of immigration or through parents and grandparents. It did not matter either way.

Always having a story to tell, he then went into a long-winded banter about the origin of her name. From my observations, and as I tried to get to the end of the register aisle and out the door as fast as my legs would allow me, his words of wisdom were completely lost on her. There was no getting around him. Just like the cashier, I was stuck listening to another round of blarney. She most likely had absolutely no clue as to what he was waffling on about. That or she played a fantastic poker face as there was no response or emotions displayed while she scanned his soup and entered his buns onto the checkout screen. That was about to change.

His conversation with her continued and took on another form I have heard several times before about his life back home and in Canada. This is offered up to everyone and their dog whether they want to hear it or not.

"Do you know that I spent twenty years in jail?"

Obviously, he had gotten her attention this time with that remark since her eyes went wide and she finally responded with, "You did?"

"Oh, yeah. I'm serious. I spent twenty years in jail! You don't believe me, do ya? Huh?"

I wasn't sure if I should inform the girl that I was his probation officer and had him on a short leash, or if he had been released on a day pass from the nearest mental health institution and I was assigned to accompany him while he was out in the community. My moment of wishful thinking was immediately busted by his next comment.

"Actually, I have spent fifty years in jail in total. Fifty years!"

I didn't think the skin wrapped around our eyeballs could recoil any further into the backs of our heads until my eyes went much wider than what hers were, in disbelief since my father continued to tell his wee story. I stood beside him, completely mortified, wishing for the heavens to open and strike me with lightning or have an alien aircraft beam me up and whisk me away for cranial testing. My thoughts then shifted to perhaps asking why the man standing next to me and speaking with a thick accent from some faraway land, was telling her this. Then again, since my own voice sounds much the same as his, I likely would have been caught on as acting a flippin' menace and perhaps more so than my da.

The total came up on the screen and as my father went to pay, he saw an opportunity to pounce yet again. I knew what was coming but there was no escape. As I mentioned, with hindsight being as clear as day, I should have asked for a paper bag to put over my head to conceal my identity.

"It says I get forty-two dollars back."

The cashier shook her head ever so slightly with a look of contempt before checking the readout on the debit and credit pin pad. Not willing to let up, my da launched again.

"The machine is never wrong, is it? I'm telling ya, it says I get forty-two dollars back" before he broke into a sly grin.

As the cashier sheepishly handed my father his till receipt, he finally let her in on his story.

"I worked with the Trustees in the Remand Centre, teaching the inmates how to cook. I'm a chef of fifty years. I worked on ships back home in Norn Iron and sailed the world. I even sailed into your part of the world, in 1959, where your name comes from."

Why he told her this was not only lost on me but on her, too. It didn't faze him whatsoever, though, as he continued with his banter and without missing a beat.

"A ship is just a large, floating jail, so it is. I spent thirty years at sea as well. So, fifty years in jail altogether."

As the cashier offered my da a plastic bag for his messages, I quickly took this as an opportunity to stuff the four tins of soup and two buns into it so I could run away as fast as possible with smoke in my trail, perhaps to never return to that grocery shop ever again. Little did I realize but should have been aware, my da's antics would not stop there. He was just getting warmed up.

Our next stop was to have a cup of coffee together at a local restaurant that has served billions and billions. We had only just parked the car when

 Four Green Fields

my da saw two fella's that are associates of one of his former colleagues from jail. Seeing one of the two had crossed the carpark to his own vehicle while the other was still on the footpath, his unfiltered mouth went off again like a foghorn. The targets were locked into his sights.

"Here. Does your friend not want to help an old man cross the road?"

I couldn't believe what I was hearing. The response was swift while I kept my own head on a swivel as if I were playing a hockey game and seeing which way the body check was coming from. The fella who had crossed the carpark burst into a loud fit of laughter while his friend, who was probably closer in age to that of my father, gave an immediate response of his sincerest disapproval which echoed across the carpark.

"Ahh. Shut up!"

His rant continued for my da to shut his mouth, peppered with a few choice and very colourful swears. Thankfully, I did not have to referee the bantering erupting **Beneath Golden Arches** (yes, another shameless plug to a poem featured within my third book, ***One Cross to Bear: Humanity through Narrative Prose***.)

After this was complete, again my da took the lead, providing his usual approach of shock and awe to the cashier. Having witnessed this on several occasions, I always take a careful measurement if I should run to the register and make his order for him, cutting him off before he can speak, head to the farthest table so I can hide beneath it, or place the order at the self-serve kiosk. Somedays, I have even thought about leaving my car running in the carpark so I can run to it, jump and slide over the hood Starsky-style, and squeal my tyres out of there before they get a look to see who is with him.

Wallet in hand, my father moved in, prepared to use his dark, Jedi mind powers on the unwitting Guest Experience Leader (GEL), a sweet, lovely, engaging young lady by the name of Natalie. To her credit, Natalie has the patience of a saint. My da made his move.

"It's our first time here today so it should be free."

This time, there was a response from behind the screen that came with a nervous laugh.

"What was that?"

"It's our first time here today so it should be free."

"Oh. I'm sorry, sir. I can't do that for you."

My dad would not allow Natalie to recover and went into his next mode of unfiltered dialogue.

"Come on. You're not a very nice person, are ya? Are ya?"

Seeing that he was not going to get the engagement or the response he had hoped for other than a smile and a face that was turning red, my da went about to make his order which, in itself, sank like the Titanic. I can only share with you that being his son and having to go through this for the gazillionth time, it was like every other time. Purely agonizing!

"You're gonna gimme an extra-large coffee, triple-triple. You're gonna gimme another extra-large coffee, double-double. And you're gonna gimme three pancakes, three orders of three each."

I put my hands over my face and almost as if I were following a set of carefully crafted police instructions, stepped back and away from the counter. There's been numerous occasions I have asked and reminded Chuckie Our Da to watch his manners. If I received one dollar for every time I've had to explain him telling serving personnel they are "gonna gimme" is not polite, but demanding and inappropriate, I'd seriously have a small fortune on my hands. As my ma would say to us, she may as well be talking to the wall.

My da grew impatient while Natalie entered his selections as he repeatedly tried to scan his card as method of payment. Eventually, the order was successfully entered.

"That'll be $36.58, please."

My da was finally caught off guard and left rendered almost speechless.

"What? How much? Why's it so expensive? That can't be right. The last time I was here it was only $13.00. Why so much?"

Overhearing there was an issue and seeing a hungry crowd had gathered behind my da, I stepped in to figure out what was going on. When trying to order, the way he asked Natalie for his pancakes made it sound like he wanted twenty-seven in total. It would have been much easier if he would have asked for three sets of pancakes since there's already three in each tray. Words we were often told as kids – "I can't take you anywhere" – fluttered through my exhausted mind. If he held his tongue and choice of words when we first arrived and focused on the task at hand rather than trying to wind everyone up, the chaos might have been avoided. But that wasn't good enough for him as he erupted into his next round.

"Can I pay you next week?

Natalie responded, "Excuse me? Can you do what?"

My da repeated himself. "Can I pay you next week?"

Natalie looked at him with shock and said, "Oh. No, sir. We are not allowed to do that. I am only new to this job."

My da was relentless and kept winding her up further and said the last time he was in, the other girl who served him gave him his meal for free. He continued with his unfiltered engagement.

"Come on. You're not a very nice person, are ya?

Just as he had done in the other shop, he locked eyes on to her nametag.

"What's your name? Natalie? I have a niece called Nathalie. She has the letter haetch in her name and she's nice. Not like you."

At this time, I decided to step back in and asked my da to stop actin' the maggot. My fear was since there was a manager standing nearby who had heard my da say he gets his meals for free, one of the staff was going to end up getting reprimanded or losing their job completely.

Sitting down at an empty table, complaining the butter was too hard and the syrup not warm enough, my da finally decided to tuck into his plate. It didn't last long, though, as he told me he wasn't really all that hungry and left quite a bit of food untouched. Seeing that a staff member had come around to clear some tables, much to my dismay, he stated another one of his infamous lines.

"Since I've only eaten half of my meal, I get half my money back."

This was met with more looks that a deer caught in headlights would give. The staff member finally gave in and responded they weren't able to fulfill his request, giving him another opportunity of getting his claws in once more.

"What kind of a place are you running around here? I want to speak to the management. I'm going to report you."

Dying with embarrassment, I set about to quietly finish my meal and busy myself with a few sips of coffee. My da, however, does not sip, but rather gulps it down. Remember, this is an extra-large with three creams and three sugars. Heart attack central, anyone?

There is a method to his madness of emptying his cup as fast as he can. He takes the lid, throws it in the bin, and heads back up to the counter for a refill with the same measurements while asking for a new lid. I dare not leave my seat at that time, because who knows what comments are being chucked in the direction of the serving personnel. This is my moment of respite from the torture.

He refuses to drink his fresh java in the restaurant. Instead, he brings it home, splits it into three servings, and microwaves it when he fancies a cup later that day. I know he lived through a period of rations back in the Second World War, but in the 21st century as well? Providing that I too have finished my cup before we leave, he goes through the same routine of

 Four Green Fields

dumping the lid and ordering a second cup of heart attack central for the following day. I admire his sense of a penny saved is $2.36 earned – the price of an extra-large coffee.

As I was driving him home, my da said, "The days of chivalry are long gone." He went on to tell me that his mummy would tell him to be "nice to the old ladies" and immediately provided a firm example. While on the bus, if it was full of passengers and he himself was sitting and a lady got on, his mummy told him he needed to vacate his seat and allow the lady to sit down. Fair enough.

My da then went on to say he also used to help old ladies cross the road. As he did, he told me he would leave them in the middle of the road and go on his own way, saying, "Let them fend for themselves."

Feckin' hell! I swear if I had a mouthful of coffee when he made that statement, it would've been sprayed all over my windshield!

Thus, if anyone out there currently reading this story wishes to adopt my father, please send me a personal email. I don't need any details, just use the code name, "Chuckie Ar Daption." Satisfaction of embarrassment is fully guaranteed. Please note this adoption is final and no refunds will be accepted. I do ask, however, that you take this opportunity on at your own peril as this author assumes no responsibility whatsoever for his antics or your individual level of personal misery!

Not only have you been provided with an Irish language lesson here within this wee story, you have learned that Mark and I are still scratching our heads on how to figure out the unfiltered comments that rolled out of the gubs of our da's. J.P. is up next and will continue with similar madness that he also experienced.

But, before you get to that, I am sure that if Chuckie Our Da gets a hold of this story, your second Irish language lesson starts now and could very well be uttered from his unfiltered mouth:

Póg mo thóin.

Repeat after me: Pogue Mo Hone.

Quite simply translated into English, it means: Kiss my arse!

"Insanity does not run in my family. Rather, it strolls through, taking its time, getting to know everyone personally."

\- **Darynda Jones.**

When I read my co-author's story about his father being inappropriate and cursing in church, it brought back memories of my own father. My father could do or say anything at any given time, without warning. Part of me believes in Mark's theory that men like our fathers acted inappropriately because they wanted to see how people would react. That was definitely the case with my grandfather, Danny Houton. My father however, was a different kettle of fish. I am convinced that my father did not possess the shame gene.

My father was born and grew up in New York. Over the years I would pick up bits and pieces of his earlier life from the stories he would tell when he was in a more sharing mood. There was so much more I wanted to know, but we had an extremely strained relationship and were always at logger heads with each other. I had to take the helter-skelter pieces of his life jigsaw and try to make the pieces fit, but there were always large gaps. As a result, I never really got to know the man who was my father.

Although he was not very successful in any of his endeavours, it didn't stop him from having a go. Whether it was building and rejuvenating jaunting cars from a by-gone era (an era in which he did not participate), or building a covered wagon, identical to the ones that you would see in an old western film, to becoming a songwriter, there didn't seem to be any limit to the man's imagination. Today, we hear so much about the importance of failing from the top CEO's. The belief is that from failing, you learn. I'm sure my father would have liked to hear that instead of the negative remarks he got from my mother when his plans did not come to fruition. I could have admired him more if he hadn't been so abusive during my childhood years and as a result, I think it turned me into more of a rebel than I might have been, had circumstances been different.

Growing up in Ireland, surrounded by our mother's relatives, I realized that the insanity which I most probably inherited from my father was not one-sided. The Houton side, from the wilds of Malin Head, were not only as crazy as my father, but doubly as wild. It has been my experience that growing up in a crazy family brings about a plethora of feelings and thoughts. When you are really young and not effected by outside influences, you don't notice your family's eccentricities. Later on, when you experience other children and their parents, you begin to wonder why yours is so much different.

Speaking for myself, I then started to wonder why mine had to be so different. Later on, after much physical contact – not only from your own family, but from school yard brawls, you realize that you have to defend your crazy family. Then there is the final phase, where you accept who you are. I have been in the final phase for quite a while now.

pissing off the priest

"When the Gods wish to punish us, they answer our prayers."

- **Oscar Wilde.**

I suppose as Catholics go, we could be considered as "fair weather Catholics." From an early age, we attended all of the big holy days; Christmas, Easter…definitely Christmas and Easter anyway. Later on, we started attending more ordinary Sunday masses.

When we went to Mass in Malin Head, we rarely ever even made it inside the door. Whether we hung with the local men outside the back door or made it in, the Big Yank always went for the condensed version. That meant that when people started to go up to communion, I slipped out of the pew (if I had made it in through the front door, which was few and far between) and went in the opposite direction – out the back door. It would be nearly another ten years before I would have a clue as to what took place after the communion was over.

I can see how this does not sound like a breeding ground for a very stringent Catholic lifestyle, but something happened to the auld fella when he declared himself a writer. He didn't embrace the faith or "find Jesus" so to speak, but he insisted that we would go every Sunday morning to Mass in Bocan Chapel. I don't remember any of us being that bothered – I was the likely voice of rebellion, but it was only an hour out of my day on a Sunday morning, so I went with the flow. I figured we were making the transformation from fair-weather to all-weather Catholics and there didn't seem to be any harm in it.

That was until he whipped out the Sunday newspaper in the middle of the Mass and started reading to his heart's content. The bastard. Never before, nor since, have I witnessed a grown man sitting in the middle of church, on a Sunday morning, reading a Sunday newspaper like he was sitting alongside the banks of a canal, passing the time. I was literally on the edge of my seat. I expected the Priest to look down at any minute and single him out. Every minute that passed was like a minute spent on death row. Not only did I have to worry about the Priest, but there were my school mates to consider. How the hell would I explain his actions when I didn't understand them myself?

I don't know how we got through that first Sunday Paper Mass, but we did. I wouldn't give him the satisfaction of saying anything to him, but I was dying to know what had possessed him. The old lady was totally blind to any and all of his faults and to look at her, you would think that all fathers read the Sunday paper during Mass. The brothers and sister were too young to notice anything out of the ordinary. What an example he was to them. I was just as puzzled by the Priest's lack of interest. This was still the time when the local Parish Priest laid down the law more forcefully than the Police. I figured that he had to know the Big Yank was mental and everyone knows you ignore a mental person as best you can. Every Sunday from then on, he read the paper instead of listening to the Priest.

You would think that reading a newspaper in Church was bad enough, but with our auld fella, there was no telling where his depravity would end. You might very well ask; "what else could he possibly do to embarrass his family more than by reading the Sunday paper?" The answer was, he decided that he was going to have priestly powers. What I mean by that, was he brought a roll of "Silvermints" into the chapel with him and he waited until the Priest was giving out communion before sharing them.

Now, if you had never seen or eaten Silvermints, you might not grasp the significance of this. Silvermints are round, thick, white mints which melt in your mouth. They actually look like a fatter version of a communion wafer. It was no coincidence that he decided to pass around his mints at the exact time the Priest was handing out Communion. To further strengthen my theory, he asked his children to stick out their tongues as he placed mints on each of them.

When I saw this, I nearly had a heart attack. Was he looking to have a showdown with the Priest? Did he think he was some kind of Priest? Whatever was in his head, I would have given anything to find out. He told us about a game he used to play when he started driving – it was called "chicken." Young lads would drive their cars at each other, from opposite directions and the first to swerve out of the way would be the loser. It struck me that he was now playing "chicken" with the priest. I did not take any of his mints, though the others all did.

All of this occurred *inside* the chapel, of course. Outside was a different story, but just as twisted. My father could never be on time for anything in his life. Timeliness had no significance for him whatsoever. Years before his reading the Sunday newspaper in church stunt, he would drive us to primary school in the morning a half hour late and we only lived a little over a mile from the school. I got so fed up always being late and getting picked on by the class and then the teacher that I actually volunteered to walk to school. It wasn't an easy matter to "volunteer" either. I had to convince him I wanted to walk in order to get fit for playing school yard football.

For a man who was always late to everything, he now started to get to the chapel on a Sunday morning a half hour, or more, early. Yes, *early!* The first time I didn't pay much attention, but I did wonder why he parked inside the yard of the chapel. It was a small country chapel with a wall around it and two big wrought iron gates in the middle. There was plenty of parking on either side of the road, but he wanted to park *inside* the gates, practically on top of the front door. Everybody knew that the only one who got to park inside the gates was the local parish priest, Father Duffy.

Before you go thinking that our old fella wanted to show off his fancy car, let me assure you that it was anything but. Our old Mark 2 Cortina was so rusted out that the driver side floor board was just a big hole. My father had to jam the lid from a biscuit tin into it to keep his feet from falling out on to the road. We never washed it. In fact, I'm sure the dirt was the only thing holding it together. Fr. Duffy, on the other hand, had a very nice new motor, but he wasn't able to park it in his spot as some crazy man always beat him to it. I often wondered what the priest thought as he pulled up to his workplace on a Sunday morning and saw a beaten-up banger parked in his spot. To make matters worse, our father always made sure the gates were closed behind him after he drove in.

wait 'til your father gets home!

"No human being believes that any other human being has a right to be in bed when he himself is up."
- **Robert Wilson Lynd.**

With those six petrifying words, the Imperial Death March theme from the Star Wars film *The Empire Strikes Back* may as well have begun playing while we awaited the arrival of Darth Vader…

"Greg… search your feelings… I'm yer da!"

Then and there, life as my siblings and I knew it was about to change for us in an extremely drastic manner. More so perhaps for my older brother and myself. This usually occurred right after our insufferable behaviours exhausted the limits of our ma's patience. The damage was irreparable. We had succeeded in our attempts to drive her over the cliff on more than one occasion. Our fate was no longer in her hands, but in the hands of Chuckie Our Da!

As I alluded to in my introduction, my father had spent the first fifteen years of my life at sea. For about two or three weeks out of every year, he'd come home. Although he took pride in his work fixing up houses in Belfast that had been blown up, as well as ensuring his own wee castle was his joy and pride, it was the only time we'd see him. It also signaled doomsday for us all.

Our ma had corresponded all the years he was away by pen and paper and wrote several letters each and every month to him. My da, on the other hand, with his methodical and intricate system of keeping every file, pay stub, or piece of correspondence he's ever received since he was a child (he maintains this pattern to this very day), would save these letters and bring them all home in his suitcase when he was granted leave.

Of course, the first night was always brilliant for us to see him, as my mum would bring my siblings and me on what seemed to be the long, grueling drive over to Larne. We'd stand there and wait for the Sealink Ferry to get in, watching him disembark from the gangplank, all the while being bloody freezing as the Irish coastal winds cut us to the bone.

We'd make our way home again, excited for whatever presents he had picked up from the various ports he stopped at during his voyages. My da would go out and come back with a tin of Coke, a packet of crisps, and a chocolate bar for each of us from the Beverly shops at the bottom of the Carnmoney road. As there was an off-license there, he could buy himself a few tins of beer and a wee bottle of scotch for our ma, along with a couple of bars of Cadbury Fruit and Nut. We couldn't have been happier with the gifts we received and our spoils of sweets, which we would take no issue or measurement in stuffing our gubs with.

The magic continued as we were given a chance to stay up a little bit later and granted the opportunity to try and take advantage of the situation by using our endearing Irish charms against our da, who was now very much at home with us all. Yet those six words of mass destruction my ma had threatened us with still rang out like church bells within our heads.

The four of us crawled all over him, praying our efforts at affection would help soothe away from his memory all of the bad behaviours my ma had captured within those countless letters. We'd use every single trick a Belfast child could think of against their father in the hopes he wouldn't beat us half to death.

No matter our efforts, and although written well after our time as children but to use this wonderful analogy created by one of my most favourite of authors, J.K. Rowling, we could not summon the brilliance of Hermione Granger or Harry Potter and use a Time Turner to go back in time to make all of our wrongs right. Simply using our fingers and pointing an imaginary wand at his suitcase while uttering the words, *"Accio ma's letters"* would not work either. And although there were times that thoughts had drifted through my mind of running to his suitcase and eating those letters if it meant escaping a perilous death, I couldn't muster up the courage, as that would have led to a fate worse than what was already in store for us all.

We had to resort to giving him kisses on his stubbly face, as he hadn't shaved before coming home, but that was more like trying to snog a hedgehog. In our minds, our measures of subtly planning how we were hopefully not going to have to plead our cases in front of the judge, jury, and executioner, had seemingly paid off. Our charms and affections worked. We were happy, as was my da. Life was brilliant.

But then it was time to meet our maker. Our plans died with the night's sleep.

On the first Saturday morning he was home, due to his own naval schedule and during the waking hours of the dead, my da dragged our weary arses out of bed instead of allowing us a wee lie in a bit longer within our toasty kips. Our bed sheets were torn clean from our bodies while we lay shivering, trying to shake off the night's sleep and focus on what was happening. "C'mon, get up, you've got work to do," followed our rude awakening.

We were not allowed any cartoons. No speaking while the BBC news was on. And if the school lockers he had built for us were not immaculate by naval standards (even though we did our best to keep them clean), our belongings would end up out in the front garden for us to fetch in our pajamas and bare feet, as our guddies had also been bunged out the front door and into the garden!

Our friends didn't need to watch cartoons either, and they could have saved their parents from buying a TV license by gathering on the front street while watching our belongings flying through the air. This would be followed by four skinny wee friggers fighting among themselves as to who owned what, scavenging to pick up their school supplies and incomplete homework assignments.

There was no mercy from Lord Vader also lovingly known as Chuckie Our Da. He did not bring his thumb and forefinger together almost in a pinch with his arm outstretched, using his dark Jedi mind powers against us while taking deep breaths. Just the very sound of his voice, the look in his steely eyes, and the dark hair on his arms was enough to frighten the shite out of us all! Thankfully he did not have a Lightsaber, otherwise we'd all have been struck down and our crumpled cloaks would have ended up in the front garden, along with the rest of our belongings.

Cue Obi Wan Kenobi: ***"Alice. You will give Charlie shite!"***

"Wait 'til your father gets home." Those six disturbing words always signaled doomsday for us, as the empire really did strike back! Although, when my da's older sister, my Aunt Alice, learned about the torment her wee brother unleashed to us as children when he came home from sea, she gave him a piece of her mind. In doing so, she gave me peace of mind!

 Four Green Fields

Nosehead Versus Chief Littlefoot

"We think we're living in the present, but we're really living in the past."

- **John Banville.**

I used to joke with my dad that he was "rock candy with a gooey center" – or tough on the outside but mushy and sentimental on the inside. When I was a kid, he would rub his whiskery cheek against my cherubic one and we would both laugh while I struggled to escape the chafing, then he would kiss the same cheek and tell me he loved me. A minute later, he would give me a hard time about something, anything, just to get a rise out of me. As I mentioned, I was a sensitive kid and took these jabs personally until I realized it was just another way he showed affection. I didn't come into my own until I was in my early twenties. It wasn't easy because I was often dueling with an Irish Don Rickles.

Slagging in America is called "firehouse humor", a merciless brand unique to the manliest men, which involves desecrating anything the other holds sacred, then laughing unguardedly until the victim thinks of an equal or hopefully greater insult.

In this respect, Belfast, Northern Ireland, where my father was born and raised, was one, large firehouse. The put-down artists who mastered the art of verbal devastation were both feared and revered. My dad was one such master, as evidenced by his perpetual black eyes. As a youth in Belfast, he almost always had a fresh one while the last one was still yellowing.

This instinct toward disrespect is both the cause and effect of the two main stereotypes about the Irish – drinking and fighting. The drink loosens their tongues, then the punches start flying. As Brendan Behan wrote, the Irish "have a wonderful lack of respect for everything and everybody."

During my most awkward teenage years, if I developed a zit, I could always depend on dear, old dad to zero in on it and say something like, "Are ya growin' another head there, laddy?" He loved an audience so comments like these were usually made when my girlfriend was with me, and followed up with something like, "Oh, by the way, a geologist called. He wants to measure your pimple to see if it's a hill or a mountain." My girlfriend struggled not to laugh but my brother and mom laughed heartily, feeling no compulsion to spare my feelings, as I writhed in embarrassment. A good time was had by all, except me.

I envied my older brother Paul for his ability to smile benignly and even give a little chuckle when he was the subject of this kind of abuse. Sometimes he would even retaliate with insults of his own. But I was still too young and afraid of the old man to try that. Paul finally took pity on me one day and said, "Look, you can't let him see he's getting to you or he'll just lay it on thicker. Either smile and shrug it off or start practicing some comebacks. You've got to earn his respect, man!"

That was great for him but, aside from my hypersensitivity, or perhaps because of it, I had a problem my brother didn't have – blushing. I was plagued by it. As soon as I felt the slightest embarrassment, I became a human thermometer. The red would rise upward from my neck until it looked like my head might explode. It was startling to witness. Of course, my dad would capitalize on this, too, by saying something like, "Why are ya blushin' like a wee schoolgirl?" Then I would turn from red to light purple and he would say, "Look out! She's gonna blow!" He would even run out of the room for effect. Everyone couldn't help laughing as I sat there with my ears burning.

This was probably my dad's way of toughening me up, and eventually he did. I just wish it would have happened sooner.

I finally employed my brother's advice one Thanksgiving evening after dinner. We were all sitting in the living room watching *It's a Wonderful Life* on TV. I had kicked my shoes off because the house was too warm when I

 Four Green Fields

sensed his eyes on me like Superman laser beams. I slowly looked over and saw him with that self-satisfied, pre-insult look on his face, and immediately knew he had lined up a real zinger for me.

Preparing myself, I warily said, "What?"

"You have the most underdeveloped feet I've ever seen on a man," he replied very matter-of-factly.

"Really?" I said. "That's it? That's all you could come up with?"

He smiled proudly and said, "Mm-hm."

I tried to ignore it and went back to watching the movie but, as expected, he wasn't finished.

"You know, if you were a Native American, they'd probably name you Chief Littlefoot."

My girlfriend started laughing and said, "Wow! He's right. I never noticed how tiny your feet are."

That did it. Turning my woman against me was the last straw. Fortunately, I was ready for him this time, and had even rehearsed a few zingers of my own for just such an occasion. I said, "Well, you have the most overdeveloped nose I've ever seen on a man."

He was shocked for a moment, then said, "Have you ever considered working for a circus sideshow? You could be Mark, the Man with Baby Feet."

Struggling to stay calm, I replied, "It's a wonder you don't have a bad back from lugging that schnozzola around everywhere."

Even more shocked that I was finally fighting back, he got meaner, like a cornered animal. He said to my girlfriend, "I hope you have big feet to balance his out, darlin', because if you don't, any babies you two have are going to inherit those freakish, wee stubs."

This is the point where I normally would have blushed and surrendered, but not this time. The peasant was revolting against the tyrannical king, and I already had my next boulder loaded into the catapult.

"You know, pop, that beak of yours could double as a weapon in a gang fight. You could swing it around and take out five, six guys, easy!"

Everything degenerated from there. He repeatedly called me Chief Littlefoot and I countered with Nosehead, Bad Back, and Weapon Face in rapid-fire succession until my mom yelled, "That's enough now, boys. Can't we just have a nice, quiet Thanksgiving?"

Unaccustomed to such resistance, he resentfully went back to watching *It's a Wonderful Life* as an uncomfortable silence permeated the room. My brother gave me a silent, secretive smile and thumbs-up. I had called the old man out and held my own for the first time.

I felt great about it until the next morning when my mother called and asked, "Why did you have to call your dad a Nosehead?"

"What's wrong?" I asked.

"I caught him in the bathroom this morning examining his profile," she explained. "He was massaging the bulb. I asked him why and he said, 'Paul has disappointed me in a lot of ways but he never called me a Nosehead."

I couldn't believe it. The insult king was insulted. I said, "If he can't take it, he shouldn't dish it out" but felt guilty later and called him to apologize. We had a good laugh about it. However, after that night he was much less inclined to insult me, either because he was proud I had finally become a real man, or he just didn't want to be called Nosehead again.

My dad passed away in December of 2014. In fact, he left years earlier due to Parkinson's Disease and Dementia. They took everything from him, including his wit. I wish he were here to take the mickey out of me once more. Oh, how I would enjoy it.

Leprechauns, Giants, & Banshees

Uncle Alfie to the Rescue

"If you cannot get rid of the family skeleton, you may as well make it dance."

- **George Bernard Shaw.**

My father felt that leprechauns, banshees and the like were created or at least perpetuated by the non-Irish, particularly Americans, more than they were by the Irish themselves. However, he didn't feel the same way as a child, largely because of an uncle who filled his head with all sorts of wild tales. I was blessed to meet him on a trip home shortly before he passed away. What a character he was. I will introduce you to him through a story from my father's memoir ***The Other Belfast – An Irish Youth***, retold by myself for the purposes of this collection.

My dad must love the irony – as a child, when he would start to tell his stories, I would often say, "I heard that one already!" But when he was diagnosed with Parkinson's Disease and was starting to forget, I asked him to tell me the stories again so he wouldn't forget them or who he was – or more accurately, who he had always been to me. Now that he's gone, I tell his stories for him, and am proud and happy to do so.

I daresay his youth in Belfast from 1935 to 1957 was a far sight more interesting than mine was in spread-out, impersonal Los Angeles. We also moved fifteen times before I was fifteen years old so I didn't have the benefit he had of growing up in one place and developing lifelong or at least youth-long friendships. Maybe it was homesickness that made my parents chase the end of the rainbow moving so much. Maybe they didn't even know what they were looking for. It was hard on my brother and I at the time. My brother Paul was three years older than I and started getting into trouble in his early teens. I did, too, though nowhere near the degree my brother did. He would later spend eight years in jail and die of a drug overdose at the age of thirty-seven. He went from a fair-haired athlete to a heavily-tattooed, toothless convict. Only I remembered the boy I played baseball with in the street under a cheerful sun when we were clean and everything was still possible.

However, I am my father's son, too, so I inherited some of the madness Belfast imbued him with, as well as his more sensible side that sustained him in business. This inherited sensibility kept me from plummeting into the abyss many times when my wild side had taken me to the brink. My brother didn't seem to get any of that. He went wild early and stayed that way.

But the times we act sensibly don't make for good stories. We don't write about how comfortable a bed was when we go to some exotic location. We write about a drunk bus driver of an overcrowded bus on a windy mountain road. Conflict is the essence of drama. Thus, the mad side of me led me to create some stories of my own, but how can I beat my father hiding under a table with his mother and sister while a Nazi blitzkrieg roared overhead? How can I compete with the wannabe Al Jolson's lined up on one knee up and down the street, performing for the line waiting to get into the Park Picturehouse? How can I overshadow Buck Alec and Silver McKee, the hardest of hard men Belfast has ever known? My dad told me about these characters and his adventures on the streets of Belfast; streets which seem to both create and inspire writers, as is evidenced further by the fascinating lives of my two fellow authors and their ability to relate their experiences.

Like most Americans, I love all things Irish – north or south – and proudly put my leprechaun (King Brian) on my front porch every year. I look forward to the day when my daughters are old enough to withstand the banshee and ghost chariot in my favorite Irish-themed movie co-starring a leprechaun of the same name, *Darby O'Gill and the Little People*, a movie made even more enjoyable by the fact that Uncle Alfie was exactly like him. So, without further ado, here's my story about him.

My parents came to Canada then America from Belfast in their twenties. I returned with them when I was three but didn't remember much except a few faint impressions, so in the summer of my sixteenth year, they decided it was time for me to meet my Irish relatives again. I was a typical teenager, more interested in going to the beach with friends back home in California than I was in visiting somewhere summer seemed to have abandoned. However, my sour attitude was obliterated when I met my father's maternal uncle, Alfie McKee. He was so irrepressibly cheerful, my adolescent ennui didn't stand a chance.

As a boy, my father struggled futilely to connect with an unhappy and work-obsessed father. Every day, his da would come home, hide behind a newspaper, and mumble "shut up" to his mother, who was usually complaining about inadequate funds to fuel her shopping addiction. They never acknowledged birthdays or Christmas and never told my father or his sister Olga they loved them.

It was the Great Depression but an even greater one existed within the walls of his home. My dad made the most of it by finding some happiness with friends, but it was a sad life for a boy. Then he met his Uncle Alfie. He was ten years old and needed a strong but loving hand to guide him. It was perfect timing.

On the day they met, my dad was playing marbles (or "marlies" as he called the game) on the sidewalk with some friends. Alfie came roaring up the street on his Royal Army motorcycle with sidecar, wearing a leather jacket, skullcap and aviator goggles. He stopped next to my dad and his friends and turned off the engine. They all stared in amazement at the exotic visitor. Alfie was always off on some adventure so my father had never met him.

He took off his goggles and asked, "Would one of you boys be John Sidney Rickerby?"

"That's me," my father said, a little scared.

"Well, you're just the one I'm looking for then!"

It was like Hagrid finding Harry Potter. Alfie walked over, reached into his pocket, took out a gold coin and handed it to him.

"That coin was given to me by a leprechaun," he said. "It's yours now."

My father examined the coin. The edges were irregular, and it was covered with strange symbols.

Alfie continued, "I was ridin' through a forest one night when I saw the wee man standin' in the road. I swerved to avoid runnin' him over and crashed me bike into a ditch. Knocked meself out cold. When I awoke, I found this gold coin in me pocket - the leprechaun's gift for sparin' his life."

My father and his friends were entranced. He found out years later the coin was actually from ancient Rome and common to collectors, but by then it didn't matter because he had spent some important years with what he believed was a magic amulet in his pocket.

"I see I interrupted a game o' marlies," he said. "D'ya mind if I join ye?"

They eagerly accepted. Alfie sat on the sidewalk with them.

"But ya haven't any marlies," one of them said.

"Ach, sure I do," Alfie replied. With that, he unceremoniously scooped out one of his eyeballs, wiped it on his jacket lapel, cocked it with his thumb and forefinger, and sent it scooting along the sidewalk, capturing three marlies in the process. My dad and his friends were equal parts mortified and fascinated. Alfie noticed them staring and asked "What?" as if he didn't know. They all pointed at his disembodied eye.

"Oh, that? Don't be frightened, lads. It's just an old injury. Here, have a closer look."

He handed them his eye and they passed it around.

"Aren't you afraid of scratching it," one of them asked.

"Ach, it never fooled anyone when it was new, either," he joked. "Now then, I think I'll say hello to that sister of mine. Can I have me eye back?"

They returned it to him. He polished it, spit on it for lubrication, popped it back into the socket, and walked into the house. My dad followed him inside and watched him tease his mother as she prepared tea. He winked at my dad occasionally until her annoyance turned into laughter. His charm was irresistible. As my dad grew up, Alfie became more of a father to him than his own was able to be, giving him advice in romance and helping mend more than one broken heart.

When I met Alfie, he had white hair and was wearing khaki's, a navy-blue greatcoat and a fisherman's cap. He looked like Popeye in his later years. I received the same advice from him about girls that my father had decades earlier, and needed it because I had asked a girl named April back home to "go with me" only days before I left. She had closed her eyes, expecting a kiss, but I was too shy to deliver it. I was kicking myself over it and told Alfie about it. He said, "Listen, son, no matter what girls say about wanting nice, polite boys, what they really want is one who'll give 'em a respectable kiss with no apologies." I stared at her wallet-size school photo that night and decided to kiss her properly when I got home.

We were all relaxing on the beach one morning when Alfie said to me, "D'ya want ta hear how I lost me eye?" I eagerly said yes. I knew the beginning of a good story when I heard one. He looked out to sea for a moment and said, "My regiment got a few day's furlough. A few other fellas and I were staying in a cabin in the forest. They all went to the village one night but I stayed home. A few hours later, there was a knock at the door. I opened it but nobody was there. I closed the door and turned to see a human skull by the fireplace, still with wee bits of hair and skin on it. I took the poker, stuck it into the skull's eye, and threw it back outside. The next day, I lost the very same eye. It was the skull's revenge!"

I practically fainted. What a story. A few days later, I was having lunch with my parents and Alfie's wife, Flo. I mentioned his story about the skull. She laughed and said, "Ach, he didn't tell ya that old yarn, did he? That's a load of malarkey. The eejit lost his eye because he forgot to duck during a hand grenade training exercise."

Normally, I would have been upset about being lied to, but Alfie told the story with such aplomb, I laughed along with everyone else.

When I arrived back home, I went to my girlfriend's house, planning to be braver, as Alfie advised. She opened the door, said "I don't want to go with you anymore", then slammed the door with no explanation. I cried all the way home. I later learned a "friend" had been telling her lies about me while I was gone to win her for himself. I was heartbroken to lose her, but also over the betrayal by a friend.

April would tell me over a decade later that my ex-friend didn't get anywhere with her either, but for the opposite reason – he was too forward – or as they would say in Belfast, he was always trying to get her knickers off. She finally sent him packing, too. I sure wish she would have told me sooner, though, because I was in a miserable state for months after that abrupt dismissal.

Alfie called that week, during the sad end of my sixteenth summer, and asked to speak with me. He wanted an update about the girl. I told him what happened. He said, "Ach, I'm sorry, son. I know it hurts, but neither of them are worthy of you. You go and find yourself a girl who'll appreciate a fun, kind-hearted young man like you."

I felt better immediately. That's all a teenager really needs – someone who really cares about them, not some jaded adult who will write off their real heartache as trivial, overly dramatic, puppy love. Alfie had been there for my father when he needed him most. Thirty years later, he was there for me, too. When he passed away, we cried together. Alfie had helped raise us both.

caᴠe ḣill

"Vision is the art of seeing things invisible."

- **Jonathan Swift.**

The next three pieces of reflective prose I am sharing all come from my third book, **One Cross to Bear – Humanity through Narrative Prose**. I wrote twenty new compositions over a two-week period while on a road trip to Alberta, Canada with Ciarán. As I mentioned, he is a goalie of ten years and was invited to participate in a rookie camp with the WHL Calgary Hitmen.

From Alberta to Belfast, the Cave Hill was a bit of a mystery to us as kids, as were much of our surroundings in Newtownabbey. Nevertheless, we passed under this basalt formation more than enough times on our journey along the Antrim Road while going into Belfast to visit our granny, aunties, uncles and cousins, or just for a day out in the center of town. Unfortunately, we never really paid much attention to the significance of it.

It seems the longer I have been away from my homeland, the more I have placed an emphasis on trying to find out as much as I can about the history of it all. Efforts are made to go back to so many childhood places to try and reclaim the lost footprints of yesteryear and the memories that were left behind there along with those who helped to create them in the first place.

If this magnificent formation could indeed reveal the secrets that have been kept by it throughout the centuries, I can only imagine what stories the Cave Hill would have to tell. That includes trying to come to an understanding regarding a dark period known as 'The Troubles', if that is at all possible...

Cave Hill

In original Gaelic, Beann Mhadagáin,
According to Irish mythology.
Spanning the modern province of Ulster,
The ancient territory of Ulaid.

Lying peacefully on the mountainside,
Stories of rebellion overheard.
No matter the history each century brought,
You've never spoken a word.

The rugged look of a sleeping giant,
With resemblance to Napoleon's Nose.
Upon discovering your splendid formation,
The Travels of Gulliver arose.

Towering above the City of Belfast,
Outstretched along the Cave Hill.
Safeguarding the sandstone castle below,
Yet your body is peacefully still.

Looking out towards Titanic's dry dock,
The building of bow and keel.
The cranes of Samson and Goliath,
The banging of metal and steel.

Saying farewell to her birthplace,
Towards her maiden voyage of death.
No hand was raised to wave goodbye,
You never even muttered one breath.

Peregrine falcons soar your mountaintop,
With grace, they scour the sky.
Their prey dead locked, blood now spilled,
Yet you've never blinked an eye.

Exploring each secret hidden within you,
Only for those who dare to be brave.
McArt's Fort ruins at your highest point,
The treacherous entrance to each cave.

In all the years I've been away,

My heart it hungered to be near.

Hiking upon your sacred ground,

I believe you know I'm here.

The landscape that you've shown me today,

Scrabo Tower, the Mountains of Mourne.

Breathtaking views beside our sleeping giant,

The view, my memoir, you'll adorn.

Giant's Causeway

"The experiment of poetry, as far as I am concerned, happens when the poem carries you beyond where you could have reasonably expected to go."

\-   **Seamus Heaney.**

One of the greatest wonders of the world to behold is that of the Giant's Causeway, situated within the Nine Glens of Antrim.

Every time I speak to people who say they've gone to Ireland for a vacation, I find myself asking if they decided to go to the north of Ireland. Sadly, and more often than not, it is met with a resounding 'no' as tourists tend to hit the streets of Dublin and then head around to the south and west from there. The beaten path of tour buses and local attractions always take precedence.

There aren't many who decide to take a trip up to the north, unfortunately, due in part to the residual effects of 'The Troubles' as well as the yearly marches that take place. Friends of mine from both sides of the community tend to leave during that time, as it quickly becomes fueled into an inferno of hatred along with the fires that light up the night sky and burn within the communities that celebrate. Exactly what are they celebrating? Burning pallets stacked 80' high for a battle from 1690? Yet people tell me to stop living in the past and writing about my experiences?

Regardless, I have gone to this stunning location on several occasions, starting as a child on a day trip from school, returning as an adult to show family and friends around, and in my dreams. As you will see from my next piece of reflective narrative prose, it never ceases to amaze me there is always something just waiting to not only take my breath away, but the breath of each person who dares to stand among the folklore and legend of our Irish giant…

Giant's Causeway

Standing your ground for countless years,
Along the North Antrim Coast.
Ferociously battled by Atlantic waves,
Irish legends and myths to boast.

The basalt rock that lies within,
Offers unbridled splendor and pleasure.
Stepping stones, the Wishing Chair,
So many myths to treasure.

Fionn Mac Cumhaill was his name,
Standing sixteen meters tall.
The Irish Giant we know him as,
In truth, was actually quite small.

For Benandonner, a rival giant,
From across the sea of Moyle.
Residing on the Isle of Staffa,
His lair overflowed turmoil.

Benandonner stood much larger in size,
Yet Fionn was rather brave.
He built a pathway across the sea,
And over to Fingal's cave.

For here he'd met his bride to be,
A giantess all the same.
With our Fionn she fell in love,
Oonagh was her name.

Exhaustive work, the Causeway built,
Columned stones of honeycomb.
Fionn promptly fell asleep,
Before welcoming Oonagh home.

A war of words was brewing,
A challenge for a fight.
Bigger and stronger was Benandonner,
Giant footsteps in his might.

As he walked along the Causeway,
North Antrim in his eyes.
Oonagh bundled up her husband,
A giant now in disguise.

Approached did Benandonner,
The challenge his first test.
Asking where the "coward" was now,
To show him who was best.

Not ready to accept defeat,
Oonagh pointed to her guise.
Seeing the swaddled baby giant,
Fear swept right through his eyes.

"If that's the size of your baby,
His father must be quite huge."
And in his wake, the causeway ripped,
Benandonner sought refuge.

Fionn stands watch now over his land,

Be respectful when you approach.

Do not challenge a trial of strength,

Or upon his land, encroach.

For within his home, you'll find his boot.

And be cradled in its size.

Look directly up above you,

And see his majestic eyes.

Now nestled within his footprint,

Your presence, notably small.

Choose a note, play the basalt keys,

Organ Pipes stand dauntingly tall.

Or light a fire, and keep him warm,

Smoke through the Chimney Tops.

Then pluck a string upon his Harp,

The music never stops.

The backdrop set, the story told,
He's waiting right here for you.
Our Irish Giant, Causeway home,
The legend of Fionn Mac Cumhaill.

Banshee of Dunluce Castle

"Your feet will bring you to where your heart is."

- **Irish Proverb.**

Having had the wonderful opportunity of standing on the grounds and within the ruins of this once mighty structure, which is located a short jaunt away from the Giant's Causeway, I assure you the legend of Maeve Roe, now a Banshee, is very much alive.

A hot sunny day with nary a wind blowing through yet suddenly, an icy cold chill pierces throughout your entire body. Goosebumps light up like welts on your arms and legs. All the while the hair on the back of your neck is standing to attention like a soldier waiting for orders. That is just what you will experience when you first enter onto the grounds before exploring the secrets that have been kept within the historic walls of this family fortress.

Again, when speaking with people who have chanced a trip to the North Antrim coast, they will often say they took a tour to the Causeway. And after learning the histories of our Irish Giant, they pass on by this beautiful castle, which is an utter shame. They have no idea on what they're missing out on. If they are connected to their inner energy and the flow from it, then they will understand the story I am about to tell and how they can reach out and enjoy what secrets lie within. Not only can this be considered a haunting experience, but one of a spiritual awakening.

Thus, if ever you are home in Ireland, make this a day trip. Do not be frightened if an icy blast of cold air passes straight through you. It is simply one of the inhabitants letting you know that they are aware of your very presence in their home, and that they are keeping watch…

Banshee of Dunluce Castle

Its Celtic name, Dún Libhse,
And the stories it once did boast.
The kitchen walls now lie in ruins,
Below the rugged North Antrim coast.

Atop a rocky promontory,
Dunluce serving its duty.
This fortress precariously perched,
Surrounded by picturesque beauty.

Transformed from fortress to castle,
Yet balanced majestically.
A mighty medieval stronghold,
Against an unforgiving Irish sea.

Once occupied by Lord MacQuillan,
At war with the O'Cahan clan.
To cement his place in history,
He hatched a deviant plan.

An offering to marry her cousin,

To Richard Oge, her hand set to wed.

His fiercely beautiful daughter,

Maeve Roe, would rather be dead.

The love of her heart was Reginald,

A bitter rival to her father's power.

In his attempts to displace this union,

Locked his child in the north-eastern tower.

Longing to be in her lover's arms.

Maeve Roe's mindset quite fraught.

Spending lonely days and nights trapped here,

Sweeping the floor, completely distraught.

While Lord MacQuillan raided a rival's land,

One stormy, windy night to dare.

Beneath Dunluce, in the Mermaids Cave,

He ensured Reginald would be waiting there.

Four Green Fields

Released from the desolate turret,
By a servant who carried out the deed.
Leading her down to pending freedom,
A consequential escape they would heed.

Their rowboat smashed to smithereens,
By wind, rock, and turbulent wave.
As Reginald's body washed ashore,
Maeve Roe sank to a watery grave.

A wailing cry of sorrow heard,
Her legendary ghost now born.
As each MacQuillan met their fate,
Their pending death she'd mourn.

The years that passed thereafter,
Servants would always cower.
Never gathering dirt nor dust,
She swept MacQuillan's tower.

During stormy nights for centuries,
Blanketed by rain-soaked cloud.
Alone, down by the rocky shore,
Stands Maeve Roe in a White Shroud.

Delicately embark upon these windswept ruins,
Explore the secrets that are hidden within.
The spirits of those who still remain here,
Their presence will make you whim.

Tread carefully upon their sacred ground,
While the sun shines down on you.
Suddenly awoken by an icy chill,
Ghosts of yesterday pass straight through.

Forever looking out from her prison tower,
Awaiting her rescuer, an eternal hassle.
Maeve Roe's troubled soul, trapped within the land,
The Banshee of Dunluce Castle.

The Troubles

Following in my Father's Footsteps

"Anyone born and bred in Northern Ireland can't be too optimistic."

- **Seamus Heaney.**

I fly to Belfast for the first time alone and walk the wet streets, thinking of him, how much he loved this place. Sixty years in California and he never gave up on her.

It's just a city like any other. Why couldn't he forget it? Sure a man could love any place if only because that's where his life happened. That soil caught his blood and sweat and most sacred tears. The love is only deepened if that land is troubled. A place can be like a wayward child - their mistakes and troubles only soften our hearts all the more.

I pass chips in the façade of a hotel wall, remnants of dark days. I pull up my collar and wander away from the city to a quieter neighborhood. I pass a group of children playing and hear in their joyous whoops and already thick Belfast accents the life I might have had. The sun splits the clouds. A sun shower rainbow forms over us like a giant ribbon.

And in that moment, I understand why my father never stopped caring about Belfast, and why he always stopped to talk to the children. It had more to do with these little heirs to these sacred streets than it ever did with him.

PRODS AND TAIGS

"We all want progress, but if you're on the wrong road, progress means doing an about-turn and walking back to the right road; in that case, the man who turns back soonest is the most progressive."

- **CS Lewis.**

(From The Other Belfast – An Irish Youth)

"Ireland is a country in which political conflicts are at least genuine: they are about something. They are about patriotism, about religion, or about money: The three great realities."

~ G.K. Chesterton

No book about Northern Ireland would be complete without at least some mention of "the troubles" between the two tribes of "Nor'n Iron" – the "Prods", also known as the Protestants, and the "Taigs", also known as the Roman Catholics. The Prods are a majority in Northern Ireland, especially around the capital city of Belfast, and outnumber the Catholics two to one.

In conversation, Protestants will routinely refer to Roman Catholics as "Taigs". No one can seem to agree on the origin of this term, though the most popular theory is that it is derived from the common Irish male name of the same spelling, or the surname of Teague, as the term "Paddy" came from "Patrick". Another common Protestant slur of Catholics is the term "Fenian", undoubtedly a reference to the Irish-Catholic Fenian Brotherhood, a secret revolutionary organization in the United States and

Ireland in the mid-19th century dedicated to the overthrow of British rule in Ireland. The appendage "bastards" is also common, as in "Taig Bastard" or "Fenian Bastard".

When I grew up in Northern Ireland, the term most used by Protestants in referring to Catholics was "Mickey's", probably because many Catholics are named Michael. The use of the term "left-footer" is also popular. For example, when inquiring about someone's background, the question is often asked, "Does he kick with the left foot or the right?" It is known that Prods kick with the right foot, Catholics with the left. When using the pejorative "Fenian" or "Taig", Prods often do so with a contemptuous curl of the lips or a scowl to accentuate their distaste for "those people."

Despite the colorful use of epithets in referring to Catholics, the response from Catholics has been either mild or comparatively unimaginative. The worst put-downs I've ever heard a Catholic use toward a Protestant are "Prod bastards" or "Orange bastards." Catholics just don't seem to have the desire to create as many colorful descriptions of Prods as the Prods have for them. I think the answer can be found in how each community views the other. The Prods, while a majority within Northern Ireland, are the true minority in the whole of Ireland with all of the attendant fears common to minorities who consider their community under siege.

Most Protestants have long believed that the Catholics are intent on the destruction of the Northern Ireland State and the Protestant way of life. This fear eats at the soul of the Protestant community in Northern Ireland and is the source of their hatred of Roman Catholics. The Catholics, on the other hand, know that time and history is on their side and that sooner or later they will prevail and Ireland will be "united and free". The prospect of this eventuality terrifies Orangemen.

Another example of the bitter hatred the Prods have for the Taigs can be found in the nature of Orange music or "party" songs. One of these songs goes as follows (with apologies to the author of "Galway Bay."

If you ever go across the sea to Ireland,
Be it only on the Twelfth Day of July,
Just to see again the lily and sweet William
And to watch the Orangemen as they walk by,
And if there's gonna be a fight hereafter
And, somehow, I'm sure there's going to be,
We'll make the fenian's blood flow like water
Down the Belfast Lough into the Irish Sea.

Another song goes –

Do you think that we would let
A dirty fenian git
Destroy a leaf of the lily-o?

Alongside the political divide, which has to do with the future of Northern Ireland or lack thereof, there are other divisions. Catholic schoolchildren attend Catholic parochial schools. Protestant children attend state schools. Some efforts have been made to have Catholic and Protestant children attend non-denominational, mixed schools but with only limited success. There are also exclusive Catholic sports such as Irish football and hurling in which Protestants do not participate. One of the few common interests the two communities share, however, is soccer. In the past, certain teams had a Catholic following and others an exclusively Protestant fan base. The division even extends to the national newspapers. Catholics will receive their version of events from the Irish News and Protestants from the Belfast Newsletter. Both tribes, however, will purchase the Belfast Telegraph, which attempts to remain somewhat neutral.

Where one lives is often an indicator of one's religion. Working class Catholics and Protestants tend to congregate within their own communities. These communities have unofficial but strict borders. A common practice during periods of communal violence was to raid the other's territory and toss Molotov cocktails through parlor windows, a particularly despicable practice given that the victims had little enough in worldly possessions. During the height of the troubles, the authorities erected tall fences between the two communities to deter cross community raiding.

The worst of the violence and the greatest degree of hatred is found within the working-class neighborhoods in Belfast, Derry and other Northern Ireland cities. The middle and upper classes remain aloof from and experience less of the effects of the conflict. There is little difference to be found between a rabid, working class, Roman Catholic nationalist and a working class, Protestant fanatic. Neither can find any good with the opposite side.

The provisional Irish Republican Army, the IRA, a mostly Catholic group vehemently against English presence and rule in Ireland, drew its recruits from the blue collar, nationalist neighborhoods and their counterparts in the Protestant community from the Protestant ghettoes. They are mirror images of one another.

A solution to Ulster's political and religious divide would bedevil even the most rational thinker. For the fanatics, it's impossible. Yet apart from a few psychopaths on each side, the working-class people caught up in this conflict are basically good people confused and torn apart by history. As a community, Northern Ireland's Protestants and Catholics contribute more to national charities per head than any other group within the United Kingdom.

Of the two groups today, the Protestants exhibit the greatest degree of pessimism. They feel betrayed and let down by the British government whose perceived "concessions" to Ulster's Catholic minority has weakened the Protestant power base. The common sentiment now heard around Northern Ireland is, "The Catholics are being handed everything they want." The beloved Royal Ulster Constabulary has been restructured and is now the Northern Ireland Police Force. With the peace process, IRA gunmen guilty of murder are being prematurely let out of jail, although the same is true of Protestant militants. Former IRA militants are now political leaders in the prominent Catholic parties in Northern Ireland. They draw handsome salaries from White Hall while in the past they drew only guns. The hated Roman Catholic tri-color flag now flutters over former Protestant neighborhoods in Belfast. The British "sell-out" is well underway.

The sad fact is that Northern Ireland is an embarrassment to Britain. The claims of the Ulster Loyalists for inclusion in the U.K. as British subjects are unwelcome. The absorption of Northern Ireland by the Irish Republic would free the British of any financial obligation to Northern Ireland. Thus, for the most part, the Protestants are on their own. However, for the sake of the health and sanity of the people of Northern Ireland, a settlement is mandatory. If they can only put their history and their divisions behind them, as appears to be the case with the recent agreements, they can turn Ulster into a decent place to live in and bring up children. It would be an even greater place than it already is if they could combine their talents for the good of all the people of Ulster, particularly the children, who are always the innocent sufferers of the ignorance of their parents. Whether the two communities have the will and the courage to change things for good and all remains to be seen.

As a Protestant, it pains me to say this, but one of the main hurdles to achieving a lasting peace in Northern Ireland is Protestant gloating about ancient battles through the constant parading of Protestant power by the Orange Order. The Twelfth of July Parade is a prime example of this. In any other country, such ancient victories would be nothing but a sidenote in the history books, only vaguely recalled by anyone but history buffs. For instance, the Fourth of July in the States is more of a national holiday for independence than it is a celebration of victory over the British. In fact, most Americans now love all things British. In the case of the Protestants, however, the defeat of the Catholics is the core of their sentiment, and the Orange parades are a demonstration of the supposed superiority that the

Protestants hold in the north. Protestants even used to walk along the wall bordering the city of Derry and throw pennies down into the Catholic ghettoes where the poor Catholic's were living, obviously a very demeaning act. Until this kind of behavior stops, there will be hatred. And as long as there is hatred, there can never be complete or lasting peace.

The main reason for all the Protestant celebrations is the strong emotional attachment they have to the soil of Ulster; to the six counties. It's almost ethereal how they feel about it. There are many reasons for the problems between the two groups - the Celts and the Anglo-Saxons (the Celts being the Catholics and the Anglo-Saxons being the Protestants) - religious, ethnic, historical, political, even racial, but it all boils down to who controls the territories. In that sense, the conflict in Northern Ireland is a turf war. Getting the British out of Northern Ireland will not solve nor end the problem. There are still the Protestants to deal with. In fact, the English wouldn't even be there if it were not for the Protestants, who are still their subjects and who number approximately one million out of about one and a half million in Northern Ireland. The British would dearly love to cut the tie once and for all. There is no benefit for them in having Northern Ireland. It has ceased to be of strategic importance to them. Funding Northern Ireland to keep it up to the standards of the mainland is an economic drain financially. They would love it if the Protestants gave up but that's not going to happen in the foreseeable future. The British are also too proud to be chased out of Ireland by a bunch of ragtag revolutionaries like the IRA.

Growing up in such a divided environment, I absorbed some of these attitudes by osmosis. Nobody ever sat me down as a child and gave me a detailed history. In fact, we were not even taught Irish history in school as Protestants. The Catholics were taught Irish history and had a keener sense of their own background than we did. It is still that way today. So through the attitude of our parents and the people in the neighborhood we lived in, all we were taught was that we were Prods, that the Catholics were against us, and that they were no good and could not to be trusted. We were taught they were feckless and lazy and did not have the qualities of thrift, hard work and cleanliness that the Prods had. Ironically, these were and are the very same comments made about blacks by racists in the deep south of the United States. The mass generalization inherent to prejudice is always the same, no matter where it is or who it is directed toward.

ĸamiĸaze catwalĸs

"Out of Ireland we have come, great hatred, little room, maimed us at the start. I carry from my mother's womb a fanatic heart."
- **William Butler Yeats.**

Since I was raised in Newtownabbey, which is just northeast of Belfast, I guess I was somewhat protected to a lesser extent from 'The Troubles'. However, with the building of a council housing estate just beyond the perimeter of what was considered our once peaceful neighbourhood, we very soon found ourselves facing the same rubbish as what we would witness on the evening news.

Even as I reflect on this right at this moment, I don't dare put the name of the district into print because I feel it is undeserving of any sort of recognition whatsoever other than to say it quickly became a very bitter bastard shitehole. It was given a nickname to reflect the people who lived there. The same occurred when we went to Belfast to visit family and began to get repeatedly targeted by individuals who were not a part of our friendship circles.

For whatever reason, those who moved into and lived within the shitehole district (quite often by burning Catholics out of their homes by throwing a Molotov cocktail through their livingroom window) felt they had the right to bring their views of hatred into our area, even though we were from a mixed community and, for the most part, got along very well without their involvement or input. This may have been due in part to our choice of music, as there were different genres that went out of their way to beat the living daylights out of one another, depending on whether you identified as being into mod, skinhead, teddy, punk, or my own choice of music, heavy metal. Quadrophenia was alive and well during this time and led to several clashes on buses and in the streets depending on the clothing choices people displayed.

In order to get ourselves out of sticky situations — and there were certainly more and more of them occurring on both a daily and weekly basis — my brother, Joe, his mates (who were a part of the Woodford Heavies), my best friend from childhood and school, Denis, and I would teach ourselves how to navigate the streets of our community by barely stepping foot on to them. We would call this going for a 'catwalk'.

Starting from the back garden of our own house, Joe would teach me how to cross in and out of approximately fifteen houses which made up our street as well as the street behind us as the houses backed on to one another. We did this by climbing fences, sneaking behind fir trees that lined the bottom of gardens, and hiding behind sheds.

Leaving the safety of our back garden, we would first climb over the brick wall into the neighbour's house. Once there, we would sometimes see the neighbours just outside their back door, talking and having a feg, all the while doing our very best to not be seen. This would lead to a moment of panic for if we were caught, we would be told that we "were dead" or "in for it."

But we did not stop there; we continued into neighbouring gardens and streets to learn which routes were safe and which were not. Some fences were taller than others, while some would certainly not support our weight. We looked to see which walls we could access to hide on top of a garage roof while waiting for our tormentors to go on by, or to simply scope out the rest of the neighbourhood and see what other places we could hide in should the need ever arise. The countless occasions we practiced honing our skills became a second, and necessary, form of survival.

As we made our way along the Woodford Road, we would run up to the chain link fences that surrounded a neighbouring school — which was built to serve the newly created shithole district that also housed our tormentors — and learned how to jump the fence while diving over it into

a forward roll once on the other side. This would help us get a few strides
on our pursuers once we managed to get back into an upright stance after
clearing the chain link. Being quite a bit smaller than Joe and Denis, I often
found myself getting hung up on the top of the fence at times and would
be left with serious abdominal bruising. I never learned my lesson. Perhaps
it was because I was so stubborn and wanted to ensure I could do what
everyone else in our circle of friends could.

One night a large group of us were out messing about in the streets
about half-two in the morning. We were hanging around the Woodford
shops when we saw a paddy wagon coming straight up the Woodford
Road for us. These were used by Northern Ireland's police force, the Royal
Ulster Constabulary (RUC). Although we would see them up and down the
streets of family members who lived in Belfast or when check points were
set up, which was pretty much a daily occurrence, we certainly weren't used
to seeing them in our neighbourhood unless they happened to be stopping
outside of the houses of officers who lived in our district.

They were very ominous looking vehicles and had the same colour
scheme associated with "The Daleks" from the British television show
Doctor Who, which only added to our fear. After we made the call to each
other, we all bolted in separate directions as we did not want to get picked
up or interrogated by the peelers. We had heard sayings around Belfast
such as "Help the RUC. Beat yourself up". None of us wanted to find out
if they would do that for us or what state they'd leave us in even though we
were doing no harm.

Joe and I took off along Woodford Crescent and dove over a wall at
the top of Woodford Drive that had a heavy, full growth of fir trees behind
it, but it was about a three-foot drop to the garden below. I hit the ground
with a hard thud and as the pain wreathed through my guts, we pushed
ourselves up against the wall. There was nowhere else for us to go as this
was a corner lot with a wooden fence surrounding it. Joe whispered to me
to not breathe or move, a feat we had practiced several times before.

 Four Green Fields

The trees provided us with excellent cover, as only a moment later we heard heavy boots walk above us with one of the men saying, "I'm sure some of them went this way." We must have lay there for a good twenty minutes, holding our breath and waiting for one of our other mates to give everyone else the signal that the coast was clear. Even then, we weren't sure that it was safe to come out of our hiding places and stealthily moved about to be sure we weren't walking into a booby trap or ambush.

Another tactic was to go to the Woodford shops and scale the large number of steps to the hairdressing salon located on the second floor of the building. We would teach each other how to climb over the wall and grab onto the pipe that stuck out of the wall beneath our feet on the other side, which was likely used to house thick plumbing lines. We never stopped to think how crazy or dangerous this was as one wrong move or misstep would have certainly spelt death by falling straight to the carpark below.

We lowered ourselves down to the pipe and hung from it with our arms outstretched above our heads before letting go and dropping to the surface below again. We practiced this so often that it too almost became second nature, as well as perhaps a sideshow for those who didn't believe we could pull such a feat off without breaking our necks in the process. The twenty-to-twenty-five-foot drop demonstrated the extreme measures we were willing to take to get out of whatever situation we found ourselves in.

Although in those days I saw myself as invincible, when I last saw and photographed that wall, I cringed at the thought of trying it again as I did in my childhood days which I did without a second or educated thought. Perhaps the kamikaze in me has since come to understand the meaning of that word and now chooses to be cautious, something which was seriously lacking in my childhood. But when faced with several unwarranted beatings due to our religious upbringing, as well from the wankers who lived in the bitter bastard community and were nothing more than a pack of shitehawks looking for their daily dose of "actin' the tough man", it became a method of survival. We must have been considered outlaws, or imminent threats, and were hunted as such.

The sad thing is, my ma's mum - our granny, Mary Devlin - lived in that shitehole district long before it became such. She had a wee flat next to another pensioner whose grandchildren went to our school. Our visits were wonderful until the mindset came about that Catholics were to be burnt out. Her identity in that district remained secret right up to her death in October 1992.

Donegal and Derry

"In Northern Ireland, helicopters are not usually used to promote poetry."

- **Seamus Heaney.**

I grew up on the Inishowen peninsula of County Donegal. It was and still is a spectacularly beautiful area, surrounded by miles of white sandy beaches and green rolling hills. Being at the very top of Ireland meant that we were fairly much isolated from the rest of Ireland, especially the Republic. Derry was our neighbor. Industry was few and far between. Farming was the main occupation, whilst other employment opportunities such as house plasterer often involved working across the border in Derry and other parts of the North.

As young boys, we were not all that concerned about employment woes. In fact, we didn't care at all. Our father was a chef and he worked in Buncrana. His restaurant was in McCartan's shirt factory, where most of the women around Buncrana also worked. All my brother and I wanted to do was to play and climb things. Every Saturday, our parents would drive us up to Derry city where we would shop for hours, get treated to fish and chips, and finish off the day by going to see a film at the Odeon cinema on the Strand Road.

After the film, our father would stuff all kinds of food under our clothes, under the car seats and even under the baby brother's blankets. Although it wasn't spelled out, we were in fact smugglers. During our first summer of smuggling, Derry was like Donegal, only with more shops, people and cars.

The following year, everything changed. We still smuggled food down from Derry City to Donegal for our father's restaurant but, overnight,

British soldiers started to appear on the street. With the soldiers came armoured cars, tanks and barbed wire everywhere. Bombs were going off and Molotov cocktails, more commonly referred to as "petrol bombs" in Ireland, were the order of the day. People were being killed and the war was real. It was not like the make-believe games which my brother and our friends used to play, where we were either cowboys or soldiers and tree branches were our rifles. Even though we were young, we had some kind of an idea what was going on.

When we walked along the streets on a Saturday, we would always quicken our step walking past a soldier. It wasn't that we were afraid of them, but we knew they were being shot and none of us wanted to get in the way of that.

Donegal and Derry

Soldiers' guns are big
In Derry
Not like
A boy's stick
In Donegal

We walk fast
Past a soldier
In Derry
Just in case

We play
Cowboys and Indians
In Donegal
Soldiers don't play
Make believe in Derry

Petrol is for cars

And barbed wire

Keeps cows from straying

In Donegal

But not in Derry.

Fenians and Milk Bottles

"If history repeats itself, and the unexpected always happens, how incapable must Man be of learning from experience."

- **George Bernard Shaw.**

(From The Other Belfast – An Irish Youth)

"Tourists have nothing to worry about in Ireland. The Irish love everyone . . . except each other."

~ A comment made to my son, Mark, by a Belfast cab driver.

My father, Jack Rickerby, had good, close Catholic friends at his work at the railway, and he always made exceptions for them when he castigated the Catholics as a group.

During a vacation back home one year when I was in my forties, he and I went to a soccer game at Windsor Park. We took a bus home and were walking the several blocks to our house when he said, "I can always spot a Catholic house."

"Oh yeah? How can you do that, da?" I asked.

"By the milk bottles," he replied.

"Milk bottles? What do you mean?"

"They're always dirty. Catholics are lazy bastards. They don't wash out their dirty milk bottles before settin' 'em out on the steps for the milkman t'pick up."

"Really, da?" I said.

I thought this was an interesting anthropological observation on his part and I pondered it as we walked along.

"I was visitin' a Catholic friend'a mine one time," he continued, "and 'is wife put out a saucer'a milk fer the cat. The cat turned its nose up to it and do you know what she did then?"

"I don't know, da. What'd she do?"

"After the bloody cat got through sniffin' at the milk, the oul' doll picked up the saucer and poured it back into the bottle! I never saw anythin' so disgustin' in my whole life! There's Catholics for ya! Only a fenian would do somethin' like that – pour milk a bloody cat sniffed over back into a bottle fer human consumption."

Playing the devil's advocate, I argued, "Well, maybe the cat didn't actually drink any of the milk." This threw my da into a fit of anger.

"Ach, it doesn't matter if the cat drank the milk or not! The milk was fouled just by the bloody cat sniffin' at it, ya eejit! Don't be daft!"

"Okay, da. I guess you're right."

To accentuate his point, he pointed out dirty milk bottles on various front porches and clean bottles on others, saying, "Catholic house, Protestant house, Protestant, Catholic, Protestant, Protestant, Catholic" and so on. The more dirty milk bottles he saw, the more his disgust and contempt mounted, until he had finally worked himself into a seething rage. It was obvious he could not conceive of a Protestant family anywhere in the world leaving a dirty milk bottle on their porch.

When we arrived home, I noticed that there were three empty milk bottles on our own front doorstep with a film of congealing milk inside all of them.

I said, "Jesus, da! Look! Catholics must have taken over our house!"

He gritted his teeth, stormed into the house and didn't talk to me for two days.

Belfast City Asylum

"In a war situation or where violence and injustice are prevalent, poetry is called upon to be something more than a thing of beauty."

- **Seamus Heaney.**

It was not until we had left Belfast that I myself started looking back to try and understand what all the fighting and violence was about. But this is not something that we ever did. We simply took the times and our surroundings as being very natural, even though I would eventually learn that there was nothing natural about it. It was a political war which had been disguised under a religious veil.

The norm became that people simply got on with their lives and went about their daily business. But in leaving behind our beloved community, neighbourhood, our country and our stolen identities, others took great pleasure in trying to flush out of us all that was going on back home. At house parties, the questions were endless:

"Why do Protestants kill Catholics?"

"Why do the IRA blow everything up?"

"Why is there so much violence?"

"Why do you not tell the paramilitaries to stop their campaign?"

It became extremely tiring hearing these questions being asked continuously. I appreciated people trying to understand it all, but we were kids who had nothing to do with it. We were removed from the savagery by our parents. It was their goal and aspiration to provide their children a life absent the violence which had taken hold of our community, city, and country. The insanity did not belong to us, nor was it ours to explain.

Years on, I still try to make sense through my reflective writings, including these next three compositions. Along with a story, the second poem, *Stranger to my Land* is featured within my very first personal memoir, ***Through the Eyes of a Belfast Child: Life. Personal Reflections. Poems.*** but as a poem in my second book ***An Irish Heart: Poetic Memoirs of a Belfast Child.***

The first and third poems here, ***Belfast City Asylum*** along with ***In the Name of Religion*** are sobering compositions in my third book, ***One Cross to Bear: Humanity through Narrative Prose.***

Sadly, the thing I never seem to realize when I am writing each of these pieces is not only do they have a direct personal impact on me, they also reflect the common attitudes of the time. In the 1970's, my cousin, Stephen, was a youngster playing on a street one day in the district my mum grew up in when, without any warning, a rubber bullet was fired up the street and made a direct hit. Stephen lost colour vision in one eye as a result and spent his life living with what could and should very well have been a preventable injury. Senseless incidents like this left me and a lot of others wondering why the troops put their feckin' guns away and take their insensitive war as far away from our wee country as possible.

See, people asked me questions for which I didn't and still don't have answers for. I am angry for the events that occurred. A lot of innocent people were caught in the crossfire, including women, men, children, toddlers, babies, and tourists. Mothers and fathers, sisters and brothers, lovers and strangers.

Thus, as I sit here writing this, I have the strangest feeling that when you read this, you'll be doing the exact same thing I am – shaking your head in complete and utter disbelief. That will most likely be followed up with tears after you chance a read of these next three compositions regarding the sanitarium you were welcomed to in my introduction, along with the passenger ships that sailed into Belfast each day . . .

"Once you attempt legislation upon religious grounds, you open the way for every kind of intolerance and religious persecution."

- **William Butler Yeats.**

Belfast City Asylum

Hunger Strikes and petrol bombs,
Paramilitary brigades.
Sectarian ideology,
Marches, and parades.

Political interference,
Stormont makes its stance.
Warring factions, steadfast minds,
Can you please give peace a chance?

Constant interrogation,
Our prayers, they never last.
A warning call, the bomb explodes,
Innocent lives caught in the blast.

An Irish city, torn by war,
Armed British soldiers patrol.
Check points placed, with razor wire,
Rubber bullets fly out of control.

Victims shot on their front porch,
Execution: point blank range.
Burnt out homes, shattered lives,
Will this hatred ever change?

Bunting strung across lampposts,
Curbs painted red, white, blue.
Bonfires reach up to the sky,
Tri-colours burned right through.

Kick with your left or your right foot?
Are you Orange or are you Green?
Are you Catholic or a Protestant?
For the Pope or with the Queen?

Say one letter in the alphabet,
Sing the Sash My Father Wore.
Right, just as I suspected,
You're the child of a Fenian whore.

Each July, year after year,
Ireland's north goes up in flame.
Will our land ever know freedom?
Or be a Nation once again?

Lay down your arms; put away your guns,
One thing we'll learn for sure.
It's time this Belfast City Asylum
Finds a harmonious cure.

Four Green Fields

Stranger to My Land

In my beloved town of Belfast,
Off goes yet another devastating bomb blast.
In the streets the people lay dying,
Over their bodies, their families start crying.

In a land that is run by hatred and rule,
Fragile people are made to feel like a fool.
Where the citizens would like to have the choice,
Freedom of speech, the language in their voice.

Both sides, for their marches and silly parades,
Look like nothing more than a game of charades.
While they walk so defiant, they chant and they shout,
"Soon we will get all of those other bastards out."

While we know the place is well overrun,
By ignorance, who shall hide behind a gun.
They target all innocence that lock into sight,
They continue their torture by day and by night.

When people do apply for a job,
Noses are turned up just like a snob.
"We will only hire from our own kind,
You're fully qualified, but not what we had in mind."

There are many armies that walk the street,
They point their guns at certain people they meet.
They know whose side that they will take,
Their sincerity can be determined as nothing but fake.

To the people that live on the non-sectarian road,
When they ask for assistance, they are left in the cold.
The safeguards that were put into place,
Will shower them with bullets and spit in their face.

I wonder if my country will try and make peace,
Will the guns stay silent? Will the violence cease?
Will people no longer hide behind a frown?
Will they finally have freedom from the bitterness they drown?

My closing word to the nations of the Emerald Isle:

Hold your heads high, and be proud when you smile.

Now is the time for the healing seeds to grow,

Give a chance to be united, and not for what you know.

In the Name of Religion

Our once peaceful neighbourhood,
When religious views were mixed.
People helped one another,
Things were always fixed.

Simple discussions of right and wrong,
Never a concern about one's fate.
Reproachful words weren't spoken,
Opposing backgrounds could relate.

We all came together as one,
And knew each other by name.
Childhood games of Kerby and Red Rover,
Never riddled by guilt nor shame.

Out of the blue, a drastic change,
When a new district came to be.
Suddenly we found ourselves at war,
Labelled foreign in our community.

Hate not within our nature,
Upon others, no words to condemn.
We did not hurl slanderous insults,
Yet were now referred to as 'them'.

Just simply an Irish family,
Growing up with many a friend.
Denominational views cast against us,
We truthfully could not comprehend.

The streets on which we freely played,
Now turned into a battleground.
Twisted minds, standing next to us,
Into our jaws, their fists would pound.

Collecting debris was the next event,
Just prior to the Eleventh night.
Although we'd always participate,
The stack we weren't to light.

For what we would come to learn,
"Those Catholics are all the same."
The eradication of our identity,
The symbolic gesture of flame.

Effigies of His Holiness, the Pope,
Recklessly chucked into the fire.
Things would go from bad to worse,
Quite honestly, they were dire.

When Hunger Strikers began dying,
"Our kind" weren't allowed on the bus.
It would not be the last time, though,
Torment would be brought against us.

Since our school uniforms gave us away,
We would be chased everywhere.
Abhorrent words spewed without cause,
Cut our hearts out, they did swear.

Thrust straight into Nellie's Dam,
Not one would show a frown.
My sister now deemed a target,
Her life, they tried to drown.

"We are not Irish Soldiers,
Nor did we fight the battle of Boyne.
Learn your bloody history, wee lad,"
Only to be met with a kick to the groin.

Despicable slander, it grew in spades,
As the cancer continued its sprawl.
"Fuck the Pope, Kill All Taigs Dead,"
Said the writing upon the wall.

The immeasurable times they muttered,
"You're the child of a Fenian whore."
The very next moment, we always knew,
That we had to escape once more.

Sneaking around our darkened house,
That night for us they came.
Hushed voices, barely making a sound,
Survival now the name of the game.

Catwalk through our neighbourhood,
Back gardens or rooftops the same.
Our senses always on heightened alert,
Persistence our second name.

Within the Doagh Road Forest,
A thirty-foot plummet or more.
Taking a risk, the tree trunk snapped,
Dumping me to the pine-needled floor.

Back up and into a panicked sprint,
I followed the muddied terrain.
Across the river, near the waterfall,
I began running once again.

Four Green Fields

Now a grown man and Social Worker,
Battling constantly when I dream.
The scars from evading my tormentors,
These nightmares my recurring theme.

The mothers who fell into the streets,
As the blood of their children flowed red.
Cradling their near lifeless bodies,
Before a priest declared them dead.

Now read these words, I'm not alone,
In the damage that has been done.
Please tell me once, what have you solved,
The conflict has never been won.

3,700 lives claimed by The Troubles,
Sectarian oppression and undue violence.
Frequent desecrations of human rights,
Fully supported by political connivance.

And all in the name of Religion,

No Surrender is what you claim.

A continuous war, no heroes to greet,

Time to lower your heads in shame.

Four Green Fields

Stolen Identity

"Anybody who has the courage to raise his eyes and look sanely at the awful human condition … must realize finally that tiny periods of temporary release from intolerable suffering is the most that any individual has the right to expect."

- **Flann O'Brien.**

While speaking to an audience of punters at the Dublin, Ohio Irish Festival where I was signing books along with other brilliant authors who hail from America and Ireland, I was truly honoured to have a couple of them sitting in the audience. J.P was one lad. Although his experiences of travelling into County Derry, Northern Ireland were of a very different nature in his family's bid of survival, he was definitely exposed to what many young women and men such as ourselves saw during 'The Troubles'. One other lad was from County Tyrone; his name is Colin Broderick. They both sat quietly listening to the presentation I gave about my experiences growing up just on the outskirts of Belfast.

As Colin listened, he shared that he never knew there were others outside of Tyrone who had faced similar experiences to what he and his family did. It helped me to come to the realization there are plenty of us who have had those same traumas painfully cast against us, for mere virtue of growing up in the land of our ancestors. We were targeted because of a religious identity we didn't ask for and our sense of self was systemically removed because of where we were innocently born. Both of these crimes were conducted under a veil simplistically referred to as 'The Troubles.'

I never did get a chance to say cheerio to Colin at the end of the book signing. As he would later explain, he wasn't one for painful goodbyes, something I have been guilty of myself far too often. He chose to instead slip away quietly after all the festivities had wrapped up. But, Colin left an everlasting impression on me. This included him speaking to a human condition called Post Traumatic Stress Disorder, or PTSD as it is more commonly referred to.

I was left in awe by his statements, pondering how many of us are living with this yet are oblivious and have gone undiagnosed with this condition as we see it as being 'normal'. It helped me understand why I often run, fight, and get shot in my dreams – experiences I wrote about earlier. This reflective piece, as featured in my third book, was composed in his honour.

Stolen Identity

Today is the day that I must go,
To deliver my baby, there's much you should know,
My dear child, I fear what lies ahead,
The bombed-out cars, the rifled dead.

Guard you from violence, the hatred out there,
The political upheaval, their decisions unfair,
My options are few, to protect you from war,
This identity imposed, it pains my core.

Critical perspectives, yet these are untrue,
Of the persons we are, but this I must do,
When you come to ask how I chose your name,
You'll not understand the harm or shame.

I promise to shield and protect you from pain,
But that promise I make, acknowledged in vain,
There will come a time, that they will know,
You're an Irish soul, now labelled their foe.

No matter my efforts in protecting thee,
My heart it breaks for what you will see,
Derogative words will be cast against you,
Despicable, racist, discriminative too.

When that day does come, and you start school,
The friends around you, their intentions, now cruel,
For the colours of your uniform, will give you away,
The measures I've taken will begin to fray.

My hope for you is harmony and peace,
The violence to stop, the bitterness cease,
Yet sectarian seeds, they viciously sow,
Generational brutality continues to grow.

The gruesome horrors, it's what they do,
Their targeted loathing forced upon you,
Cultural genocide is all that we know,
Our people they drown in grief and sorrow.

Four Green Fields

My child so precious, so undoubting, so pure,
The cruelty abundant, there's much to endure,
Humiliating taunts, the ongoing curse,
Our nation divided, progressively worse.

Nine months nurtured inside of me,
I pray someday, our people are free,
The troubled history, raw to the bone,
Our voices fall silent, the fractured unknown.

Enter this world, a gift without sin,
An innocent life, let your journey begin,
To this tragic play, you may add a verse,
Welcome, my child, to Ulster's curse.

ULSTER

"The worst sin toward our fellow creatures is not to hate them, but to be indifferent to them: that's the essence of inhumanity."

- **George Bernard Shaw.**

When my father, John Rickerby, left Belfast for Canada in 1957 to seek greater opportunity, he wrote to my mother, Rosaleen, every week for two years until she too left Northern Ireland. They were wed within a year. My brother, Paul, was born in Ontario. My dad landed a job in New York and they lived there for a year. After several years, was offered a job in Southern California. My mother was pregnant with me when they made the cross-country trip, taking the opportunity to see some sights along the way.

The adjustment to California living was not difficult. We had many happy days on the beaches and my father often rented campers to take us to Pismo Beach and the woods of the great northwest. It was an idyllic time. So idyllic, in fact, that nobody would have thought twice about it if my father forgot all about Belfast. But he never did. In fact, the troubles that worsened as time passed only endeared him more to his hometown. As mentioned previously, he became a peace activist to assuage this worry and sorrow for his beloved Belfast, and received death threats by those who disagreed with him but didn't believe in intelligent discourse.

As a child, I couldn't understand why anyone would want to kill my dad. I didn't understand the conflict in Belfast but neither was I too young to know that blowing up buses was wrong. My schoolteachers told me "two wrongs don't make a right" and "treat others as you wish to be treated" so I couldn't understand why so many adults had such difficulty living up to these philosophies.

 Four Green Fields

I'm not sure who originally said it, but my father often repeated the line, "If you think you understand the Irish troubles, you're not well-informed." He would also quote an old Ukrainian proverb - "When the banner is unfurled, all reason is in the trumpet." These lines seem to reflect the bewilderment most feel about the troubles and their persistently lingering legacy, and it is perhaps this frustration that caused my father to write the poem "Ulster" wherein he reminisces about the sweet and simple pleasures he and his mates enjoyed in simpler times, before the seeds of hatred he witnessed led to hatred's inevitable endings – bloodshed and destruction. He wrote this poem during the height of the troubles in the 1970's. This poem tells a very different story from what the world often and quite sadly saw happening in and around the north of Ireland.

As you have read, Greg has captured some of those experiences as seen through his eyes in excruciating detail, beautifully told through his writings. It is true that we are condemned to repeat that which we allow ourselves to forget. Experiences like those Greg has survived (often just barely) during this period of horrific bloodshed cannot and must not be forgotten, nor should they be written off as "living in the past." The young must be warned and guided gently toward peace. This was my dad's attempt to do both, and my sharing of his poem is my attempt to make him proud of me, even if beyond the grave, by promoting the causes of peace and brotherhood that were so dear to him.

ULSTER

There are those who say that Ulster
is a place of hate and pain.
but many who have left it
would still go back again.

The strangers do not see
behind the bombs and flames and smoke
and fail to see the character
of the kindly Ulster folk.

But we have memories of the days
when we were young and gay,
of carefree romps through Ormeau Park
or over Cave Hill's Bray.

The Saturdays at Windsor,
the Sundays by the sea,
the bathing belles at Pickie,
the sands at Donaghadee.

Four Green Fields

Our best suit pressed and ready
and we were Plaza-bound
but first a stop at Mooney's
and pints bought all around.

The Sunday morning papers,
the bacon and dip bread,
then a dander to the castle
where all the scores are read.

Back to work on Monday,
the weekend's tales are told
while the oldsters smile and chuckle
as our youthful tales unfold.

A new girl in the office;
she's a quare wee bit o' stuff.
Is she going strong, you wonder,
as you act so big and tough.

Those were the days; there is no doubt,
as my memory wanders back.
That is what we all recall,
not the rifle's crack.

Will it ever be the same, you ask.
Will today's kids ever know
The simple life we all enjoyed
a long, long time ago.

Yesterday's Footprints...

everlasting homesickness

"In life, we all have a cross to bear and a very unique story to tell; we just hope that someone will take the time to listen."
-   Greg McVicker.

This reflective piece of narrative prose will take you back to where my own journey first began - when my father and mother made one of their most difficult of decisions to leave home and relocate their children, by way of immigration, away from all the sectarian hatred and targeted attacks which we were subjected to each day back home in Northern Ireland.

We had nothing to do with any of it, yet always found ourselves on the receiving end of it all. Though I still regret that this occurred, it created what has become a lifelong and desperate desire to find my way back home again, but without all the shite that came with it.

Although I am still haunted by and continue to struggle with the memories associated with this, it is by far one of the most courageous offerings of personal sacrifice my parents have ever had to make, not on their own behalf, but for the love, safety, and protection of their children. They left their lives and their own families behind for our benefit.

Little did any of us realize at the time that it would begin a period of eighteen solid years of homesickness for me. Although I was told by some to "get over it already", they have no clue about the agony I experienced, nor do they understand it is something that simply does not go away on its own. It is a lifelong heartache, one of cherished memories and painful reflections. This does not only happen with me living on the other side of the world now, but every time I go home.

Everlasting Homesickness

Roman Catholic, unqualified,
Only one job could be had.
On floating jails, cast solid steel,
He set off a young lad.

On British ships, far away at sea,
Tireless hours my father spent.
Home each year, two meagre weeks,
Farewell and off he went.

An undying love with distinction,
Bequeathed so naturally.
A beautiful gift of breathing life,
Into my sisters, brother, and me.

On the war-torn streets of Belfast,
My mother would stand her ground.
Amongst the debris of bodies from bombs,
Her children would not be found.

Burnt out homes, Hunger Strikes,
Recruited by sectarian brigades.
Political bloodshed, blanket protests,
Paramilitary funerals and parades.

My folks explored their options,
Possibilities were rather few.
They felt they had no other choice,
But to restart life, brand new.

Return from vacation, August '84,
Undesirable decisions contrive.
"We must leave behind our families,
To help our kids survive."

The backdrop outside so bitter,
With my siblings huddled around.
A secret placed upon our souls,
"Next year we're Canada bound."

Nothing could've prepared me,
Or the pleaded cries I'd beg.
The news they broke to us that day,
We were immigrating to Winnipeg.

"No one out there needs to know,
Better keep this to yourselves.
Although we move out next July,
It's time to pack the shelves."

The shock it rippled through my mind,
"What exactly does this mean?
My life is here in Ireland,
Awaken this nightmare dream."

Their chosen words, spoken so clear,
They shushed my panicked voice.
Words of hatred muttered between each breath,
I cursed my parents' choice.

"To love and freedom is where we'll go,
There's no reason to be sad.
Our promise to you, once we get there,
Our happiness will be clad."

The life and land I loved so dear,
Suddenly came crashing to a halt.
To walk away from our wee house,
On my parents, I placed all fault.

For I did not want to leave my home,
Or the trusted friends I had.
Regardless of my pleaded hopes,
"Button your mouth, young lad.

For you'll walk the streets without torment,
And will enjoy a peaceful place.
Do not weep, my little one,
Put a smile back on your face."

 Four Green Fields

And while the days were growing short,
The months passed quickly by.
Packed supplies, a hateful heart,
The silent tears I'd cry.

Before I found myself uprooted,
I wanted to run away.
Shy of fifteen, a delicate age,
Homesickness was here to stay.

The Doagh Road Forest, the Boghill Dam,
All corners of Newtownabbey.
Everything cherished and loved so dear,
I wanted to take with me.

While standing up at Knockagh Monument,
I scanned the horizon below.
Carrickfergus Castle, Belfast Lough,
Perhaps my Uncle Jimmy will know.

The constant reminder, the forms we filled,
I continued to make my fuss.
"No one will take care of you, Greg,
You are relocating with us."

Regardless of the options I gave,
My focus fully dwelled.
Like church bells ringing in my head,
My angry protests quelled.

No matter of my hopeful plans,
Those dreams were constantly dashed.
Resentful of my mum and dad,
Our words they often clashed.

"Put this life behind you, son,"
Was what I was frequently told.
"Forget everything that you once loved,"
My father would repeatedly scold.

Four Green Fields

The time did come, one final bash,

A chance to say goodbye.

Out on the street, we all ran free,

There were no tears to cry.

Among invited party friends,

The Harp it flowed so strong.

No adults did ask questions,

There was no right from wrong.

I'd sneak back in to our wee house,

And emerge with several tins.

Gulp each pint, the bitter taste,

Drowned out our previous sins.

My first time tasting Guinness,

Brought my palette to its brink.

Continued booze, no remorse,

For how much we all did drink.

Although the craic was ninety,

Out on our street that night.

The seconds continued ticking away,

To boarding that dreaded flight.

A pain so deep within my heart,

Is something I couldn't foresee.

The following morn, possessions shipped,

Across the Irish Sea.

The final night before we flew,

Nothing but carpet for my bed.

No pillowed comfort, an emptied shell,

Like a cemetery built for the dead.

A threadbare home is all we had,

My parents will never forget.

As I slept that restless night,

I cursed them without regret.

The plane took us to foreign land,
Searched hopes for a better life.
Although my parents did this for us,
My heart was filled with strife.

Aunts, uncles, and cousins to greet,
Yet they were perfect strangers to me.
Homesickness beginning to take its toll,
Back home, my heart longed to be.

Going to class, failing all grades,
Illegal phone calls placed from school.
Immeasurable taunts, slanderous terms,
Countless people were cruel.

The Halloween dance, drunken stupor,
No one would understand or care.
My foot split open, a hospital trip,
I begged for return airfare.

My parents their hearts were breaking,
For they felt their choice was wrong.
In taking me away from our country,
The place that my soul does belong.

Excessive drinking, a troubled start,
There was nothing for me to boast.
The letters I wrote, then sent away,
I constantly checked for new post.

Letters and calls once abundant,
Had trickled to a halt.
My belief was that being separated,
Is where we would lay fault.

Seven years on, though time stood still,
I finally made my way home.
No longer a lad, but now a grown man,
And everything was gone.

Four Green Fields

My granny lay still in her coffin,
And the drink it flowed so free.
As much as I did fully participate,
I ached for my community.

But what a shock when I got there,
Nothing felt right at all.
Standing now as a full-grown man,
Everything seemed so small.

My friends grew up, some moved away,
And one young lady got wed.
Attending the reception in Cushendall,
Jumbled thoughts all through my head.

For time had not stood still for me,
Or waited for my return back here.
I paused for though, yet nothing made sense,
Things now were more unclear.

The only thing that was constant now,

The Troubles, they remained.

Guns, bomb scares, and murals on walls.

The ignorance sustained.

My heart it wept, long last my return,

But nothing was ever the same.

There I stood, a man of two countries,

Stolen identity made up my frame.

To this day, I continue to fight,

Since that island still calls my name.

Before I exhale one final breath,

I'll return to that nation again.

Four Green Fields

Donegal Fishermen

"May the holes in your nets be no larger than the fish in it."

- **Irish Proverb.**

You have to be hardy to make a living fishing the Atlantic Ocean, when the waves and the wind are mocking you to "take them on." So it is with the fishermen of Donegal. As if the elements were not life-threatening enough, many of these same fishermen also play Russian Roulette by going out on their boats after a hardy bout of drinking, and many do not believe in wearing life jackets. The thinking is that the ocean needs to claim what is lawfully hers and if a man is washed/blown overboard, he becomes the property of the sea and it is his fate not to survive.

There is one particular family in Malin Head who have been fishing the treacherous waters of the Atlantic for generations. The sons are big, broad men with long, curly locks of hair and strong, red beards. As a boy, they always reminded me of Vikings.

Indeed, I have no doubt that we have a fair bit of Viking DNA in us. The men who now harvest the ocean are without a doubt related to those wild men who plundered our shores more than a thousand years ago. Instead of swords, they are now armed with lobster pots. They are at one with the sea, as they are with the soil.

Donegal Fishermen

Lashing gales
Drive
Crashing waves
At any time
Of year
The wild men
Of Malin Head
Fish the Atlantic
Unknowing
How to fear

Modern day Vikings
Plunder
The waters
Often for small
Rewards
Scraping the sea
To feed

Sons and daughters

Far cry

From the Nordic Hordes

Who pillaged

Lands

With the upper hand

Invaders

From frozen fjords

Fishermen now

Push out boats and plough

The angry seas

With lobster pots

Not swords

Time Out

"We make out of the quarrel with others, rhetoric, but of the quarrel with ourselves, poetry."

- **William Butler Yeats.**

Most of the poems which I write and have written are influenced by the Irish countryside – weather, seasons, mountains, fishing, agriculture, national topics - and as such they are observations and reflections, mostly without a humorous element. When it comes to weather, for the most part, it is wild and unpredictable throughout the whole country.

Having grown up in the most northerly tip of Ireland – Donegal's Inishowen peninsula, our weather was that much more unforgiving. Sunshine was an infrequent visitor, while lashing rain and wild winds were constant companions. Although it is a small Island, we used to refer to Southern Counties like Wexford and Waterford as the "sunny South East."

Time Out percolated in my mind from a story which took place in the West of Ireland. Several decades ago, an Irish Policeman (Garda) claimed to have seen a former Taoiseach in a bush, alongside the road. The Taoiseach of Ireland is the equivalent to what most countries refer to as a Prime Minister. The Taoiseach in question was called Jack Lynch. While Jack Lynch was alive and well at the time of the alleged sighting, there is virtually no chance that he was sitting in a ditch in the middle of nowhere, simply passing the day. There was however, a far greater chance that the Garda in question had been under pressure and was having what might be described as a bit of a "meltdown."

As I contemplated having worked, lived and visited bustling cities around the world, such as New York, Washington D.C., Dublin, London, Shanghai, Bangkok, Mexico, etc., it came to me how much we can get

 Four Green Fields

wrapped up in our day-to-day lives and forget to take a deep breath. Then I took it a step further and wondered what would be the reaction if Jesus were to return and decide that He wanted to take a time out in a remote area of Donegal? Would He be ogled as he passed the time sitting in a ditch? His Mother, Mary, visited Ireland in the past when she appeared in Knock, County Mayo. What if His Mother convinced Him that He should drop in on the Irish – somewhere nice and peaceful like Northwest Donegal?

The Wild Atlantic Way, may just be "the way."

Time Out

I once knew a man
Who swore
He saw Jesus
Sitting on a ditch
In Gweedore

"Stone mad"
Was the local opinion
What would bring Jesus
To the back of beyond?
And I thought
The mother was fond enough
Of Ireland
And furthermore
Maybe He needed
A break

Some turned to the Priest for advice

Were they being visited

By Christ?

He thought the Lord

Had better things to do

With his time

Not to mention

Better places

But he'd bring it to the Bishop's attention

Next week at the Galway Races

So many questions

But nobody stopped to think

That Jesus

Can do as He pleases

And if He's so inclined

To spend some time

Sitting on a ditch

In Donegal

Then so be it.

Everyone deserves a break.

scattered youth

"The completely solitary self: that's where poetry comes from, and it gets isolated by crisis, and those crises are often very intimate also."

- **Seamus Heaney.**

When I left my home and community in July 1985, I vowed that I was coming home and that nothing would ever keep me away. Somehow, someway, I was coming home. I would never lay claim to the land or what I perceived to be my forced relocation by way of immigration to Canada. It was not my home or native land!

Needless to say, when I made my return trip home after seven long and agonizing years had passed, and my family's reunification was only because of the death of my granny, my heart was to be broken that much further. I was not prepared for what I was about to behold and learn. My hatred for Canada grew.

My young friends had grown up and were moving full steam ahead down different paths. They no longer hung out together as one crowd and barely saw each other. They were now men and women living their own lives.

My perfectly preserved memory was completely shattered, for time had not stood still as I had thought it would. The precious memories and dreams from my youth that I had held so tightly onto for seven years were scattered upon my return home.

The last person I wrote to had moved over to England for her job. Although we remained in contact for years, I never received a final response to my longest piece of correspondence; a fifty-four-page, handwritten letter along with thirty-six photographs to her. I would learn that she was settled into her career and had a well-defined British accent, completely different from what I knew and associated her with. She eventually got married and moved on in her life and career pursuits.

Everything I knew and longed for had eroded, and there was absolutely nothing I could do to change this. Yet I clung to those memories of years gone by while trying to block out the bitter portions, including the hatred that had started filtering into our neighbourhood from those who came from the council housing district that would question us before starting a fight. I felt so bloody cheated by this. As if I ever had control over it.

Over the years thereafter, I was left with many questions but never received answers. What happened to my friends and our youth? The life I longed for was gone.

Sadly, to this very day, now as a grown man and successful in my careers as a social worker and an author, I still yearn for the times and friends that were left behind when we uprooted. There are days that I beg to go home and lose myself in the wilds of Ireland, yet there are also those days when I completely despise what I return to when I step foot back into my wee community, for nothing has ever been the same. That was the exact case most recently when I flew home to accompany my dad to the funeral of his cousin, Eamon. Unexpectedly, my eyes were fully opened on this trip!

The only saving grace I can take from this is while home and although there are those who made me extremely welcome, I decided to livestream six videos to family and friends all around the world. As several joined me online (only to be met with my true accent), I pondered out loud if they required a text feed along the bottom of their screens to understand my extremely pronounced brogue! Nevertheless, I brought everyone into my neighbourhood and to the areas I frequented as a child. Places which have haunted my mind since I left them all behind on July 19, 1985.

I did this in part to promote this wee book, as well as to provide myself (and others) the opportunity to visit those places anytime. Not only within my memories, dreams, and writings, but now also on my social media page.

scattered youth

Recollecting my thoughts
Of the years gone by.
Looking back to my childhood,
Heavy-breathed, I sigh.

I think of my friends,
And the places we played.
The secrets we kept,
The promises we made.

I reflect on the words,
To each other we'd say.
Tomorrow is our future,
Which now was yesterday.

With each morning that shone,
With every passing star.
Always there for one another,
We would never stray far.

Passing by along the street,
In our land of the Emerald Isle.
No matter our inner mood,
We managed to crack a smile.

Friendships were more than special,
We knew more than just a name.
Together we fought hard as one,
Never experiencing guilt or shame.

I thought our happiness would never end,
Through the days and years we'd seen.
Now fifteen years on down the line,
In a different country I've been.

Letters and calls once abundant,
Have all but come to a halt.
Should we say that being divided,
Is where we could lay fault?

We all have gone our separate ways,
New lives they have begun.
Anticipating one day we all reunite,
Before our final song is sung.

Waiting

"Ireland has one of the world's heaviest rainfalls. If you see an Irishman with a tan, it's rust."

- **Dave Allen.**

When it came to saving crops in Ireland, especially in the northwest, which seemed to have the worst weather in the whole country, it was important to try and time it correctly. Summer might wind up being a week of dry/half-dry weather, or it might be just the one fine day, or it might decide to skip that year altogether and have a go the following year.

That is not to say that those of us who had to manually save hay and turf had it easier when the weather did not cooperate. Far from it, in fact. Saving hay for winter feeding when the weather was poorly meant that one had to work longer and harder in order not to lose the crop.

I remember my father looking out at the non-stop rain and knowing that the hay was past when it should have been cut. It was the only time when we spent money on hiring machinery, so it was necessary to book the farmer, as everyone around was in the same boat. We could only hope the day the cutter would come would be dry enough to allow the work to be finished.

If we were lucky, we'd be able to turn the hay (by hand of course) from one side to the other over a few days. If we were unlucky with the weather, we could be turning those fields day after day until it turned into weeks. If we could have imported bottled sun from Spain, we would have made a fortune reselling it.

Waiting

Waiting for a dry spell
To cut
The hay
Knowing that a spell
May be
But a day.

Dear bought work
Small farm
In Donegal
Cattle feeder
Winter heater
One size fits all

"When's the best time
To visit Ireland?"
Asks the tourist
"When it's not raining"
Says I
Like some weather Jedi

And still

The small farmer

Waits

One never knows

When fine days chose

To stop by

With a few of their mates.

The Enchanted Isle

I was born and raised in the good ol' U.S.A.
But my heart also belongs to a place far away,
An enchanted isle of leprechauns and banshees,
Of shining, green fields, craggy hills and bent trees.

Where constant sun showers illuminate the grass.
Their emerald beauty dazzles the eye as you pass.
The thatch-roofed cottages speak of simpler ways
And cause the mind to drift back to quieter days.

The beauty of the land stuns you into reverent silence
And makes you wonder how there could be any violence.
I wish every man on earth with a troubled heart and mind
Could spend some time there to get them both realigned.

I could live there forever if I were given a choice.
The peaceful silence makes it easy to hear God's voice
It's in the whispering of the wind as it stirs the trees.
Your heart and soul are invigorated by every breeze.

A rainbow forming over a glade's babbling brook
Makes you abandon whatever you're doing to look.
The water's teeming with life and the bank is, too.
It's like a storybook, and the main character is you!

You don't need to be Irish to love the "Emerald Isle".
Whether north or south, you'll receive a bright smile
From the kind-hearted folk, the nicest people on earth.
They've survived much adversity with humor and mirth.

In fact, the Irish have a greeting, unique to them alone.
I can't describe it; you would simply have to be shown.
It's a wee turn of the head and an impish wink of the eye
That seems to say, "Isn't it lovely, friend, just to be alive?"

So come along with me now to a quieter place,
A land that forgot to join this mad human race.
There are some fine people I'd like you to meet
Just over that hill there and down the next street.
You just might recognize them as family because
Half the world's Irish, and half wishes it was!

Mark Rickerby

The Bogman

"I think of the bog as a feminine goddess-ridden ground, rather like the territory of Ireland itself."

- **Seamus Heaney.**

In rural Ireland, the majority of homes were heated from fires and ranges which burned solid fuel – word, turf or coal. Turf was the first choice for many as it was cleaner and less expensive than coal. When we were growing up, everybody cut their own turf by hand. Families would work in the bog together, with the father cutting the moist blocks of turf and his wife and children spreading it out on the turf bank to dry. It was hard work, but necessary to keep the house warm over the long winter months.

Once the moist peat had been turned over and crusted, we would stand four to six 'bars" of turf leaning against one another, so that it resembled something of a "Teepee" frame. This was called "footing" the turf. That formation allowed the wind to blow through and continue the drying out process. The next stage was to put two to three footings together, making a "clump." Eventually, the clumps got larger and signaled that the turf was ready to be brought home and built into a stack.

My father, who was always inventing something that a horse or donkey could pull, designed a cart without wheels. The body of the cart was a car bonnet ("hood" in the U.S.) from a Morris Minor. The bonnet would be turned over, at which time it resembled something of a large mixing bowl (you could also use the same device to mix mortar when building). To the sides of the bonnet he attached two shafts, which could be harnessed onto our donkey. The donkey would be led by his bridle and the cart would glide along the heather to the spot where the turf stack would be built, thus preserving and protecting the turf during the winter months.

The task of cutting turf fell to me at an early age – in my early teens. It was back-breaking work. My poem depicts a man in the bog getting on with the task. One needed an abundance of patience, knowing that the cutting and saving would take all summer long. These days, turf cutting by hand is rare due to the machinery which came about in the 90's that sucked up the wet turf and then spewed it out in long liquid-like lines. That is how the phrase "sausage turf" came about. Those same machines were the very reason that cutting turf is now prohibited in many areas as the government feared bogs would run out in much the same way as an oil well would run dry.

Ironically, many of us now look back on those days with a mixture of fondness and satisfaction. Whilst it was a laborious task and seemed to be never-ending, we persevered and fought through the pain, enjoying the spoils of war – basking in the warm glow of a turf fire on a long winter's night.

"Moderation, we find, is an extremely difficult thing to get in this country."

- Flann O'Brien.

The Bogman

Bent back

And thrusting arms

In an up-and-down motion

Like a blacksmith's bellows

Pushing and lifting

On a creaking handle

With paining muscles

Like a town fellow

Never imagined.

The moist brown

Of the peat

His driving

Thrust enters

Cooling the edge

Of a razor sharp blade

Silver beads of sweat

On a furrowed brow

Fall on the turf cutter's slane

Mission man

Without distraction

Plunging deep

For each extraction

His rhythm

As unchanging

As the sameness

Of his cutting

Never reaching a frenzied climax.

Donegal Boys

"A good storyteller never lets the facts get in the way."

- **Dave Allen.**

Growing up in Donegal decades ago, young boys (and girls) didn't have a lot of toys, but there were alternatives which did the job quite well. A stick could very well be used as a sword, and it could double up as a gun when needed. "Cowboys and Indians" were a staple part of being out playing in the fields.

My grandfather taught us that crabs hide under rocks at the edge of a Donegal beach. Then he shared a secret with us – how to bend a nail into a U shape and tie it around the end of a pole. This homemade "hook" would then be stuck in under those rocks and pulled out when a crab got caught.

And if you wanted to feel like a true Viking, there was always a turf stack to summit or a tree to be climbed. The hard part was always coming back down. When we were out in the fields chasing rabbits, setting home-made snares, or climbing house roofs and turf stacks, we were in our element. We hardly ever seemed to worry about getting hurt, although that was an ever-present possibility.

By the same token, we could never understand why our parents seemed to get so bent out of shape if they somehow happened upon our escapades. Looking back now, I realize that those long days, evenings and nights were some of the best times we would ever experience. We had absolutely no responsibility (but oh, would that come later) and the world, as they say, was definitely our oyster.

Being a typical Irish nomad, I took to wandering around the world. I'm not sure that I was searching for anything - maybe one day I will be able to answer that - but I was content to discover faraway places and cultures.

Sometimes that discovery came as a result of a chance meeting, or a missed connection, or hearing a story about a place that I didn't even know existed.

Other times, the discovery involved a war, or a region in uprising, or the result of a catastrophe. The one thing I never got to find out was, what happened to the boys with whom we played and went to school?

In America, everybody seems to first of all go to a prom (in Donegal, we had prams, but we had absolutely no idea what a "prom" was) and then later to school reunions. I'm not sure where they start, maybe at the ten-year mark, but they go back after twenty and thirty years, at least. I've never been to a school reunion and at this stage, I don't think I ever will. Hopefully those young boys who shared tree branch rifles with us are still around and have children of their own who have as active imaginations as had their fathers.

Donegal Boys

Jagged rushes
For St. Brigid cross
Whin bushes
Mountain moss
Wind with no sense
Of direction

Stoney roads
Dust when dry
Bent nail
"You'll lose an eye"
Hunting rock crabs
With your Grandfather

Dig for worms
Food for fish
Blow on a dog's nose
Make a wish
Climb a tree
And not break your neck

The old people talk
Laugh and spin yarns
The young one's fight
Climb the turf stack of Farrens
All bones intact
No harm done

Right wild eejits
They said we were
Hard to know now
When it's all a blur
What did they expect
From this Viking blood?

My Road

My Road is a poem about taking the road less traveled. From as far back as I can remember, I always had a fiercely independent streak. This despite the fact that I grew up in a setting where the head of the house was the only one allowed to exercise his independence. Which is quite ironic, since children learn from their parents and I could hardly help wanting to be an independent type. My father himself introduced me to an unorthodox, alternative lifestyle when he inducted me into his cross-border smuggling operations between Derry City and North Donegal when I was nine years of age.

Later on, however, I was to be ostracized for thinking independently when it came to mapping out my future. Basically, I could be anything my parents wanted me to be. Needless to say, this caused a fair amount of resentment and disillusionment among the troops (me) and set the scene for an internal revolution in the hills of Donegal between myself and my father.

During my adult years, I assumed various roles of significant responsibility. All the while, though, I carried out those duties with an independent attitude, which very rarely endeared me to the various supervisors whose paths I would cross. Actually, some of my best work, in the most trying of circumstances, turned out wildly successful due to the aforementioned attitude.

My path has seldom known smooth sailing. Often it feels as if I am in a light currach, being tossed around by the rough waves of life. Dark and stormy nights usually outnumber sunny blue skies, but this is the path I have chosen. I stay true to myself and forge ahead.

It is the only way I know.

My Road

Saw a quote
About roads
And one
Less traveled

No need
To wonder
Why many
Wander the other

The path
Of my journey
Is over-grown.
I must
Machete my way through

Twists and turns
It heaves and churns
Like a currach
In a gale.

My road has seas

Dark and wild

Like a Donegal night.

I stay on my road

It leads me

Even when it bleeds me,

It is my road

To the end.

"Death leaves a heartache no one can heal, love leaves behind a memory no one can steal."

- Inscription on an Irish headstone.

In loving memory...

White Feathers

Today, I went to the doctor to see,
A follow up from my chemotherapy,
The news, far from good, and so I was told,
A gift of White Feathers would begin to unfold.

"When life is challenging, your loved ones are sad,
Because they know the results could be bad,
In times of heartache, and downright despair,
White Feathers appear from out of thin air."

In that instance, there was nothing more I could do,
But think of the life that I've cherished with you,
Moments of yesterday flashed through my mind,
In good times, and bad, White Feathers we'd find.

Reflecting on one memory I'd refused to frame,
After our team had lost the championship game,
When suddenly, a gift fluttered down to my knee,
"A White Feather," you'd said, "from Heaven, to thee."

"It's a treasure, so it is, from up high above,
A message carried on the wings of a dove,
From your Guardian Angel, who wants you to know,
White Feathers, they nurture us, in times of sorrow."

As I looked to the ground, and cast a blank stare,
Sure enough, they appeared, from out of thin air,
Two tiny gifts from Heaven, landed either side of me,
White Feathers, their message, my destiny.

Accepting this news; previously panic and fear,
I've fought courageously; my time is now near,
You'll never walk alone, this I do swear,
White Feathers will let you know that I'm there.

Believe in us, and the journey we've bared,
The tears we've cried, the laughter we've shared,
Without warning, when you awaken, in the days ahead,
White Feathers will fall to the foot of your bed.

If met with grief, times seemingly are tough,

Life's little challenges; things appear rough,

Please understand that we're not far away,

White Feathers are we, guiding you through each day.

Composed in loving memory of Tommy McManus,

Karen McVicker, and John McManus, Sr.

even heaven can't hold us

My father died four years ago at the age of eighty-one, but I actually lost him years earlier as Parkinson's Disease and Dementia whittled him away to nothing mentally and physically. During most of his final year, he didn't even remember me.

Before the diseases had taken their toll, I took him golfing when he felt up to it because he had always loved the game. I was terrible but that didn't matter. I wanted him to play better than me anyway. I wanted to remind him of who he used to be. On one of those days, during one of his more lucid moments, he said, "I know you worry about me, son, but don't. You know I'm a tough, old bird." Even in the throes of those diabolical brain diseases, he was worried about me.

But it was true. He *was* a tough, old bird. He survived emotionally empty parents and a Depression-era childhood in Belfast. As a teenager, he became a semi-professional boxer and reserve police officer on some very mean streets. He lost almost one hundred pounds and his entire stomach to cancer when he was forty-five. But, despite all these challenges, he never became one of those men who finds trouble everywhere and never realizes he's the one creating it. He became the polar opposite. He made people laugh everywhere he went. He sang and told jokes, which he had an endless litany of, so his friends could forget their troubles for a while.

After emigrating to Southern California, he became known as a singer, story-teller and M.C. for events in the Irish community. He also worried incessantly about Belfast during the worst years of The Troubles. In the 1960's, there was an expression, "If you're not part of the solution, you're part of the problem." So he became part of the solution, writing and speaking widely to American audiences, doing his best to increase tolerance and respect on both sides of the spectrum. He knew that terrorism and violence override other evils and only serve to inflame the will of one's adversaries.

The Irish are famous the world over for two dubious and legendary traits – mean tempers and never shrinking from a fight. So of course the troubles dragged on forever. Knowing themselves better than anyone else, everyone in Ireland should have seen that coming. But sure there's never much intelligent reasoning in hatred and rage.

As I mentioned in a previous chapter, everyone told my da he should have been a professional singer. Many just assumed he was. He was *that* good. But the first job he ever got when he became a father to my older brother and I was an insurance claims adjuster and that's what he was trained to do. He eventually opened his own company, and it flourished for almost fifty years until he was dragged into retirement in his mid-seventies.

Though he had no formal education (he got a job at fourteen to support his parents), his business stayed afloat while companies run by highly-educated men rose and fell. His edge over them was his personality. Nobody ever called his office without getting a joke and some friendly conversation. He was quite literally "the life of the party" at work and at the pub. He was also so honest I used to call him "the last boy scout." So watching everything he was gradually disappear during those last five years was nothing short of hellish. He even began to lose his singing voice, which was like Van Gogh getting uncontrollable tremors in his painting hand.

Much is said about "accepting the inevitable" when someone is dying. Though steeped in denial, one of those moments for me was when I realized I hadn't heard him sing in months. It was always his greatest joy and the last stronghold of his mind against the brain diseases assaulting him. In pure desperation, I bought the best karaoke machine I could find and tried to sing his old "party pieces" as he called them – the standards. And he gamely tried, but he knew his voice wasn't as good as it used to be, and he refused to settle for less. It was a sad day. I left the karaoke machine at his house, but he never used it.

A month before he died, he fell and broke his hip in four places, then spent four agonizing weeks at a hospital with a staff that made so many mistakes, I lost my temper and had a security detail assigned to me until the day he died. Our relationship had often been strained, but I cried like a baby during his final days.

I had helped him finish his memoir about his youth in Belfast before he got sick so I knew all he had gone through as a child. His parents never told him they loved him, never acknowledged Christmas or his birthday, and were generally too wrapped up in their own problems together and as individuals to give him and his younger sister much attention. Compared to them, he was a tremendous father.

In his book The Prophet, Kahlil Gibran wrote, *"Ever has it been that love knows not its own depth until the hour of separation."* So it was on the night of my father's death, as I waited for the morphine drip to stop the heart that had survived so much. I cried into his neck, forgiving every mistake and hoping he had forgiven mine, praying for him, telling him I loved him over and over, and that it was okay to leave. The doctors said the morphine usually worked much faster. His words returned to me, "Don't worry about me, son. You know I'm a tough, old bird." I begged him to stop being so tough and finally escape from his broken body.

After he died, and still today four years later, I have had a terrible time getting over not only his death but also the terrible suffering of his final years. I don't understand how a man who was so kind to others had to die like that, slowly erased, degraded in every sense of the word, unable to shower or go to the bathroom alone. I was as angry as I was sad. I cursed God. A more faithful friend said, "It's okay. God can handle it." I answered, "I don't want God to handle it. To hell with His strength. I want Him to be crushed like I am."

During the month or so after he died, I had a particularly bad night. I hadn't slept and was lying in bed as the sun came up. I whispered, "Dad, you told me you were a tough, old bird. Prove it to me now. Find a way through whatever separates heaven and earth and let me know you're okay. I need to know you're free of those horrible diseases. I need to know you're singing again."

I have two daughters, Marli and Emma. At that time, Marli was four years old and Emma was eighteen months and just starting to talk. A few minutes after I said that prayer, Marli came into the room and said, "Dad, what does claim mean?" I asked her to repeat herself to make sure I was hearing her right. She said it again. I asked her why. She said, "Because Emma keeps saying the word 'claim' over and over again."

I jumped out of bed and looked at her as she played with toys on the floor. I heard her say the word one more time before she went on to something else. I sat next to her and asked her to say it again but she just stared at me. The only other word she could have said that would have let me know equally well that my father was speaking through her was "Belfast", the name of his beloved hometown. But he knew I would associate him with that word because of his career as a claims adjuster. He was always talking about claims and the interesting people he met handling them.

I felt much better after that day. My father was tough enough to crash the gates between this world and the next. But it didn't stop there.

I was gardening one sunny day recently when the sadness and anger crushed me again. I don't know what the catalyst was. Maybe it was because it was the kind of day my father would have loved to go golfing on. Again, I asked him for some kind of sign. A few minutes later, I moved the trash can I was dumping leaves into and was astounded to see a puddle on the ground beneath it in the perfect shape of a shamrock, the symbol of Ireland. I was so dumbstruck – or gobsmacked as they would say in Ireland – I ran to get my phone and take a photo of it. It had evaporated a little before I got back but I was still able to capture it. I showed it to my wife, children and several friends that day and they were all amazed by it, too. Here it is –

 Four Green Fields

Another time, my daughter Marli and I were walking our dog Pixie and guessing at what her date of birth might be. My sadness was heavier than usual that day, too, but I was doing my best to conceal it. The first date Marli picked was May 11th, my father's birthday.

There have been other coincidences not related to my father, such as my first-born being delivered at 10:17, the same number as the date of my brother's death (October 17th) and the number of the room my mother-in-law was in (1017) when she died several years before the granddaughter she would have loved so much was born. The most recent was on December 21st. I was driving and saw an older lady running for a bus and miss it. I asked her if she wanted a ride and she said she was going pretty far - to a town called Panorama City. I said I was passing by there and could take her. I ended up dropping her off at the hospital where my father died on December 21st the previous year!

Cynics would call these events coincidence or the product of an overactive imagination, but even they would have to admit the evidence is mounting that the other side is real, and every now and then, if they see us suffering, those we have lost can find a way back, perhaps with God's permission, to let us know they're well and waiting to see us again.

The Irish aren't world-famous for their tenacity for nothing. But apparently, that resilience and grit isn't limited to the mortal world. If God didn't give my father permission to visit me on those occasions when my crying was loud enough for him to hear, I'm sure he was tough enough to sneak away and break through whatever separates heaven and hell to let me know that grand mind of his has been restored. And if I could find my way to him as well, I'd leave right now and traverse galaxies just to hear him sing one more time.

Whispers in the Breeze

"Memory, in widow's weeds, with naked feet stands on a tombstone."

- **Aubrey de Vere.**

I returned to Belfast a second time after being away for thirteen years. However, I was not coming back for a funeral as I had done six years earlier with my mum and aunt after my granny passed away from a massive heart attack. This time, I was accompanied by my daughter and wife for a family vacation. Yet they had their own country to return to. They had no intention of staying beyond the three weeks we were there. For me, however, the life I left behind and longed for was met with more grief, homesickness, and a desire to stay there for up to six months. It never happened.

A few days before we were to return to Canada, I stood with my four-year-old daughter at the grave of her great-grandparents. As kids, we had spent a lot of time visiting my granny in Belfast as well as when she moved around the corner from us. Close, yet now so far away.

Lost in a trance, I gazed at their headstone, and it dawned on me I was following a process that many others do. Standing in a lonely graveyard, reminiscing on lives once shared before their untimely passing. Untimely because I wished I could have spent more time with them before their death, because of all the things I should have said to them but now would never had the chance, because of things I did I wished I could take back, and because all these things didn't fit with my schedule until it was too late. As such, I found myself asking my granny and granda for their guidance and prayers from beyond the clouds that day.

Looking out towards Belfast Lough, I reflected on my life, their passing, and that one-day my loved ones would be doing the exact same while standing at the foot of *my* grave - pausing to reflect.

Our lives are fleeting glimpses of time; we never know when our journey ends or a new one begins. Those we love, the heartache we experience, and the memories we carry until we meet again…

whispers in the breeze

Realizing my innermost fears,
Choking back the steady stream of tears.
Not knowing your time had come,
Without you I feel so numb.

Just a whisper in the breeze,
Brought my world down to its knees.
The day that you were called away,
Paradise is where you now stay.

When the days do come to pass,
I call upon your bed of grass.
Comfort inside knowing you're there,
Looking up at my vacant stare.

The silence I exchange with thee,
Speaks volumes, I'm sure this you'll see.
My shadow casts across your grave,
While I stand so lonely, I stand so brave.

Now the days they seem so long,

In your arms is where I belong.

I close my eyes and hear you speak,

You call my name; my legs feel weak.

Together we promised that we would grow old,

We thought our happiness would never unfold.

I kneel at your feet with my head hung low,

Thoughts in my mind you already know.

This quality time with you I spend,

Will hopefully help my broken heart mend.

Feeling guilty when I turn to leave,

Returning home I continue to grieve.

When my term approaches death,

Time to exhale one final breath.

I wonder if others will fall to their knees,

When my name whispers in the breeze.

Laying to Rest

"Do not resent growing old. Many are denied the privilege."

- **Irish Proverb.**

Poems come about in many different ways. Sometime a thought or a mere kernel of a thought nibbles at a writer's sub consciousness, waiting patiently to be extracted and delivered onto a page. Other times it feels as if a tsunami of words and feelings are about to burst the banks of one's mind. I think it is more unusual for a poem to be carried around incognito for several years, only to pour forth one day with no warning whatsoever and write itself.

I know the exact time and place when **Laying to Rest** was conceived. It happened when I looked into my father's coffin, in the front room of a bungalow in the far North of Donegal and I had to finally admit that he was gone. His death was especially surreal for me, as I heard of it quite by accident. Forty-eight hours before, I was three thousand miles away and only returned to Ireland to attend my father-in-law's funeral in Mayo. They died within two days of each other, having only ever met once.

Laying to Rest was born three years later, fifteen miles outside of Dublin. I'll never forget that day. Officially, I wrote the poem, but it felt like all I was doing was holding the pen, as the poem wrote itself. I never stopped writing from start to finish. I might have changed three or four words, not even changed the words, but changed their position. As soon as I had written the very last word, I knew it was done. At that exact moment, I felt a heavy weight being lifted off my shoulders. I had become so used to feeling weighed down, that I stopped noticing.

Prior to its current publication, I could count on one hand the number of people who have read this poem. It has taken a while, but I feel it is now time to share it with a wider audience.

Laying to Rest

On a warm summer day

In the back of a Mark 2 Cortina

I first heard the words "Multiple Sclerosis"

I was too young to understand

That some doctor from Pakistan

Just sentenced you to death

"What does that bastard know?"

You wanted to know

"Some student over here for experience."

In a rage

You questioned his parentage

And diagnosis simultaneously

We all agreed with you

For a while

Wanting to believe

You hurt your back

In the bog.

But in the back of my mind

I had doubts

I thought it naïve

To believe

The chiropractor coming down from Derry

Every Tuesday morning

Could restore your limbs

Like some modern day Lazarus

I once tried to share

This fear with my mother

"Mr. Anderson knows what he is doing"

She assured me

"The neighbours all swear by him."

I figured it was worth

Ten shillings a week

To ease her mind

I never doubted

The massaging messiah again

Except to myself.

I wondered over the years

If you knew

Your cause was lost

In the dead of night

Did you fight back tears

Was it a living hell?

You had twenty years to contemplate

In the end

You knew too well.

It's ironic to think

How you always wanted

To go out like a light

In the blink

Of an eye

So to speak

Instead you spent your time

Like a convict on death row

Wasting away in your crumbling body

Four Green Fields

Of a cell

You could have told me

There'd be no Governor's reprieve

Foolishly I believed

You'd live

To a belligerent old age

Typically we fell out

As your world was falling in

Like love

Bad blood is blind

I should have been able

To read the signs

Your attempt at reconciliation

Written in a shaking hand

Was a sure indication

The Pakistani's prophesy

Had come true

It crept upon you

Like woodworm
Riddling your bones to dust

I didn't know
Thought there'd be loads
Of time
To mend the gaps
Make it right some day
Stubborn as bog fir
I did not budge
Besides, I had my own problems
Three thousand miles away

Heard of your death
Quite by accident
Thought at first
It must be some mistake
I was too thick to visit
Before it was too late

Four Green Fields

Still don't know why I wasn't told
"Had your own life to live"
Was my mother's excuse
Maybe she got
Her own back on me
For turning my back on you
But I didn't, you know
I was just waiting
For the right time

Not for time
To run out

How We Survive

If we are fortunate,
we are given a warning.

If not,
there is only the sudden horror,
the wrench of being torn apart;
of being reminded
that nothing is permanent,
not even the ones we love,
the ones our lives revolve around.

Life is a fragile affair.
We are all dancing
on the edge of a precipice,
a dizzying cliff so high
we can't see the bottom.

One by one,
we lose those we love most
into the dark ravine.

So we must cherish them

without reservation.

Now.

Today.

This minute.

We will lose them

or they will lose us

someday.

This is certain.

There is no time for bickering.

And their loss

will leave a great pit in our hearts;

a pit we struggle to avoid

during the day

and fall into at night.

Some,

unable to accept this loss,

unable to determine

the worth of life without them,
jump into that black pit
spiritually or physically,
hoping to find them there.

And some survive
the shock,
the denial,
the horror,
the bargaining,
the barren, empty aching,
the unanswered prayers,
the sleepless nights
when their breath is crushed
under the weight of silence
and all that it means.

Somehow, some survive all that and,
like a flower opening after a storm,

they slowly begin to remember
the one they lost
in a different way…

The laughter,
the irrepressible spirit,
the generous heart,
the way their smile made them feel,
the encouragement they gave
even as their own dreams were dying.

And in time, they fill the pit
with other memories
the only memories that really matter.

We will still cry.
We will always cry.
But with loving reflection
more than hopeless longing.

Mark Rickerby

And that is how we survive

That is how the story should end.

That is how they would want it to be.

MUM'S LAMENT

"Mothers hold their children's hands for just a little while… And their hearts forever."

- **Irish Proverb.**

"The seat check in winner at the game was section 308 row 3 seat 11. Granny is making her presence known."

– **Caitlin McVicker.**

While putting this book together via text messaging, emails, and telephone calls between the three of us, there were a tremendous number of interesting developments. The one that surprised me the most occurred this morning when I awoke to a late-night email from Mark, which he had sent just a few hours before. He shared the beautiful and poignant story **Even Heaven Can't Hold Us**. I will fully explain the significance of that shortly. But, another one just occurred this very moment which I entered above as the opening epitaph shared by my daughter, Caitlin.

As I read Mark's email, I was shocked to learn that we are connected by way of special dates and numbers of significant meaning to us both. As Mark said, atheists and cynics often trying to write off supernatural events as coincidence, such as when our loved ones send little messages to us from beyond the skies. My composition **White Feathers**, which you have now read, speaks to those little gifts sent to us by our loved ones to let us know they aren't so far away.

I have also experienced unexplainable occurrences, as you will see from the stories told within this reflection. For me, coming to terms has happened several times over after losing loved ones and cherished friends, including one gentleman who inspired me greatly - Tommy McManus.

One of the most difficult days of my life was when I said goodbye to my mum, Catherine Philomena McVicker (nee Devlin). She was a warrior in her own right who fought for her beliefs and for the protection of her children during a political war, as you have read in the section titled *The Troubles*. She watched over us day and night and raised us with good intentions, only wanting to see the best for us. She put her family ahead of herself while fighting a courageous battle against a silent killer.

With my dad at sea sending home his pay, my mum was left to raise four heavily asthmatic children. Even though the British government made the decision to pay mothers to stay home and raise their kids by way of adding extra years onto their pensions, this was an endless task. She made sure our Christmas and Easters were filled with joy and our birthdays were incredibly special. It was always a treat to look forward to the cakes she would make for us along with ice-cream, crisps, fizzy drinks and sweets.

My mum nurtured and cherished her family to no end. This was accomplished while managing a single income to pay a mortgage, keeping a roof over our heads and clothes on our backs, shopping, gardening, driving my siblings and I to endless of doctor's and physiotherapy appointments, never-ending errands, laundry, cooking meals, meeting teachers along with helping us with our homework. Her countless attributes included picking us up from our shortcomings all the while helping us understand the critical life lessons which were associated with those.

Fast forward to January 31, 2005. Although I was not fully aware of her medical condition, I went to visit her in the hospital. According to my younger sister, Angela, approximately nine years earlier her illness was diagnosed by her doctor when the complications began making their presence known. The x-rays showed spots on her lungs. As a result, she was placed on three units of oxygen. Just as Mark wrote about his beloved father, John, it was incomprehensible to me why she needed these supports when she had a heart bigger than the world and did so much for everyone else. It just didn't seem fair.

It was torturous seeing her connected to an oxygen tank. She spent countless hours during the night tending to our needs, interrupting her sleep patterns to put Vick's Vaporub on our chests, and providing us with inhalers to help us breathe. The damp, Irish climate was brutal for chronic, bronchial asthmatics, especially when all of us had been diagnosed with this since both of my parents carried the gene for it. My siblings and I were hit with a double-whammy. I dare not try and recall the number of asthma attacks we fought. Wondering if each attack would be the one I wouldn't survive as I gasped for air was horrifying, especially for a child.

On the morning of February 5th, 2005, my mum called while I was in-between classes at the University of Manitoba to tell me that my Uncle Thomas had passed away in Belfast. I was standing in the middle of a large hallway at the time, and my legs buckling beneath me as she shared what happened. Because my mother couldn't possibly travel, the decision was made that I would go home to represent our side of the family.

My father went to the bank and extracted funds to pay for a plane ticket home. My mum informed me that she and my dad needed me back in Canada to help them and I promised I would but did not comprehend her hidden message. Perhaps she thought my homesickness would keep me there as it had almost done every other occasion I went. But that wasn't why she told me.

Just as I had done once before, I flew home in preparation for an Irish wake. This time I was not accompanying my mum and her sister, Maureen. Although it is always a delight to touch down on Irish soil, there remains a persistent, bittersweet lump in my throat which planted itself on the day we left in 1985.

Upon making my way to my Aunt Josephine's house, a feeling of dread suddenly descended upon me. Met with the familiar black ribbon on her door signifying a death in the family, I walked into the house to find my uncle in the same place my granny was when I flew home for the first time in 1992. It all seemed so wrong. As he lay in his coffin, the hulking frame of a gentleman I knew as my uncle had shrunken so much, I barely recognized him. Gone was his full, wholesome and handsome face, replaced by gaunt flesh as thin as paper.

We proceeded with the wake services over the next few days. When the day came, after saying all our goodbyes and placing the lid on his coffin, I walked outside and waited for my uncle to be carried out of his home and out towards the street.

In traditional Irish fashion, everyone took a lift of his coffin, placed him upon their shoulders and, while marching side-by-side, carried him up his street. It was a familiar occurrence for me, with two to the front and two to the back, only to be replaced by four more pallbearers every thirty feet or so. As we did, my aunt walked behind, leading the procession.

After the undertaker took the lead, I snapped a picture of three brothers, my cousins, walking arm-in-arm behind the hearse which carried the body of their beloved father towards the church on the Crumlin Road, the same church my dad's family attended in years gone by. A sudden memory burst through my sadness – a tale about my uncle who took the helm of a horse-drawn carriage for his niece. Suddenly, the horse got spooked and took off, which sent the carriage crashing along with my uncle and his niece flying. This tale also made headlines in the local paper. It was as if he had jumped into my grief-stricken mind and stayed for a moment before the reality of another Irish rain, of the meticulous finish of the coffin with Christ's sullen face carved into it, began staring back at me. I cursed death with every step and the incessant rain that seemed to be punctuating it.

The celebration of his life was said. Again, and having been blessed (or perhaps cursed) with the gift of the gab, I was offered the opportunity to speak a "few words" about my uncle. (Would someone please describe 'few'?) I apparently talked for such a long time because when the priest retook the altar and I my seat amongst my family, my cousin, Karl, told me how proud he was of me. On the other hand, my Aunt Josephine informed me that the priest almost considered finding the rarely used St. Patrick's crook somewhere in the ancient storage room of the church, used while watching flocks of sheep from centuries before, to pull me off of the altar. Although I had finally relented as if I were a lawyer making my closing statements in court, it lead to several fits of laughter among those in attendance at the gathering afterwards. I guess if ever done, a scan of my gall bladder would reveal blarney stones, although I have never even been to Blarney Castle or County Cork to kiss that great big stone.

Afterwards, we all headed down to a local pub to have a few jars and sandwiches, as everyone had gathered to share their memories of my uncle. Some slowly left, while others stayed well into the late hours of the evening to celebrate his life or mourn his passing. I myself had left hours before as I was wrecked from the jetlag as well as from rushing around the university to ensure I had everything to get me through while overseas. As such, I made my way up to our Stephen's house, my cousin, to put my head down for a few hours before returning to again join the group gathered at the pub.

The following morning, after a night of serious drinking which would usually require several buckets of water to flush the alcohol out of our kidneys, my cousins and I decided to go out for a hearty Ulster fry. This is another one of the tasty meals I miss from home – consisting of sausage, bacon, tomato, eggs, soda bread, potato farl, black and white pudding, toast, and to some, a side of baked beans all with a pot of tea to wash it down. The joy of being in the company of my family greatly alleviated the sadness I felt over my uncles passing.

On our way out, still laughing from the conversations we were having inside the pub, our Stephen suddenly disappeared into a florist. Because it was Sunday, February 13th, and because of the massive heart thumping in his chest, Stephen came out with the largest bouquet of red roses any of us had ever laid eyes on. When asked what his plans were for them, he explained that since Valentine's Day was the following day, he wanted his mummy to know she was appreciated and that she wasn't alone. Since the large gathering of people at the wake would no longer be there upon our return, the house would be empty and eerily silent. He didn't think this was right for my aunt and wanted to bring her both comfort and warmth.

Suddenly, our laughter and jokes turned to massive lumps within our collective throats, thinking at how, in a blink of an eye, Stephen had turned his sadness into a celebration of his mum. A very unselfish thought, one which brought pure happiness to my Aunt Josephine's heart when he arrived back at the house. He let her know on this special occasion that, although only just widowed, she was very much surrounded with pure love. A beautiful gesture by an amazing son. He fought his own grief and put his mum ahead of it. Little did we know, heartache, immeasurable suffering, and inconsolable grief was about to strike into the depths of our very hearts again in the form of a brutal, unforeseeable tragedy.

Thirty-six hours after we had laid my Uncle Thomas to rest, and only six hours since I had last said goodnight and thought I would see him the following morning, word came that Stephen had been murdered while having a quiet pint and mourning the passing of his beloved father at a local pub. I dreaded the thought of putting further stress on my mum due to her breathing difficulties, but there was simply no way around this. I had to tell her and my father.

Unbeknownst to me, my mum had been discharged from the hospital and sent home. She was resting, adjusting to being connected to an oxygen tank and hose 24/7. Even though I was six hours ahead of them, upon hearing the long-distance rings go off at four o'clock in the morning, and although my dad took the call, my mum knew something was terribly wrong and came to the phone. Since it was my duty to tell her, I asked her to please sit down first. I explained I would have to stay in Ireland a while longer and deal with this unexpected death, with details about the murder still coming in. Even though my university studies included a course called *Families across the Lifespan* as part of my preparation to enter the field of social work, nothing could have prepared me for this.

 Four Green Fields

While I was on the phone, two of my cousins returned with the grim news that we were hoping was not true. One gave me the slightest nod of confirmation while the other went in with a look of pure determination on his face. I didn't say a word, although my mum was on the phone when the news broke within milliseconds of me getting the all-knowing nod. The ear-shattering wail which immediately filled every inch of available space is something I will never forget for as long as I live. A mother's cry of heartbreaking sorrow coupled with all the other events that had already and were now unfolding second by each gut-wrenching second, was heard by my mum. I couldn't hold her on the phone any longer and said I'd call her back later. However, she took the lead responsibility of letting our family in Canada know that another gentle soul was taken from us without rhyme or reason.

Just as Mark wrote in expressing his anger and frustration to a higher being when his father was taken from him and wanted Him to be just as crushed as Mark was, my cousin did the exact same thing, screaming at the top of her lungs, swearing at God as she now not only lost a father, but a brother as well.

My own thoughts swirled like a tidal wave. Why was our family chosen to be targeted? I challenged the Creator to explain His reasoning for it. Through gritted teeth, I cursed God Himself –

"Do you enjoy ripping the hearts out of families when they're at their lowest point grieving and trying to put their lives back together? Would you, the so called Almighty, show whatever presence or form you choose to come in, whether it be a burning bush or a rumble from the heavens, and explain your friggin' position?"

No!

Not only did our endless list of questions go fully unanswered, funeral planning which had just come to an end suddenly started all over again, including another Irish wake which did not come with the celebrations we normally had to ease our grief while reflecting upon cherished memories.

We had to bury a young man with his father whom we had already laid to rest. A cruel reality. "Thank you, Creator," I cried," for your unwelcomed hand in destroying us further! Should you not be responding to prayers?"

Memories of the photograph I snapped of the three brothers, arm-in-arm, walking behind the hearse of their father's coffin a few days earlier unexpectedly came flooding back to me. This same scene would almost be fully re-enacted, only this time it was *two* brothers arm-in-arm following their brother back to that same church and on to join his dad. This was not followed up with a celebration of life but a quest to find answers.

After all the events were done and I had to leave my family behind, I left for Canada completely wrecked, destroyed, and shattered after having flown home for one funeral, returning after attending a second burial and service. But the Almighty was not done with me just yet and seemed hell bent on inflicting more grief.

I was back in Canada a few months and had continued with my studies at university. On Sunday, April 17, it was approximately 7:10 p.m. when I went to see my mum who was staying on a unit at the Riverview Health Centre with patients learning to live with Chronic Obstructive Pulmonary Disease (COPD). After walking into her room with my own wee family, nothing could have ever prepared me for this, either. The first words she stated laid me flat out as if I had been sucker-punched and left breathless:

"Greg love, I'm terminal."

The shock and disbelief were incomprehensible to my heart and mind. Why was I not told sooner? Why was this happening? What did I do to deserve yet another blow? Why was life so horrible and cruel? Not only were my questions endless, my mind very quickly cast back to the three words shrieked by my cousin towards the Heavens and the Almighty when she learned of Stephen's murder. "Fuck you, God!"

Rather than scream the same or similar damning and unfiltered but extremely warranted choice words, I walked straight out into the hallway

  Four Green Fields

and paced several circles, not knowing how to take the news my mum shared with me and my family only seconds before. They all remained in the room while my mind spiraled into a complete meltdown. I had no idea she was that far advanced with her illness. Panicking, I went back into her room and asked if she said was true, if she was having me on, how long would she have to live, and a multitude of other questions that people ask when they find out their loved one is literally dying right before their eyes. This, however, was extremely upsetting to her, which was certainly not my intent. I needed to know what the hell was going on.

My mum tried to reassure me the specialists who work with this disease were well on top of things, and that she would likely have twenty to thirty years still in front of her. She said this to try and set *my* heart and mind at ease, although she knew the actual questions to the questions were completely different from the answers she gave. We stayed for two hours but needed to get the kids, Caitlin and Ciarán, to their beds. After giving our farewell kisses and hugs goodnight, the shock was beyond overwhelming and wrecked my brain as we drove. I needed to know so much more.

Upon arriving home, I researched everything I could about this disease. The results gave no comfort. I first searched for a definition of Idiopathic Pulmonary Fibrosis (IPF), Idiopathic was described as being "of unknown origin." Anyone diagnosed with this disease has approximately ten years to live. With the provision of oxygen which my mum had begun taking three months earlier, a person's lifespan is reduced drastically to five years, with the average outcome being two years, eight months.

My mum was in a unit for persons learning how to live with COPD, yet to my understanding her diagnosis was the complete opposite. In providing a very simplistic explanation, a person who has COPD can inhale oxygen into their lungs but has a difficult time exhaling it. With IPF, the effect is the exact opposite in that sufferers of this condition can exhale easily enough but have an extremely difficult time catching their breath. They quite literally suffocate.

Since she had only been on oxygen for a very short period of time, I believed we had at least another two-and-a-half years to fully enjoy our time with her and could do everything in life we never had the time to do. I wanted to spend every waking minute telling her how much we loved and cherished her for all the wonderful things she had done for us over the years. I wanted her to know how grateful I was for her having the gut-wrenching courage to leave her own mother, sisters, and brother behind to create new opportunities for her children. There was so much I wanted to do and say.

On her 65th birthday, my sisters, Karen and Angela, were over visiting our mum when she raised a glass of wine and gave a sobering toast:

"Well. Here's to sixty-five for I'm not going to see sixty-six."

Although we are never told in advance what our time allotment in life on this earth is, I would have certainly appreciated a little bit of insight, just as my mum had shared in her toast. She had less than one year left, further diminishing the already-too-short, average timeframe I researched. At this point, the online answers accounted for absolutely nothing.

Two days later, while starting the first day of a Native Studies class at University, I received a phone call from Angela asking me to meet my mum and dad. They were about to leave their family home for the hospital. I excused myself from class, raced there, and met my mum at the front doors of the emergency while my dad went to park his car. I brought her in but as her breathing was extremely labored and I heard her tell a clerk that the reason for her visit was because she could not breathe, I set about to get her information to the nurse at triage while waiting for my dad. Within a short period of time thereafter, she was admitted. Things would start to change on a monumental scale.

Over the next few days, my mum's oxygen levels were rapidly increased until they eventually reached fifteen units, the maximum administered by measurement standards in Canada. Yet there was nothing more anyone or anything could do. I was not willing to give up on her, asked for an

 Four Green Fields

emergency meeting, and offered to donate one of my own asthma-ridden lungs to her. My brother immediately followed suit and offered to do the same. In our state of panic, what else could we have done? I asked to be immediately prepped for surgery, so she could live and continue to be there for our family and her grandchildren. But there was so much we did not know, including information which was then gently shared with us but felt very much like a kick in the teeth.

In order to have a successful lung transplant, a heart transplant usually goes along with it. The donor and recipient must be deemed a match since the chest cavity has to accommodate for this. My mum was just a wee woman, standing at 4'11" while the two of us both stood a foot over her. There was nothing wrong with her heart which was completely resilient. It was her lungs that were failing at an exponential rate of acceleration.

Twenty-six days after she had first broken the news to me, on the afternoon of Wednesday, May 11th, 2005 at exactly 3:49:48, we said one last goodbye to the woman who gave us everything and left us begging for nothing. At that exact moment of time, my mum exhaled her last breath and joined her parents, younger sister, and her two brothers on the other side in the spirit world as well as other family who were deceased, including my Uncle Thomas and cousin, Stephen. Life as I knew it changed in the blink of an eye.

My first reaction was to tear the tape from the monitor which kept track of her levels until there was nothing left but a straight line. Karen exclaimed I could not do this; it was hospital property. I didn't give a damn about stupid hospital policies or their staff. For whatever reason, I wanted this final printout as I was sure the hospital would have no problem discarding it into the nearest rubbish bin as soon as our backs were turned. This recorded her final heartbeat, her final pulse, and her final breath along with the exact time of her death.

Just before she passed, I stood over her in her hospital bed and said, "Mum, I love you" four times in succession. My heart and soul literally died when she mustered up every ounce of energy to repeat those same words back to me while taking her last breaths in life, surrounded by sixteen loving family members. The grief, sadness, and despair that accompanied this was overwhelming as her passing impacted the nurses who had provided care for her.

I refused to leave her side as I did not want them taking her now lifeless body to be placed out of view from our watchful eyes. She didn't deserve that. It wasn't until 5:10 p.m. that our family made the decision we had to let the staff complete their roles and prepare her for the next part of her journey. And since we were on the Palliative Intensive Care Unit, they would need to prepare for another patient. To me, the process seemed cold and mechanical.

I guess I knew this day was coming. Just as Mark shared, we are given signs from those who have already departed from this world. A week before, while sitting on my bed, and after having returned from visiting my mum, I saw my grandparents and my mum's two brothers standing at the foot of it. My granda, John Devlin, had passed away in 1971. My Uncle Jimmy passed in 1987; my Uncle John in 1988, and finally my granny, Mary Devlin, in 1992, which was when I returned home for the first time after being away for seven years. I did not welcome their presence with open arms but swore at them and demanded to know why they were there. I was defiant and told them they were not taking my beloved mum. As much as I appreciated seeing them, I shouted it was not her turn and asked for them go back to where they came from. I really did not have a choice, for they came to release her from her suffering and needed me to prepare myself. My protests did not account for anything; it would not have been fair to my mum to prolong her suffering. Who was I to question why it was her time to venture into new beginnings, a new life, and a new adventure?

As you now know, Mark and I wrote about things happening for a reason, even if they cannot be explained or attempts are made by cynics to discredit them. Moreover, some of my mum's last words to me prior to her passing, which fell on the same date as Caitlin's text to me just now, and

 Four Green Fields

which I included at the start of this tale, were, "Greg, I'm not getting out of this hospital. I'm not coming home." I had assured my mum she was coming home. Little did I realize the truth to my words: we brought her home for her wake service and to celebrate her beautiful and courageous life under the cloak of death.

After getting permission to bring her to her house to celebrate her life in true Irish fashion rather than leave her at a funeral home, which is normally the case in Canada, the wake and other events associated with her passing are still a complete blur in my mind. But strangely enough, they remain so clear. Family and friends joined us from all over the world to participate in the celebration of my mum's life, lifting a toast over her while saying words which captured the spirit of who she was and what she stood for. We poured a glass for her spirit and placed it on top of her casket. I struggled with this set up as I had hoped to carry her on our shoulders just as I had done a few months prior with my Uncle Thomas and cousin, Stephen. Unfortunately, this was not possible.

Our mum looked very beautiful and peaceful in her casket, no longer hooked up to a machine which assisted her breathing. But nothing could ever bring her back, no matter how much our hearts broke, our minds wished, and our prayers asked. She was free to embark upon her new journey and without pain or suffering.

On the morning of May 16th, my mum would be leaving her family home for the last time, heading on to the church for final service before internment at the cemetery. It was around four a.m. when I sat down in front of the computer at my parent's house, my mum only a matter of steps away from me and composed this lament to her memory. It took two hours to write. I asked my dad and my siblings, Karen, Joe, and Ange, to review it and see what they thought. I sought their approval as every poem I had ever written up to that point was reviewed and edited by my mum. She provided me with guidance and constructive feedback when I was composing each piece, just as she did with our homework when we were kids growing up in Northern Ireland.

I asked my dad and siblings to sign one copy of the composition before placing it in with my mum. From there, I simply lay on the floor below her casket, facing her, wanting to have my time alone with her. My da came over and shook me to make sure I was alive, as he knew I was completely heartbroken over her death and was only afforded twenty-six days compared to the years she had told me. However, I knew it would be the last chance I would get, as she was leaving for the church at eleven a.m. for her final service.

I had faced my mum in a similar manner the day before she passed away. After having a family gathering at Karen's house, I excused myself to go home but instead snuck back to the hospital around ten p.m., putting my head on her pillow only inches from her face to breathe with her for over two hours. She gave me the gift of life and breath, and I wanted to share that gift with her one more time. It was difficult to breathe at her slow pace. On average, humans take thirty-six breaths per minute. With the assistance of life-support tubes, my mum was breathing only a quarter of that, nine breaths. Although I had less than thirty-five years with her, a lifetime far too short, I clutched every second afforded to me under the eyes of a watchful nursing staff. I had a personal conversation with her that night, my last chance to do so.

The church was packed, and the service beautiful. My mum was surrounded by the warmth and love that she herself had given to countless people over her years. I explained to those gathered about the development of **Whispers in the Breeze**, along with the eulogy and composition written that morning for my mum. There wasn't a dry eye among those in attendance. Somehow, while choking back tears and trying to maintain a little of the same composure she did when speaking from her heart about family who had passed, including that of my Aunt Sadie, I managed to read both pieces in honour of my mum's memory, drawing on her strength from beyond the clouds on that very morning.

Coming down from the altar, I placed my hand on the church cloth that blanketed my mum's casket before placing one final kiss to where I knew her head lay inside. I did not want to let go. It was hard to have to say goodbye, but we had to get through this for her. At the site of internment, we gave out forty roses: twenty-eight red for the adults and twelve white for the grandchildren and children who were a part of my mum's life, including one for a little girl who was named after her. Kathleen Lebel. Her mother, Tara Cahill, had honoured my mum by naming her daughter after her. This extremely beautiful gesture forever left a unique mark on us all. Tara and my mum had a special relationship in all their years of working together after we immigrated to Canada.

Upon lowering my mum down to her final resting place, I asked those in attendance to follow us in our Irish traditions and to take a handful of soil and place it on her casket, so that we could start our burial process. With the soil in my hand and while looking down to where she lay beneath me, I started by saying:

"Mna na hÉireann, mo mháthair, mo chroí, tá tú go hálainn. Go n-éirí an t-ádh leat agus go mbeannaí Dia dhuit, Mum." ("Woman of Ireland, my mother, my love, you are beautiful. Good luck and God bless, Mum.")

I'm sure she would have been so proud of how we brought her through her final moments in life with us before we laid her to eternal rest. I watched and learned from her putting her own family members to rest over the years and tried to follow those teachings with the same dignity she gave to everyone else.

As I wrote the last few lines, I realize it has now been exactly thirteen years since we said goodbye to the loving woman who was our mother, a beautiful wife, a dedicated sister, an amazing granny, and all of the other wonderful things she stood for. How odd that the date of writing this coincidentally (or not) falls on the same calendar date. Again, this life is filled with omens and messages if we are able to see them and choose to acknowledge them when we do. Although never forgotten, we often reflect upon things that are special within our hearts, especially those times we spent with her. She was truly the nucleus of our family. And today is the anniversary of her passing.

Mum, your love, your memories, and your wisdom, will forever carry on within each one of us. Thus, this lament is dedicated to the memory of Catherine McVicker, one incredibly awesome lady for her courage, perseverance, guidance, dedication, and protection of her four children, with love, as only a mother knows how to do.

If you **also** remember what Caitlin said at the start of this story about her granny making her presence known, May 11th, which is the day my mum passed, is the same day Mark's beloved father, John Sidney Rickerby, was born. My mum was born on May 3rd. And, after we moved to Canada, her house number became 308.

In addition, my son, Ciaran, was very close to his granny even though she passed when he was just three years of age. One day, he was offered the chance to pick the number for the back of his goalie jersey. Without input or influence, he asked for 38. This too has intrigued me to no end. If that is not enough, I sent the latest draft of this manuscript to Mark and J.P. for their review, only to discover the following morning that it was sent at 00:38 hours.

Although there will be cynics out there who seek to dispel this, Mark, my children, my siblings, and I often speak to how we are connected in more ways than being authors or family, as well as the special numbers that mean so much to us and appear without warning. There have been other occasions noted with friends back home who are treasured like family to me. The McManus clan of Derrylin, County Fermanagh, Northern Ireland. Their dad, a beautiful and loving man by the name of John McManus Sr., passed away and joined his daughter and son, Valerie and Tommy, a few years ago on the same date as my mum's 73rd birthday: May 3rd.

In closing and until we meet again, I send my love to you all.

Mum's Lament

Our mother's love so special,
As many folks can see.
Mum's greatest gift was giving life,
To my sisters, brother, and me.

We began as children so helpless, Mum,
Yet never a challenge for you.
No matter how little or large the task,
There's nothing you couldn't do.

Throughout the years and as we grew,
So proud of us you were.
If we needed something, Mum,
We knew you'd always be there.

You gave us so much precious love,
Which came from deep inside.
Knowing the amazing Mum you are,
Fills us with tremendous pride.

You steered us through our battles, Mum,
No one can disagree.
You guided us in darkened times,
And now we set you free.

You taught us so much wisdom, Mum,
And loved us with your heart.
A new journey you shall now begin,
For a little while we must part.

Mum, our time with you was far too short,
There's much we'd like to say.
The days ahead they are unknown,
Without you leading the way.

Although you'll look down upon us, Mum,
And incredibly sad, we'll fuss.
We take great pride in the fact that,
Your blood flows proudly through us.

Four Green Fields

Mum, we share your strengths instilled in us,
Knowing what we must do.
To continue the legacy you've already begun,
While lovingly remembering you.

Sail gently into the night, our love,
Your new beginning has come.
Although at this moment we say farewell,
Forever you are our Mum.

A wee message from Daddy too:
Kathleen, my sweet precious angel, a loving mum.
Tiocfaidh Ár Lá,
(Our day will come).

Mum, Dad is our sailor, you are our captain and ship,
And we, your children, are your crew.
With everlasting love and fondest memories,
until we meet again,
Karen, Joseph, Gregory, and Angela.

"You're Your Father All Over Again!"

"The first time I ever had a Guinness, my dad said, "Get it in you. It'll do you good." When I was barfing it all up later, he said, "Get it up. It'll do you good." He was always a man of contrasts."

- **Mark Rickerby.**

Centuries ago, Englishmen were given incentives such as land and cattle to move to Ireland in an attempt to instill "good English stock" and breed out, over time, the fierce and uncontrollable nature of the Irish. Instead, the English were absorbed into the stronger culture. Likewise, though I embraced the California lifestyle as a child and young man in an attempt to fit in with my friends, I have become more Irish every day as an adult, and that process has been accelerated immensely by writing this book with Greg and John.

It's so refreshing to be around these kind of men again – the kind of people my father surrounded himself with – who are always as quick with a kind word as they are with a joke, who are as friendly as they are fearless in a scrape, who are too full of love and life to hold it all in, and so must write and write and write to somehow let it all out, only to be filled to bursting again the next morning.

My journey from Californian to Irish would be called a "character arc" if my life were a movie. And though I joke about my father's incorrigible behavior and daily harassment of me, his character arced, too. I suppose it's inevitable, particularly for men who tend to be "hard" – or "macho" as they call it in America - in their youth, but soften as pain and loss teach them what really matters, and age and infirmity descends upon them. In this regard, the waning of testosterone is a blessing. Finally, men who spent (some might say "wasted") their youths competing with other men, measuring themselves against them in terms of strength, looks and wealth – can finally relax and let go, and maybe even realize how unimportant those things are to eternity. Love really is all we take with us when we go, and I can't recall ever hearing in a eulogy how tough a man was or how many people he beat up. Maybe that's because so few attend the funerals of such men.

My father's arc from tough to gentle is even more remarkable because of how hard his own childhood was. His parents met all of his needs – food, shelter, clothing, education – but they met none of his emotional ones. They never once said I love you to him or his younger sister, Olga, who arrived when he was twelve. He was so uninformed about life by them, he didn't even know his mother was pregnant. When she went into labor and left for the hospital, my father was left standing on the sidewalk wondering what was going on. It took a neighborhood chum to teach him about the birds and bees. He walked up to him and said, "Your mammy's gonna have a wee baby!" Shocked and insulted, my da said, "She is not!" His friend was shocked that he didn't know. Hadn't he noticed his mother growing for the past nine months? Didn't either of his parents get him ready to become a brother and prepare him emotionally? The fact that he had no clue about it is evidence enough of how extraordinarily and even bizarrely unfit his parents were. Stunned by his friend's revelations, he numbly walked into the house and sat there until his mother returned from the hospital holding his sister in her arms.

Unfortunately, that wasn't all they didn't talk about. They never mentioned birthdays or Christmas, either. The days would come and go like any other. I suppose they hoped he and his sister wouldn't remember or notice, which of course is impossible for children. Birthdays were hard enough to ignore, but every Christmas morning, they couldn't help noticing all their neighborhood friends playing with new toys on the snow-covered street in front of their house at 46 Prestwick Park Road in Belfast (half of an already too small duplex), nor could they help wondering why Santa Claus never stopped at their house.

His mother constantly threatened to put him in a home when she was frustrated with him, which terrified him because of the horrific stories he had heard about such places. God knows what this kind of harassment on a regular basis, and the knowledge that comes with it of feeling so unimportant and dispensable to one's own mother, does to a child's mind. He couldn't run to his father for his support, either, because he was even less important to him. With all her failings, at least his mother fed him well. Children take what they can get.

As mentioned in the chapter herein titled *Uncle Alfie to the Rescue*, his father hid behind a newspaper in the kitchen constantly, rarely speaking to anyone except to occasionally tell my da's mum to shut up, usually because she was complaining about his income. This concern about money somehow did not extend to her shopping habits. She had Rolls-Royce taste and a Volkswagen pocketbook.

My father invited his da to watch his soccer games every weekend but he never came. Finally, one day, he showed up. He saw him standing at the sidelines with his arms crossed, solemnly watching the game. He played his heart out to impress him but when halftime came around, he looked again and saw that his father was gone. He finished the game with a hole in his heart and walked home to find his da back behind his newspaper. He asked him why he left. Without looking up, he mumbled, "None of you know how to play football."

At the age of fourteen, my father left school and got a job to support his family at Richardson, Sons and Owden Linen Manufacturers in Belfast. He worked his way up in that company, like he would at every company he ever worked for later in life, but kept losing promotions to less qualified or even totally inept relatives of the owners. In disgust, he decided to leave Belfast and go to Manchester, England, in search of greater opportunities. He was eighteen. When his parents saw him off at the train station, the father who never gave a damn about him had a tear in his eye. Like so many men then and now, he was trapped within himself, afraid or unable to show softness even to his own child on possibly the last day he would ever see him.

Work wasn't the only reason he left Belfast. He was growing up and going out with friends at night, and his father, who never cared what he did with his time before, suddenly imposed a curfew of ten P.M. on him, which was ridiculous because they usually went to a movie that didn't end until after ten. When he would return late, his father would wait in the shadows and smack him unexpectedly. He would go to bed with a stinging cheek and a heart full of rage. He was getting too old and too big for this kind of treatment. This happened one too many times and he finally decked the old man more out of shock than intent. Being hit back for the first time sent the old man into an asthmatic attack. My father ran for his da's nebulizer, the early 20th century version of an inhaler, and gave it to him. When he recovered, he went to bed, his heart racing, knowing nothing would ever be the same again. But his father never mentioned it and stayed out of his way after that. My father had earned his independence. One night, the taxi dropped him off at home at around midnight and his father was standing on the front porch smoking a feg. As he walked into the house, he said, "Must be nice being squired about town in taxis." My father curtly replied, "Well, you have to live a little, don't you?" It was the perfect answer because his parents had demonstrated for years that they had no idea how to live at all.

He worked in Manchester for several years before returning to Belfast. Having experienced life in the big city, Belfast seemed to have shrunk. He was walking along the shopping district one day and passed a travel agency with a sign in the window advertising low rates to Canada, a land of opportunity in the late 1950's. He booked a ship on the spot. Again, his father saw him off, and though his behavior hadn't changed much in the few months that my father had been home from England, the tears were in his eyes again when he saw him off.

It would be almost twenty years before he would return to Belfast. When he did, he was in his early forties with two children and, miraculously, his father was an absolute gab shite. He couldn't shut him up. He enjoyed talking with him but couldn't help wondering where all this eager banter was when he was a kid and most needed it.

His father died shortly after that trip home. It was the first time I ever saw my father cry, and the only time he would ever cry on my shoulder. I was seventeen at the time and not used to seeing him weak or vulnerable. It was surreal but I loved him more than ever.

He loved his father the same way he loved Belfast. Belfast had failed him when he needed help most, but that was where he spent his life; that was the soil that received his blood, sweat and tears, the stage where the great drama of his life took place, so he loved it no matter how humble it was or how wayward it became. Likewise, he loved his father in spite and perhaps because of his failings. After all, we have many friends in the course of a lifetime, many children if we want to, and some even have many spouses, but we only get one mother and father.

But it's more than that. At least it was in my relationship with my father. Imperfection evokes love, not perfection; weakness, not strength. We may admire God, whom we perceive as perfect, but we love Jesus because he was human and suffered like we do. We may admire the champion show dog, but the scruffy terrier with a missing leg wins our hearts. Nobody wants a father who complains constantly and isn't strong enough to meet life's challenges, and my father certainly wasn't that. He worked with more dedication than anyone I've ever known, just as his own father had. But as the saying goes, the tree that survives is the one that's strong enough to bend. Moments of weakness and vulnerability often provide the crack that allows healing grace to enter between family members. It certainly did for me. My father was strong enough to cry in front of me. His father would have been much better off if he had been that strong, too.

As I mentioned earlier, I had only one sibling, Paul, who was three years older than me. He went seriously astray in his early teens, trying every kind of drug he could get his hands on, spent eight years of his life in jail for drug-related offenses, including getting shot in the leg during a burglary by a cop who was either merciful or a bad aim, and died of a heroin overdose at the age of thirty-seven. I moved in with my parents for a year after that and would often stay up all night, trying to convince them that Paul had made his own choices, but they couldn't stop blaming themselves.

In fact, Paul sometimes did blame him for his problems. He talked about how hard moving every two years was on him, both of us being smacked and called stupid by my father in our earliest years so often that my mother finally threatened to divorce him, and one day that was somehow seared into his memory when he asked my da to teach him how to box in an attempt to bond with him. But instead of building Paul's confidence, he peppered him with playful punches and refused to let him land one until Paul was reduced to a sweaty, blubbering wreck. My mother once told me that he pulled me out of the car as a baby during a long car trip because I wouldn't stop crying and shook me so hard, she had to snatch me away from him, fearing my neck might break. When I was fifteen, after being thrust into a new school yet again, I was being bullied on a daily basis and desperately needed to learn how to fight, but for some reason, I never asked my father to teach me. Maybe I had already heard about my brother's experience with him as a manager and didn't want to experience similar treatment. I had just seen the movie Rocky and got it into my head that not only did I want to learn how to box, but I wanted to be the Heavyweight Champion of the World someday. Talk about putting the cart before the horse! I suppose I was like any child who wants to be a fireman one day, a famous actor the next, an astronaut the day after that, etc. In any case, I approached my father as he was changing the tube in the old Magnavox TV set. He had a long-standing war with anything mechanical or electrical and, as usual, was muttering profanities and expanding my vocabulary. Timidly, I said, "Dad, I want to get into boxing. How do you think I would do?"

This was his chance to sit me down like Beaver Cleaver's dad would and say something wise like, "Well, son, boxing is a dangerous sport but also a science. It takes great dedication to become proficient at it, but you're reasonably athletic and a fast learner, so I'm sure you'd do very well at it if you put in the time and effort."

No.

Without looking up, he said, "You'd get killed."

That one hurt but not as much as it would have if it had come out of the blue. Fortunately, or unfortunately, I was accustomed to comments like this. For instance, a few years earlier, when I was ten, I was helping him wash the family car, trying to bond with pop as usual, when my best friend and father drove by, saw us outside, and stopped to say hello. My friend's parents were divorced and his father was a hyper-macho Vietnam veteran who he had an even harder time bonding with. I had joined an Okinawan karate school several months earlier but quit because the teacher was completely unhinged. He had paired me up in a sparring match with a girl many years older than me who had a penchant and talent for groin kicks. Suffice to say it didn't end well for me. When I saw the teacher laughing while I was buckled over and wondering if my only recently descended, prepubescent testicles had been reduced to pudding, I decided this was not the safest environment to learn self-defense in. My friend's father said, "Hey, Mark. How's the karate going?" Before I could answer, my father said, "He quit that like he quits everything."

If I could go back and inhabit my ten-year old body with my current mind, I would say, "Everything? I'm ten. I haven't had a chance to *try* anything yet, let alone quit everything!" But I didn't say anything. I just stood there stunned, embarrassed, heartbroken that my father thought so little of me, and confused about how he had arrived at such a final judgment.

It hurts me to commemorate these low points because there were so many high ones later, especially toward the end of my father's life, but I do so only to demonstrate that the curses his own father was afflicted with were also in him when he was younger, and to demonstrate how remarkable and even miraculous it was that he wasn't worse. After that upbringing, anyone would have understood completely if he became a raging psychopath. Instead, he improved immensely as time passed, gradually becoming more encouraging, loving and expressive. However, this growth wasn't enough to save him from the disproportionate punishment of my brother taking him, my mother and I on a trip to hell that spanned twenty-five years, visiting him in prisons, talking to him on the other side of glass partitions, seeing him surrounded by the worst of the worst in society, watching him slowly deteriorate until he became someone we hardly recognized, his life becoming increasingly unsalvageable, until the grand finale, a drug overdose in the middle of the night. When the police called my parents and told them he was dead, my mother walked away from the phone repeating "no, no, no" over and over, hoping to erase reality with the sheer strength and desperation of her own panic and denial. We all knew it would happen someday, but hoped and prayed every day that it wouldn't.

When he was in the throes of his addiction, my brother would often drift into my da's office and ask him for money. Knowing he would just go spend it on drugs, my father usually tried to refuse. My brother would say, "Okay, I'll just go rob someone and get shot or thrown in jail." The drugs had removed all shame. If there was no love, he would have had nothing to manipulate, but he knew my da loved him underneath all the disappointment and anger. My da would usually buckle and hand him a twenty, which was enough to get some dirty street blend of God-knows-what into his veins.

A year or so after he died, my da said, "Every day, I feel an ache in my chest, like I should have done more for him, showed more emotion, told him I loved him more, but all I did was hand him money to get rid of him."

When people ask me why I became a writer, I often say that one of the reasons is to exorcise the darkness that has accumulated in my soul, and almost all of that darkness came from watching my brother and father disintegrate physically and mentally, for two different reasons. My brother because of drugs, and my father because of Parkinson's and Dementia, also known as The Walking Death. I remember his confusion and frustration when it was first happening to him. I thought even then that it would be better to lose one's mind all at once then a little at the time, because the other half that's still undamaged is left wondering what the hell is going on. He gradually went from a hilarious, talented, life-of-the-party to a vacant, staring ghost.

The first time I saw the effects of these diseases, he was in a hospital with Pancreatitis. The combination of drugs and an unfamiliar location caused severe Sundown Syndrome. The hospital staff had to tie him to his bed to keep him from hitting them. The man who had always been so stable and strong was like a trapped animal. As I stood in the room alone with him, he looked at me with the eyes of a stranger and whispered, "Hey, buddy. Get me outta here. I've got money. I'll pay you. Get me outta here." It was like being in a horror movie. Nobody can ever prepare themselves for being forgotten by their own parent, or saying goodbye forever to the look of pride and love on their faces, the love they always knew, or thought, they could depend on when everything else was crumbling. But it was my father's mind that was crumbling and I was powerless to stop it.

When I would visit him at home, he would make small talk and I'd feel like things were almost normal again until he would say, "So where did we meet?"

God forgive me but I've often wished he and my brother would have just had sudden heart attacks instead, before all the suffering. It would have been much more merciful to them and everyone who loved them.

I'm proud to report that I never really gave up on either of them. I fought like hell to save my brother from his demons, and to ward off the diseases attacking my father's brain. I did everything I could not only because I loved them so much, but because I wanted to know that I tried if the inevitable happened. And in both cases, it did.

My father not only wasn't resentful or bitter about his loveless childhood, he never even talked about it. He never used it against me when I was being ungrateful or even when I lashed out at him. It would have been easy to say, "You think you have it hard? What a laugh! When I was a kid . . ." But he didn't. Ever. He was too strong to do that, and he was still too loyal to his father to criticize him.

When I was editing and formatting his memoir *The Other Belfast*, he was concerned that he was being disrespectful to his parents by writing about how they treated him. I repeated an old writer's adage – "If people wanted you to write warmly about them, they should have behaved better." But he rejected that, saying, "I don't want to get any dirty looks when I meet them in heaven."

I argued, "Dad, listen, telling the story of what happened isn't criticizing. You've got to be honest about what happened if you expect readers to care. As Neil Simon wrote in *Biloxi Blues*, 'Once you start compromising your thoughts, you're a candidate for mediocrity.'"

He finally acquiesced but part of him was always sad that he had to say anything negative about his parents, rather than the nothing at all he was accustomed to. Sometimes the truth is just too painful. Even the fact that his sister Olga never left that house or the city of Belfast, never had a boyfriend, never drove a car and became an agoraphobic recluse wasn't enough to make him complain about his parents, something she had no problem at all doing.

In an ironic twist of fate, Olga would die less than two weeks after my father did, in the same house they were both born in, but her life was so empty and friendless, her body wasn't discovered for four months. I now own that house and haven't been able to bring myself to sell it because it was such a big part of my father's life and of his memoir. It was almost a character unto itself and I have already lost too much of him. But it has always been a dark and unlucky house, so I recently listed it for sale, still with reluctance and no small amount of sadness.

Though the remoteness, lack of interest and even cruelty his own father exhibited wasn't completely absent in him, my da was a good and stable provider, sharing the same work ethic his father had, he never forgot a birthday or Christmas, and he would often surprise me with a genuinely affectionate hug or kind word. Every Christmas, our tree barely touched the ground because of all the presents under it. But like many men, the main way he showed his love was by buying us toys, and he was proud he was successful enough to do so. For his entire working life, he always made more in a year than his father ever made in ten, but he was preoccupied with work much of the time as a result.

I always think of my da when I hear a song by Marc Cohn called *Rest for the Weary* —

My father was a working man
But his work was never done
He stood behind a counter
And he smiled at everyone
He bought himself a business
Worked seven days a week
Took a holiday for Christmas
Then he fell asleep beside the tree

I remember being filled with awe and avarice at the sight of an aluminum, iridescent blue, razor-thin (and completely tacky by my standards today) skateboard in a recessed display case at my local roller skating rink. It was lit from above and had the same effect on me that the holy grail will have on whomever finally finds it. It cost way too much, about fifty dollars, but after enough coaxing and whining, my father put me in the car, drove me to the rink, and bought it for me. It turned out to be a hazard to life and limb but it was nice to look at. He did the same thing with just about every other silly novelty item I decided I couldn't live without.

As time passed, he started saying he loved me more and more often, perhaps because I said it so often to him that he had to respond in some way. In this way, I'm glad I was half-Californian and in the habit of blocking the aisles in the self-help section of bookstores all over Los Angeles, struggling to make sense of my hopelessly tangled emotions. To say I was a mess is an insult to messes. My problem was not expressing emotion, it was holding it in. I was a gusher, a hugger, a weeper. My more macho friends were often taken aback when they'd see me react emotionally to a song or poem, or get a tear in my eye when telling a story (as the Irish are famous for) but somehow I always knew that it was much healthier to release all the pressure-building emotion bottled up inside us than it is to hold it in for the sake of that unwisely perpetuated "strong and silent" image. I don't know how some men survive. In many cases, they don't, as if the emotion is raging inside them, tearing up everything in its path. In this way, I think I helped bring my dad out of himself further than he might have been able to without me.

For instance, we were driving through Death Valley to Las Vegas one day with my mother and aunt in the backseat when a song came on the radio called *Everything I Own* by the group Bread. It was written by David Gates for his father after he died. I mentioned to my father that the song always reminded me of him. He listened silently and looked out the window as it played.

You sheltered me from harm
Kept me warm, kept me warm
You gave my life to me
Set me free, set me free
The finest years I ever knew,
Were all the years I had with you

And I would give anything I own
I'd give up my life, my heart, my home
I would give everything I own,
Just to have you back again

You taught me how to love
What it's of, what it's of.
You never said too much
But still you showed the way
And I learned from watching you.
Nobody else will ever know
The part of me that can't let go.

When it was over, he reached over and put his hand on mine for a few seconds. That's all. He didn't say a word or need to. I would play the same song at his memorial service less than ten years later.

Shortly after my brother died, desperate to prove to my parents that they did a hell of a lot right, I sat down and wrote down every happy memory I had from childhood – road trips through Oregon, riding on my dad's massive back as he swam across Palm Springs swimming pools, building snowmen and riding inner tubes down snowy hillsides in Big Bear, and on and on. By the time I was done, there were hundreds of glowing memories. I watched him from around the corner as he sat reading page

   FOUR GREEN FIELDS

after page, alternately laughing and wiping away tears. I am so glad now
that I took the time to do that.

The struggles between boys and their fathers are as common as they are
legendary. But becoming a parent doesn't mean a person is finished
growing, as I'm currently learning with two girls, both under eight years
old. Children raise their parents, too. My daughters have also improved me
as a person much more than I could have accomplished by myself. As the
notorious Hollywood playboy Warren Beatty once said after he finally
settled down, "Without wives and children, men drift around aimlessly on a
perpetual, narcissistic trip their entire lives."

My daughters sharpen my focus because I want the best for them and
want them to be proud of me. They make me better because I know they
will become who I am, for better or worse, not what I tell them to be. And
if I fail as a parent, nothing else I ever accomplish in this life will matter
very much.

The final stage in psychologist Erik Erickson's stages of development is
integrity versus despair. If we live our lives well and do our best to be kind
and undo or at least atone for the damage we all inevitably cause, we die
with integrity. If we don't – if we become worse – as so many do, we die
with despair. My father died with integrity. Over the course of his life, he
won a tremendous victory over not only his younger, less patient nature,
but also over the toxic legacy of his parents, and probably their parents
before them. He became better. He wasn't always easy to get along with
but when he kissed me goodbye on his deathbed, he knew the good he did
for me far outweighed the damages caused by his loose Irish tongue. He
knew I forgave him, and I knew he forgave me for the things I said to him
in anger during our thankfully few but vitriolic arguments. As I described
in a previous chapter, even through the morass of the diseases that ravaged
his brain during his final years, and the added confusion of the drugs
flooding through his system on his deathbed, including the morphine that

would struggle to stop that big heart of his, he still reached out to me and gave me a kiss. He recognized me in the end, and he knew how much I loved him. He was dying, but he saw me crying and, as usual, comforted me.

In fact, we both improved as we got older, and our relationship did along with it. We brought each other up. What Renee Zellwegger said to Tom Cruise in the movie *Jerry Maguire* ("You complete me") is true of any good relationship. People should help each other recover from past traumas, reach their goals, and become whole.

My father conquered his demons with my help, and I have conquered mine with his. And I would give everything I own to see him again, to hug him again, even toward the end when I felt like I might break him if I squeezed too hard, when I held him and said "I love you, da" over and over, hoping everything he was would suddenly come rushing back to his mind, and that I would magically defeat the diseases ravaging his brain with sheer will power, only to be looked at by him afterward and asked, "Am I really your father?" Nobody needs to tell me to go to hell. I've already been.

We had a rough start but in the end we were in perfect sync and proud of each other. In fact, I am becoming him so much as time passes, after I tell my wife a joke or make a facial expression that reminds her of him, she often says, "Oh, my God. You're your father all over again."

And I always respond, "Thank you." Always.

It is high praise, indeed.

On Looking Through Old Photographs

Sometimes the heart doesn't know it needs healing.

Sometimes the soul just gets used to the pain.

And the path which once shone so brightly before us

Withers so slowly we barely notice the change.

For not every dream of the past can come with us.

Not every wish is meant to come true.

A whole lot of living and loving and losing

Goes into the making of a me and a you.

Not 'til we're filled can we know we were hollow.

We must cure our own blindness before we can see.

No one's born with wisdom, talent, or virtue.

We must conquer ourselves to be all we can be.

It's not just our triumphs that shape and define us.

It's our failures and fears and shortcomings, too.

Not 'til our hearts have been broken and empty

Can we savor the time when they're happy and full.

Mark Rickerby

We all dream of happiness, of fortune and fame
And in the races we run, we all want to be first
But the fact is we learn most quickly and deeply
When our lives are in ruin and the pain is the worst.

So don't regret yesterday for all of its sorrows.
Don't fret for the dark times when you lost your way.
Don't put yourself down for mistakes of the past
For they gave you the insights that you have today.

The path of today is always in our keeping
And yesterday's needn't be utterly lost.
A few dreams survive if only we'll tend them.
The bridge between then and now can be crossed!

Four Green Fields

shenanigans & storytelling

sammy

"When Jesus Christ asked little children to come to him, he didn't say only rich children, or white children, or children with two-parent families, or children who didn't have a mental or physical handicap. He said, "Let all children come unto me."

- **Marian Wright Edelman.**

One of the people I remember best from the old neighborhood and have had a lingering fondness for in my memory over the years was a kid called Sammy who lived at the other end of my street. Sammy was mildly challenged mentally and would hang around with us wee kids, though he was about fourteen years of age himself. At only eight years old, we were more mentally advanced than he was. But there was one thing about Sammy which made him immensely popular with the neighborhood kids aside from his gentle demeanor - he had a storehouse of pre-World War II comics. That is, prior to 1939 when comics began to be rationed for the war effort.

I loved reading comics. My favorites were The Dandy, Film Fun, The Beano, The Champion, Radio Fun, The Wizard, and The Adventure. Some were just comic strips, but some were stories serialized from week to week. Because paper was rationed along with everything else during the war, the stores would only order magazines and comics for customers who had placed an order with them. This meant that one had to make a commitment to a shilling or two each week to pick up three or four comics. My family couldn't afford that, but on Tuesday when the comics came into the store the delivery people would always leave a few extras on top of the ordered count. All of us kids knew when it was delivery day so at lunchtime several of us - myself, Teddy Weatherhead, Ronny Stephenson, and a few others - would dash round to the news agent's store. The store was called The Endeavor and was next to the school. When we got there, we would try to grab up the comics, which were left on the shelves for anyone who wanted to buy them. The competition was so fierce to arrive first and have first pick of the best comics that we tripped each other up as we ran at great risk of bodily injury. The preferred technique was to click the heels of the person in front with the tip of the toes causing one of his feet to get caught behind the other. It was kind of a mean version of leap frog. In our mad dash for the comic shop, we would take turns sprockling on our mouths and noses on the pavement. Then the tripper would go running past, perhaps stepping on the trippee in the process, as the former leader writhed on the ground whining about his injuries. He would get back up as quickly as he could and try to return the favor.

The serials kept us all on pins and needles from week to week, wondering what was going to happen next to our favorite characters. There was a serial story about a guy called Wilson, a real loner who lived in some moor in the south of England and dressed all in black. He just ran all day and ate natural food at nighttime. He didn't like being around people so he turned himself into a championship runner, which contradicted his loner lifestyle because one would assume he was preparing to actually compete with other people at some point. One day he was out running in the wild, desolate moors when, way off in the distance, he saw a young couple, just two tiny specks.

"This place is getting too crowded," he said to himself, and immediately moved somewhere else.

Among the comic strip characters, there was Desperate Dan, a big cowboy type with a gigantic chin covered with stubble. He was always getting into all kinds of crazy predicaments. He was the world's strongest man, able to lift a cow with one hand. His beard was so tough he had to shave with a blowtorch.

Then there was Keyhole Kate, a tall skinny girl a bit like Popeye's Olive Oyl with glasses and a long, pointy nose, so named because she was always looking through keyholes and spying on people. Another favorite was Lord Snooty. He was a rich kid with a top hat who had a bunch of scruffy-looking friends. Korky the Cat was another character in Dandy. Originally mute, Korky was given a voice in 1940. Speaking or not, Korky's antics were always hilarious. We younger kids liked Dandy and Beano. The older kids liked the Wizard, Hotspur and the Champion. The Dandy pulled no punches parodying our WWII enemies, either. Hitler was regularly lampooned and humiliated in a variety of ways.

Because of the brutal competition for comics every month, we all lusted after Sammy's collection and spent hours brainstorming about how we could get him to part with them. It was a seemingly impossible mission because Sammy never let them out of his sight. He treasured his comic book collection and would have fought to the death to protect it. One day, however, we hit upon a plan.

Even though Sammy was much larger than us, he joined us in our hockey and soccer games in the street. Sammy's mother always told him not to play too roughly with us because of his size. She yelled to Sammy from the window, "Now don't you be hurtin' those wee boys, Sammy, or it'll be too bad for you!"

Since none of us could afford hockey sticks, we used tree branches roughly cut into an L-shape instead. Knowing that Sammy was mortally afraid of what his mother would do to him if he hurt us, we pretended that he had injured us somehow and fell to the ground, screaming and yelling. Afraid that his mother might hear, Sammy stroked and shushed us, but we would just keep crying until he ran inside and got a comic book to shut us up. (Cruel, yes, but effective.) When he brought out the comic, we shut up immediately. He reluctantly handed over the comics but warned us to take good care of them. The comics were maintained by Sammy in mint condition, and he insisted that they be returned to him in the same condition after we had read them. When we brought them back, he carefully inspected them page by page for any sign of damage. If the comics were in less than perfect condition, he would chase the offending

 Four Green Fields

party, smacking him up the ears and neck until he got away. I had even gotten into the habit of lightly ironing the comics to avoid Sammy's wrath.

One day, distracted by a friend calling outside, I had carelessly left one of Sammy's comics on a chair in the kitchen. Forgetting about the comic, he and I ran off on some adventure. When I returned, I discovered to my immense horror that my mother had been sitting on it for quite some time. I found the forlorn-looking thing sitting on the chair (the comic, not my ma) wet with perspiration and collapsed in the middle with wrinkles extending outward toward all four edges. I shuddered at the thought of what Sammy would do to me when I handed it to him in that condition. Panicked, I got the iron out and attempted to give it the usual treatment. Usually, comics which were slightly crinkled from normal use needed only one light going-over with the iron, but this one was in such terrible shape, I had to keep going over it again and again while dabbing it with a moist towel. I was relieved when it finally looked straight. However, when I went to pick up the comic from the ironing board, it was as stiff and dry as a roof shingle. I had ironed all the moisture out of it. I attempted to open it, but the pages just crumbled in my hand like dry leaves.

I was a nervous wreck returning it to Sammy in this condition and attempted to avoid guilt by inserting the comic into a stack of others he had loaned me. He took them and went inside to put them back while I joined the other boys playing in front of his house. As I played, I kept an eye on the house, knowing that Sammy was in there scrutinizing his comics one by one for any sign of abuse. As expected, a few moments later, I heard a guttural moan come from the house and knew Sammy had discovered the petrified comic. He came barreling out of the house yelling, "What have ya done to muh comic, ya wee shite?"

I took flight and yelled, "I'm sorry, Sammy! It wasn't my fault! My ma . . ." trying to explain as I ran. But it was no use. Sammy was on the warpath. He chased me around the street for ten minutes, smacking me around the head and ears as I ducked and dodged, futilely screaming my excuses into the uncaring wind. This provided great amusement for my friends. I finally decided to run home and return at some later time when Sammy's rage had dissipated.

Maybe it was because of his ailment but Sammy never held a grudge for too long. In fact, he and I became quite good friends despite my torture and execution of one of his comic books.

One day when Sammy was about sixteen and I was ten, we decided to take a bike trip to Bangor, which is about twelve miles down the coast. It was quite a feat talking his mother into letting him go away for the day. She made me promise I would watch out for him. To anyone looking on, this would have sounded like a strange request, considering Sammy was older and a good foot taller than I. After winning her trust, I got my da's old bike out for the journey, Sammy got his bike, which was much nicer than mine, and the two of us took off along the Bangor Road with the wind in our faces.

The trip to Bangor was quite an adventure for two kids. We had to go through the city then beyond it to the south, down the coast past Millisle and Helen's Bay before we arrived at, glory of glories, Bangor. We rode our bikes right down to the sand. I saw the sand approaching so, naturally, I slowed down and got off my bike. I was expecting Sammy to do the same but he just sailed right past me at about thirty miles per hour, apparently trying to ride right to the ocean's edge. When the tires made contact with the sand, the bike came to a complete halt and Sammy flew over the handle bars landing flat on his back in the sand about ten feet ahead. Once the crowd knew he was unhurt, everyone had a good laugh, including Sammy.

The smell of salt water was always the first thing I noticed when I went to Bangor because it was such a refreshing change from the coal-laced air of Belfast. The promenade was always packed with people walking back and forth. Ice cream cones and soft drinks were sold from dozens of shop windows. The soft drink manufacturer then was Cantrell and Cochrane, and they made delicious lemonade. The bottle fizzed over after I pulled the cork (No twist-off's in those days!) and I held the cold bottle to my head

 Four Green Fields

for relief from the sun. And, oh, the taste! On a warm summer day, it was nectar of the gods.

After our lemonades, Sammy and I headed for Pickie Pool where all the bathing belles gathered. After we had given them all a good ogling, we walked over to the amusement park, which had swings, musical chairs, and all kinds of rides. The chairs flew around at the end of a chain. It was a lot of fun if one hadn't eaten too much beforehand, but every now and then, a kid would lose his lunch halfway through the ride. Vomit would spray outward in a giant circle, sprinkling any pedestrians who were unlucky enough to be walking below. I never saw Sammy happier than that day. I guess it was a relief to get away from his parents and feel like a normal kid for a change.

Sammy got steadily worse as time went by. About a year later, his parents must have decided that they needed some help, and they sent for the sanitarium wagon to come and pick him up. The wagon pulled up to take Sammy away. Three burly men dragged him out of the house. He fought like the devil, total confusion and panic on his face.

The men were wearing white but they didn't have a net like they did in the comics. There was nothing funny about this, either. My heart was breaking for Sammy. I wanted to run and pull him away, get on our bikes, and ride back down to Bangor where he would be safe and happy again. Sammy was strong, but they overpowered him, forced him into the wagon, and slammed the door. Sammy looked at me through the back window, tears streaming down his face. I waved goodbye, but he didn't wave back. He looked toward the house, yelling for his mother, who was crying into his father's chest.

I don't know where they took Sammy, but we didn't see him again for about two years. When he came back, he was very quiet. The other kids and I wondered what had happened to him, but he was too unapproachable to ask. There were rumors about shock treatment and drugs. Whatever they did, it didn't improve him. Sammy had become very morose, a word no one would have used to describe him before. He wouldn't talk or play with any of us anymore. We'd see Sammy sitting in the front window of his house and yell over, "Hi, Sammy!" as we walked past, but he would just glance over, sullen and silent, and look away again. We all felt sorry for him but we were scared of him now, thinking he'd finally gone completely mad and might suddenly turn violent on us.

Sammy just moped around the neighborhood, eyes on the ground, and would only mumble if we said hello to him. He didn't even seem to remember us. I always wondered what went on at that hospital to reduce him to such a state, whether something sinister had happened or if Sammy was just devastated by the fact that his parents had sent him away. I suppose no matter how mentally challenged someone is, they know who loves them and who doesn't, and that makes all the difference. Either way, I was glad that Sammy was back home.

About fifteen years later, I came back to Ireland after living in Canada and the States. I was thirty-five years old or so and I hadn't seen Sammy in all that time. In fact, for five years before I left Belfast, he had disappeared from view entirely so it was more like twenty years since I'd last seen him. I was walking down the street one day, and his mother was out at the front door talking to one of the neighbors.

"Hi, Misses Todd!" I said.

"Sidney! Are you back from the states?" she said.

"Yeah, I'm over for a trip. How's Sammy doin'?"

She yelled toward the house, "Sammy, come on out and talk to one of your friends!"

Sammy came out of the house and stood next to his mother, looking at his feet.

His mother said, "Do you know who that is?"

Sammy raised his eyes, looked at me for a second and said, "That's

 Four Green Fields

Sidney Rickerby."

I was amazed. Deep down, his mind was still working. He was completely incapable of taking care of himself, but he still remembered me after twenty years. My heart swelled with fondness for him, remembering the boy who loaned me his prize comics and took a ride to Bangor with me one sunny day twenty-five summers earlier.

Sammy had a brother, Harry, who was also a friend of mine, and a sister, Agnes. Harry and Agnes had both married and moved away. Finally, Misses Todd died and Sammy's father then had to take care of him all on his own. They sold their house and moved up the Ballysillan Road.

About ten years ago, I went home again and stopped in to visit Mister Todd, who was then in his nineties. He was still taking care of Sammy. Here was this poor, old man, almost a hundred years old, taking care of a son in his seventies and still loving him. I asked him how he did it. While some might have taken this opportunity to deliver a speech on how selfless and noble they were, Mr. Todd only said, "Well, I can't leave 'im alone, can I? He'd set the house on fire."

And that was that. He brought Sammy into the world, and it was his job to take care of him, no matter what.

Many Americans think the people of Belfast are all half nuts because of the political violence there over the years, but many of them are absolute saints. There's a warmth and kindliness and devotedness that isn't mentioned on the telly. These people are much more common than the other kind; people like Mr. and Mrs. Todd, who accepted their lot and did what the Lord and the dictates of their own hearts commanded them to, without self-celebration or complaint.

Danny Houton, Malin Head, Co. Donegal

"The Irish are very fair people; they never speak well of one another."

- **Samuel Johnson.**

My grandfather was unique. Actually, one word can't come close to describing the character that was Danny Houton. The man was a force of nature.

He came from one of the wildest places in the country – Malin Head, at the very Northern tip of Donegal's Inishowen peninsula. Locals eke out a living from the land, or from the sea, while many emigrate to England, Scotland, or America in search of employment. I don't know very much about his father, only that he was killed under suspicious circumstances when Danny was a young boy. That no doubt had a huge impact on him then and throughout his life.

The Houton's had a very large farm for that part of Ireland – one hundred acres of prime land. It had been farmed constantly for generations and never suffered any neglect. When he was sixteen, Danny married my grandmother, who came from outside of Malin town. They had four daughters and a son. While most of his brothers and sisters had emigrated, Danny remained on to take charge of the family farm. The plan was for him to inherit the land and raise his children there.

At some stage, an older sister, who was the only other sibling to stay and live in the Inishowen area with her family, talked their mother into signing over the family farm to her. Unfortunately, my grandfather was put off his own land and shortly later, he moved his family to Scotland. After my mother and her sister received their nursing degrees in Scotland, they all emigrated to the U.S.

Danny was full of mischief and mayhem and since that is the basic make up of most young boys, I looked upon him as my idol. It was he who taught me how to smoke a pipe when I was nine and how to improvise when you ran out of tobacco (you then smoked loose tea leaves), how to make a "crab catcher" with a bent nail tied around the end of a stick, how to whistle with a "lilt" and many other life-changing tricks. One trick which I whole-heartedly regretted was trying to chew plug tobacco.

When I was a boy, many older men used to chew tobacco. It came in a big lump (plug), which very much resembled licorice. My brother and I would watch in awe as grandfather and our father would break off big chunks of the tobacco and start chewing. Most men carried around pocket knives which they used to slice a piece off when they wanted to chew. Not my grandfather, though. Not for him the trappings of normal society. His way was always more in keeping with the "call of the wild." He would place a good knob of the plug between his teeth – the same teeth that he used to open beer bottles and chomp down into the tobacco, wrestling off a piece like a dog with a bone.

We had convinced ourselves that the tobacco just had to taste like licorice, since it looked identical to it. During one céilí session at a neighbour's house, we hung around the tobacco chewers' feet and must have been dropping hints about how we also wanted to chew. Looking back now, it surprises me that giving a wad of tobacco to a nine and six-year-old boy must have been nothing terribly out of the ordinary, as that was what they did. We both grabbed our swag and belted out the door, running around the corner of the house. After popping the plug into our mouths, we realized right away that it did not taste anything like licorice. As a matter of fact, it stung our lips.

Unfortunately, we had overlooked the spitting aspect, which is an important part of the tobacco chewing process. As a result, we swallowed gobs of tobacco juice. Within minutes, I saw my brother's face turn a yellowy shade of green. I'm sure mine had too, but I couldn't see it and he was not fit to talk. Violent vomiting followed and, at some stage, one of the adults came out the door to throw out tea leaves in the street and saw our poor condition. We were brought in to be cleaned up and patched together. I remember the adults laughing and saying that we would grow up to never use tobacco later, after getting such a sickening at that early stage.

Danny Houton lived to entertain people with his carry-on. I am not totally convinced that he was performing for anyone other than himself, it's just that his mad actions usually occurred when others were around to witness it. Then again, he always had a bunch of men who loved to hang around him and they were always a generation or two younger than Danny.

I started going out with my grandfather when I was around twenty. One of his mates, a local farmer and fisherman was in his early forties. He told me that none of the older men my grandfather's age (late 60's/early 70's), could keep up with his drinking and wild ways, so he had to skip a generation. Even his own cousin, Packie Houton, did not have the stamina for the wilder Houton.

After grandfather had returned to Ireland to retire, he came back to the family farm which he had left some four or five decades previously. In the interim, his sister had put it up for auction and Danny's eldest daughter, Annie Houton, a nurse in New York City, had successfully managed the winning bid and it was back where it rightfully belonged. Not one to bother himself with local authority laws, or any other laws for that matter, Danny set about building himself a house on a wee spot he picked out in the front garden overlooking the Urblereagh road. Being an accomplished stone mason, he was building it from the ground up, to his own specifications. He lived in a little tin caravan until such time as he could move into the house he had built.

Eventually the Donegal County Council got wind of an illegal dwelling being erected in Malin Head and confronted my grandfather about why he was building a house without planning permission. His response was to curse them from a height and to advise them that this was his land and he didn't have to ask anybody for permission to build on his own land. I don't know if he threatened to shoot them at that stage, but he assured his daughter, my mother, that if they tried to come and knock down his house, he would empty both barrels of his shotgun at them.

So it was in this little tin hut where I would visit my grandfather and where we would have a few belts of poteen before going out to the pub. When we returned home at 1am or 2am (often later), we'd go back to his little place for a few nightcaps. He never kept the illegal brew in his property, as the police would raid him from time to time. If they did find something outside (which they never did), he would shrug his shoulders and tell them that somebody else must have put it there. He knew they couldn't prove it.

It was on one of these cold January nights when my grandfather informed me that we were going out with a boat crew the next morning to haul in lobster pots. His old friend was the skipper of the boat. That night we had the usual drinks until the wee hours of the morning and it was decided that I was to collect him at nine a.m. We were meeting the crew in Dock's Pub (The pub was a landmark, overlooking the Malin Head pier. It was too far off the beaten track for the police so most of the time the owners closed whenever they wanted despite the law governing opening and closing times.)

The given name of the owners of Dock's Pub was Doherty, but there were so many Doherty's that it was necessary for each of them to have an identifying nickname. They apparently got theirs from living in close proximity to the dock. I collected my grandfather as planned and arrived at Dock's by 9:15 a.m. Inside, there were four men drinking at the bar – an older gentleman who seemed to be around seventy years of age and three younger men with long, curly hair and thick, red beards. This was the boat crew. My grandfather asked me what I wanted to drink and I had to bite my tongue to keep from saying, "A nice hot cup of strong tea." I hadn't had any breakfast and we only finished drinking about five hours before. In that part of Donegal, the drink is a pint bottle of Guinness or Smithwicks and a "half one." The half one is usually whiskey, but it can be anything at all. When Danny Houton wasn't drinking illegal hooch from one of his ditches, his preferred drink was sailor's rum and peppermint cordial, which he always referred to as "rum and pep."

I decided to have the same as he was having, and after two rounds (which was really four drinks each), I figured that the fishing trip must have been cancelled as it was only after 10 a.m. and we appeared to be settling in for a fairly serious drinking session. I looked out to sea when I parked the car and remarked how the waves were especially rough. I could only imagine being tossed and thrown about in a small boat. I lost count of how many rounds we had consumed, but it must have amounted to at least sixteen drinks a piece. You can imagine my surprise when, four and a half hours later, the skipper finished his drink and told us that it was time to get the boat. Apparently, we had been waiting for the 2 p.m. tide to come in.

With the churning winter waters of the Atlantic tossing us about, I had no concern about how many lobsters we would catch. I wasn't even concerned about being swept overboard. I was too busy fighting off the feeling of sea-sickness. Normally, the water would have no effect on me, but normally I wouldn't be in a small boat, on a grey winter's afternoon, having just finished a hardcore, four-hour drinking session just minutes previously. The fact that I hadn't eaten since the day before definitely didn't help.

All the boat crew were busy hauling in lobsters' pots and setting new bait for the next catch. My grandfather stood upright in the boat, with both hands buried deep in his pockets, rocking back and forth as he surveyed the agitated sea. After a few minutes he announced to nobody in particular that he was hungry. Now, when you are out on the sea with a bunch of hard-drinking, wild-looking Donegal fishermen, there is no talk of food. The only thing resembling food would be the live fish which were brought up from the deep in the lobster pots. That is where my grandfather headed in search of his lunch.

 Four Green Fields

Whistling with that tongue lilt of his, he reached down into the body of the boat and picked up a crab which was very much alive and kicking. He still had one hand in his pocket. I watched him like a hawk, having no idea what he was planning to do with the crab. After all, there was no way to cook the crab on the boat. What he did next shocked a couple of the wild fishermen as much as it did me. He bent forward from the waist and smashed open the crab's back on the floor of the boat. Then he stood up straight, raised the broken crab to his mouth, and sucked the juice out of it before plunging his fingers into the meat and scooping that into his mouth.

One of the Vikings looked at me and said, "I hope he is not a relative of yours." I looked him back square in the eye and replied, "Never saw him before this morning." Then I did my best to hold the contents of my stomach down until we returned safely back to the dock.

MURPHY'S LAW: MY FRIEND OF MISERY!

"People who lean on logic and philosophy and rational exposition end by starving the best part of the mind."

- **William Butler Yeats.**

At one point or another, we have all heard that famous adage from a fellow named Murphy, and how it applies in principle to some Law that he developed in the arse end of nowhere. My question for Mr. Murphy is how was it that I suddenly became his chosen apostle, and how another famous phrase – "when it rains, it pours" - was tacked on to his signature line just for me. Thanks for nothing, big lad!

It was October 26th when I decided I would follow through with plans to attend the 9th annual Irish Books, Arts, and Music (IBAM) Festival in Chicago, Illinois, which celebrates and highlights the contributions of Irish artists throughout the various genres that are intricately woven within the title of this prestigious event. Having been there the year before through a personal invitation from Mr. Cliff Carlson, the director of this beautiful and wonderful program, I decided I would indeed give it another go. My efforts to get there, however, became arduous to a supernatural degree.

Leading up to IBAM, I had been writing furiously and managed to pen a couple of brand new books which would be featured and launched at the Irish American Heritage Centre. The excitement of having two newly released, fresh off the press, crisp and colourful books in my hands to showcase to their audience and the amazing staff and volunteers who bring about this fabulous event would be a tremendous welcome back. Or so I thought. But what would become painfully obvious is that auld Murphy had other ideas in mind for me, so he did. And without advanced warning!

His Law made its presence known when I went to pick up the first print run of books. Peering between the pages of one, my immediate reaction is that it must have been put together by a Paddy Irishman, or perhaps someone was trying to take the mick out of me. The inside of the book had been glued to its cover upside bloody down. That being bad enough, I would also come to see that the laminated covers, brightly reflecting the overhead lighting directly above me, appeared to have significant flaws to them. I was stunned to see that the edges were peeling like the plastic wrapping that encases slices of cheese, which are one molecule away from being the same product. Plastic. This simply was not acceptable to me as I am a perfectionist in my approach to everything. Nothing less than the best will suffice for this lad. I am quite often the cause of my own demise if I do say so myself.

The printing company set about immediately to address my very valid concerns and said they would have the order rectified just in time for my departure for Chicago. True to their word, they did, although they had to undergo several other processes to ensure I would get what I was hoping for. Problem solved. Except for damn old Murphy, who still had a change of plans in mind for this unsuspecting author.

While frantically packing the night before, my father kindly offered to drive over early the next morning to ensure that I was at the airport on time for my red eye departure. Not a problem. Unless you are trying to pack two boxes of books into one suitcase and stay within the magic number of fifty pounds to prevent the airline from charging me the price of a second plane ticket for my luggage if it was an ounce heavier. And yet they persist in calling it "the friendly skies."

Packing suitcases has become like a human game of Tetris for me from all of the travelling I've done. Carefully selecting which piece of the puzzle fits where, only to find each time that my prizewinning combination has been completely wrecked by baggage handlers after arriving at my destination, and taxi drivers overly eager to dump the suitcase into the boot of their car and back onto the road so they can move on to their next fare.

I shouldn't give a damn by now but find undergoing the same process each time anyway.

Running on less than two hours of sleep that night due to the excitement of heading out to the Windy City and showcasing my latest literary baby, my father pulled into the driveway, ready to help me load up my cases. However, my excitement would soon be met with several disappointments, again undoubtedly orchestrated by that bastard Murphy.

The first was a cup of morning java served to me by a place that stays open 24 hours that was likely still in the brewing pot 23 hours earlier. It was not only disgusting, it was bloody freezing. Trying to choke it down me while nibbling on their English muffin filled with plastic cheese, circular egg, and rubbery bacon made to be the same size as the egg and the muffin itself was a bit of a chore. I ate the sandwich but had nothing to rinse my gub with since the coffee was stinkin'. And so it began...

Murphy 1. Greg 0.

We pulled up to the airport with my father doing his usual best to get me a trolley for my bags. I must honestly give him credit for thinking of my best interests, even though I informed him several times that I would not be in need of a trolley since both of my suitcases have multi-directional wheels.

Murphy 2. Greg 0.

Going through our usual process of saying cheerio, including 'all the best, have a great trip, see you when you get back', etc., off my dad went. Walking into the airport, I went up to the terminal and tried to avoid adhering to the newly-implemented process for travelers requiring them to print their own boarding passes at electronic screens only slightly larger than their mobile phones. This all the while knowing full well that the menace of a machine was going to tell me it couldn't find my ticket since it was booked through an online airline rewards program.

 Four Green Fields

As the agent floated about pressing buttons, entering airport codes and destinations, scanning passports and tagging overstuffed bags, I struggled in vain to get her attention and tell her my ticket would not print. She finally told me I would need to go to the counter, where their colleague was staring at the computer in front of them. Once there, they directed me to follow the prompts on the automated terminal.

Murphy 3. Greg 0.

Sure enough, after seeing I was getting absolutely nowhere, the same agent told me I would need to go to the counter and speak to another of his colleagues as my booking reference could not be located within their system.

Murphy 4. Greg 0.

Handing my passport to the counter agent, things seemed to go off without a hitch. Perhaps Murphy and his daft law were starting to grow weary. Could it be, I wondered, that he was searching for another exhausted traveler to annoy? But then my trip truly hadn't begun yet. This was just the beginning of my trials and tribulations.

Once my tickets were handed over and my suitcase was dropped onto the conveyor belt, I went through to the security line and began the pre-screening process. Lo and behold, everything went smoothly. My luck really seemed to be changing!

In all the years I have been travelling as an author or attending Irish Festivals to do speaking engagements, I have never had an issue. I've always been wished the best of luck with book signings by the customs agents I was greeted by. They went through their process in explicit detail but provided me their stamp of approval and off I went. Except this time.

I immediately recognized the customs official and the lump in my throat felt like it ballooned to the size of a grapefruit. The reason is that when I had flown to the Windy City a month before, I was attending the screening of a debut movie by my fellow Irish author from County Tyrone, that being *Emerald City* written and directed by Colin Broderick. Along with J.P. Sexton, we met Colin at the Dublin, Ohio Irish Festival in August, signed books with him, celebrated in a lot of mad Irish craic, banter, and humour, and promised him we would fly there to support him and his fellow cast and crew members for the screening.

However, I had previously met that same customs official and went through a grilling of about twenty-five questions about how I knew the people I was going to see, when I first met them (including friends), and other questions that are not normally posed during a pre-screen. Perhaps the new border restrictions being put in place by the administration were being squarely directed at a particular Irish author who works full-time each day as a social worker. Perhaps not. Nevertheless,

Murphy 5. Greg 0.

Yup. You guessed it. Murphy would rear his ugly head again and cause more grief for me. After presenting my boarding pass and passport, the grilling of questions from the previous month continued. Where was I going? What was I doing there? Who was I speaking to? Who invited me? And countless more.

I answered each question fully and honestly, only to then be directed to a secondary pre-screening area. This is where I was informed by another customs officer that I was not allowed to board the plane with the books I had so carefully stacked the night before, which had deprived me of pleasant dreams and a wistful sleep. In the three years I had been doing book launches and signings, I was never told that they were to be shipped in advance and that they would have to be left behind or I would not be allowed to enter. My suitcase was removed from the boarding area. Sweet Mother of God.

Murphy 6. Greg 0.

After receiving a scolding, I was directed out of the secondary screening area and back out to the front counter. Here, I would be met by the same airline agent who directed me in the first place to use the automated terminal and enter my flight information. There they all stood, bewildered at why I was now back at their area.

Frantically explaining my plight, I was amazed that they showed compassion and were shocked to hear what had just happened. They could not comprehend it either and said they would refund the $25.00 that I paid to have my suitcase on their flight in the first place. Was Murphy actually about to lose a point to his chosen victim? Not quite.

The agents informed me that there was still time for me to board my flight provided my books could be dropped off. Wonderful. Thank you very much for that piece of very enlightening news. I am going to IBAM as a returning Irish author to do a book launch, signing, and speaking engagement with nothing to show for it other than the one sample of each book that would be permissible according to the customs official. Jesus, Mary, and Joseph! How in God's name would I pull this off? Was it worth the effort?

I phoned my dad and asked that he immediately return to the airport. He had driven forty minutes to drop me off, only to drive another forty minutes back home and had just walked through the door in the nick of time to hear my frantic phone call asking him to come back and pick up my books. This between my panicked breaths trying to tell him what the hell just happened, that there was no time to waste, etcetera. I told him I would wait at the same platform area where he had dropped me off eighty minutes before.

If anyone has ever experienced possibly missing a flight which was scheduled to leave on time, they could certainly relate to this. Looking at their watch or phone screen every ten seconds while pacing a trench into the hardened concrete path outside of the airport. It is a feeling of complete helplessness and utter despair. I am sure that if Murphy was standing beside me, he would have been crippled with laughter at my anxiety. Go ahead, you miserable sod. Chalk up another point!

Murphy 7. Greg 0.

The only way time could be passed at this point was to call the person at my destination who was wondering what the hell was going on by my texts. I had stated that my books were not allowed in and I might not be boarding the plane after all.

While trying to explain this, an RCMP police officer approached me and asked what was going on. Thankfully, I immediately recognized him as a friend of mine. Our sons had played hockey together on the same team the previous year. I explained everything while I frantically searched for my father's car among the hundreds entering the airport. No such luck. I had fifteen minutes before I would need to be at the gated area for boarding. Sigh. No pressure whatsoever!

As time ticked on and I felt like my blood was ebbing away, I repacked my suitcase and placed all of the books into it minus the three sample editions I would be allowed to bring with me and placed those with my laptop. Such a sad looking carry-on bag that I had now, which only carried the weight of my change of clothes.

Airport agents came out to check on me and let me know I needed to hurry up. I searched for my father's car again and, after what felt like an eternity, finally saw the familiar shape of his headlights at the top of the road. I would have celebrated if there was a moment to and I wasn't an emotional wreck.

Without wasting any time, I loaded my suitcase into the boot of his car and informed him I would call him after landing. This would hopefully give me a chance before catching my next flight to do what was necessary to ensure the event at IBAM was not a complete disaster.

Scrambling back into the airport, through the airline agents, and on to security, I went through the entire screening process again only to be met by three customs agents who informed me to hurry up and get on the plane as the gate was closing, while ensuring that I had no books with me other than what they would allow. I wasn't about to tempt fate.

I raced down the ramp to the airplane which, to my horror, was completely full of passengers who had already boarded and were impatiently waiting for me. And since my seat was in the third row from the back of the plane, I would have to walk down the aisle and past each row of faces staring back at my reddened face, both from running down the ramp to the gate as well as from being flustered from my experiences. I silently took my seat and closed my eyes, hoping in that very moment my life would fade to black.

Murphy 8. Greg 0.

As the flight attendants went through their pre-departure checks, the plane pushed back and would have to go through a de-icing process since an ice fog had settled in the area that morning. I was fine with this, as I'd been through this several times before. And after torturing myself a few days earlier watching a program called Airline Disasters, I would rather that the wings were not iced prior to our departure. I'm sure everyone else felt the same way.

The plane sat for a while a few feet from the gate and did not move any further. The confusion of this would be interrupted by an announcement from the captain that there was a failure in the left engine. He explained they were waiting for instructions from their headquarters in Atlanta to figure out what to do next while ground technicians also tried to sort out the technical difficulties they were facing. They decided to turn the plane off as if they were simply removing keys from the ignition of a car.

Sweet Jesus. What the hell was Murphy up to now? I guess he felt that the ridiculous amount of trials and tribulations that had already occurred that morning needed amped up. Ten minutes later, the engines fired up and roared back to life again only to be followed by a second announcement from the captain.

"Ladies and Gentlemen. We were informed by Atlanta that we had to shut the plane down and start it back up. This seems to have resolved the issue as the engine light has gone out. We will depart shortly. Apologies for the delay. We hope to have you in the air soon. Thank you for your patience and for choosing to fly with us."

Are you kidding me? Shut the plane down and start it back up again? This has resolved the issue? The check engine light has gone out? What is this, a desktop computer that gets a command from IT to turn it off and on again?

By this time, I was of the opinion it was Murphy who was choosing to fly the plane and was rubbing his oversized hands with glee at the chaos and disruption he had caused. Bastard!

Murphy 9. Greg (and his fellow passengers on the plane) 0.

As the engines warmed and the flight attendants went about the pre-departure checks all over again, there was a panicked voice that occurred in the back of the plane, two rows directly behind me. This being the very last row of seating.

"Sir. Sir. SIR. Are you okay? SIR? Can you hear me? SIR!"

The intercom rattled to life.

"Ladies and Gentlemen, we have a medical emergency. If there are doctors or paramedics on board, can you please identify yourselves and make your way to the back of the aircraft. We need your assistance immediately."

After what seemed to be an eternity, suddenly an assortment of paramedics and doctors, at least five, along with an occupational therapist who happened to be on the plane, headed past me and attended to the distressed passenger.

 Four Green Fields

The plane sat for at least a half hour before a decision was made to pull back up to the gate and assistance arrived to remove the gentleman and his wife from the plane so they could receive the necessary attention. This involved removing their baggage, which would take another half hour. I was sad for the couple since they wouldn't make their trip but was happy that they would receive medical care and felt that it was best this occurred on the ground rather than in the air.

Trying to put everything into some sort of perspective, it seemed at that moment my own difficulties that morning were meaningless in comparison. Perhaps there was a reason Murphy put his Law into place. Or perhaps, I was going soft in the head thinking that he was being nice to me.

As the medical emergency was being cleared and their baggage offloaded, I decided to use the bathroom at the rear of the aircraft. Since I could not return to my seat, I was afforded the opportunity of speaking with two of the airline hostesses that were seated waiting for instructions. I decided to share with them my many disasters that had already occurred that morning. They too, could not understand why I would not be allowed to bring my books in with me, and suggested that I should look into it further. I guess Murphy didn't single them out as he did with me.

Getting settled back into my seat, it would be another twenty minutes before we would finally push back from the gate and get on our way over to the de-icing pad. Going through this process would also take a while, so much so that two hours had already passed from when we had first attempted to leave our gated area. It was likely that many of us were going to miss our connecting flights. This however, also gave me a chance to see if I could ship my books overnight to Chicago in time for the festival.

Perusing one option, it would only be a paltry $450.00 for that to occur. Unless there was some sort of divine intervention, my newly pressed releases were not going to make it after all. Once again, my heart sank into my stomach.

Murphy 10. Greg -50 (the book count that was denied).

We finally taxied out to the runway and made our departure. The flight did not take very long at all, but what I was not expecting upon our landing was the crosswinds that the plane would now come into contact with. Gliding down to the runway, it felt as if the plane was flying sideways. It touched down on its left rear landing gear, and stayed there for a moment before settling onto the right wheel. Finally, the nose of the plane came down hard and immediately thereafter the brakes were not only applied but it felt as if they had been stomped on, sending us crashing into the seats in front of us. I had been quietly watching season seven of 'The Walking Dead', but sure as hell didn't want to be chomping the TV screen on the seatback just as the zombies were doing with the flesh of the living. Chalk up yet another point for Murphy.

Lucifer 11. Greg 0.

Taxiing up to the gate, flight attendants were trying to assist with what flights had already departed and to help the masses go to the counters inside the terminals to retrieve their new boarding passes. I grabbed my bags and followed suit, grumbling and muttering to myself as I exited the plane, only to be met with smiles from the captain and his crew. Perhaps they were all delighted to have this flight behind them. I know I certainly was. But I certainly did not anticipate what else Murphy and his damn Law had in store.

Heading up the ramp and into the airport, I didn't even look at the arrival or departures screens but went up to the counter along with hundreds of other passengers who had gathered, trying to collect their replacement boarding passes. This looked like a mosh pit at a rock concert but without the music or fun. I quickly found mine and went to an area to see if the information I researched earlier online was indeed correct in that it would cost me a small fortune to ship my books to IBAM. Sure enough, the results were less than satisfactory. The next cheapest option was $400.00, but this meant my father would have to drive back to the airport again and ship them from there. Hadn't I already wasted 160 minutes of his

   Four Green Fields

life that morning in making two return trips to the airport? I wasn't about to press my luck in asking for a third attempt.

I called and informed him that although I made it to the first destination, we were two hours late. I began explaining everything that had gone wrong already - from why the books were not allowed in, to the left engine failure, the medical emergency on the plane, and then the de-icing. I also let him know about the cost that it would be for me to ship my books and that this option was not one I was about to attempt. Thus, I'd have to explain things to the festival organizers as well as those wishing to purchase copies.

Since everything else had gone from bad to worse, I thought I may as well buy a lottery ticket from a dispensary beside me. They do say that God loves a trier. Obviously, Murphy loves a fool.

After doing so, I decided to look up at the departure screen and noticed that the flight I was supposed to be on and was under the impression that I had missed was DELAYED, and was still sitting at the gate. Seriously? Was my luck actually changing? Perhaps I finally got one up on auld Murphy and decided to tempt fate.

Murphy 11. Greg 1. Finally!

I ran down to the departure gate and met with the airline agent who was standing at the counter.

"Are you Greg McVicker?", she enquired.

"Yes, I am. I didn't think I would make the flight because of some delays in Winnipeg."

"Well, we have been waiting for you and were wondering if you were going to join us. We had a bit of a mechanical issue with the boarding door and the flight has been delayed. Our technicians are working on it and the flight should be departing shortly. I will open the door for you here; you can make your way down to the aircraft."

My mind began racing.

"Wait a minute," I thought to myself. "Did she just say that they are having mechanical issues with the aircraft? You've got to be kidding me. I made a flight that was supposed to have left already due to another bloody failure? Jesus Christ_Almighty. To hell with you and your stupid law, Lucifer. Murphy. Or whatever your friggen' name is. You're still a bastard all the same."

Murphy 12. Greg 0. (I lost the one and only point I had gained!)

Walking down to the gate, I was met by one of the ground crew who, with a Cheshire Cat type smile, informed me that I must be the luckiest passenger on the planet and was able to make my flight which had been delayed. I could not hold back any longer.

"Are you serious? Have you any idea what kind of a morning I have had so far and what I have had to go through to get here?"

By this time, I began wondering if the fellow with whom had just flashed his cheeky grin at me was actually Murphy himself. Perhaps he was a Body Snatcher, had made his way to the airport, and was delighted to watch how frazzled I was from all of the crazy events which I had gone through that morning and was finally unravelling at the seams. Perhaps I should not have watched the movie based on Jack Finney's novel of the same name.

I chose to not look at his nametag or his passes because that would have wholeheartedly done me in. There would have been a scene of complete heart failure, or this author being carted off, all the while screaming Irish expletives at the body-snatching technician while watching four other aircraft mechanics trying their best to sort out the door on the opposite side of the plane that would not close. They were accompanied by four airline hostesses and one of the pilots. Jesus. Things did not look good.

Murphy 13. Greg… has completely lost his mind at this point. So much for the superstition that 13 is very lucky in Ireland. On this day, it was nothing but a horrible curse!

As I stood watching in disbelief at the staff blocking my entrance to the aircraft, I decided to walk back up the ramp, order a rental car, and drive for destinations unknown. Before I could make my move, however, the hostess looked at my ticket and waived me on to the plane. By this point, I was so exhausted, I figured I may as well continue. Murphy had gone thirteen rounds with me and scored a knockout.

Walking down the aisle and looking at the seat numbers above me, I found that I would be sitting in an exit row, beside a door, which looked like the one behind me that did not want to shut. Well, this is getting a whole lot better. A lady was seated on my left. I wondered if my friend Murphy would jump from the technician's body into hers so she too could have a laugh at my misery. She never looked up from her book.

About thirty minutes after I had boarded the plane, the captain came on to tell us that the issue had been fixed and we would be departing shortly. Hallelujah! Finally, I would be able to put this rotten day behind me once and for all. And that moment for me could not come soon enough.

The flight itself went smoothly until we started making our final approach and had to cross partially over Lake Michigan to make our turn back towards the runway. Since I always had an interest in planes and having landed at this airport several times previously, I thought that we were coming in a little too fast. Could that bastard Murphy now be flying the plane, too?

Sure enough, we hit the runway very hard. Much like the previous flight, the pilot stomped on the brakes, which launched every passenger, including me, to sink whatever remaining pearly whites we had directly into the seats in front of us. The sound of metal grinding on metal from the wheel base of the plane below us was brutal. Welcome to the Law of Murphy's Airlines. Where if anything can go wrong, you are certainly guaranteed that it definitely will! Murphy had driven his point into my skull.

I phoned the lady who would be greeting me at the airport and she asked if I had made it. My response was no, that we had to make an emergency landing in the lake and that I was standing on the wing, waiting to see if I should jump in because of how this day had gone. That comment was met with laughter, which seemed to provide me with renewed strength and to maybe not be defeated after all, although those chances to slim to non-existent.

Since I now had no luggage to retrieve, I headed directly outside. It was nice to finally be on solid ground again. While waiting to be picked up for the final leg of the journey to Chicago, I figured I would get the last word in against Murphy by ordering my books and having them shipped via a rush order to the festival site. Calling the distributor, I learned they could indeed do this for a small shipping fee which was no problem at all. Finally, I was about to get one leg up!

Jumping for joy and celebrating my changing fortune, and after placing my order, I could not believe what was in store for me. I would go on to learn the books would arrive the day after IBAM wrapped up. Talk about rubbing salt into already gaping wounds.

In hindsight, I had the last laugh over my auld friend of misery. During the awards dinner the next night at the Irish American Heritage Center, I found myself being introduced to Irish singer Daniel O'Donnell, who received a lifetime achievement award for his contributions to music and television. It was quite a prestigious honour to sit in his company, and to have an in-depth chat about his experiences growing up back home in Ireland, which mirrored that of my own in that my father was away working for months at a time, just as Daniel experienced with his.

In closing, and to my dear colleague and friend, Cliff Carlson, perhaps IBAM might consider presenting Murphy with a Lifetime Achievement Award of his own, and one that fully recognizes his mischievous Law that if anything can go wrong, it will!

Belfast Comes to Burbank

"I had a very happy childhood, which is unsuitable if you are going to be an Irish writer."

-   **Maeve Binchy.**

I was having lunch at an outdoor café with my wife and daughters one sunny Saturday in Burbank, California, when an elderly but fit-looking man walked by our table. He didn't blend in at all with the typical Burbank crowd. However, he would have fit in perfectly in Belfast. You see, he had a walking style my father used to call "a tough, wee dander" - a bit like Popeye the Sailor. I was even accused by my father of having a tough, wee dander a few times. I like to think it's the product of simply being overstuffed with too much enthusiasm for life, but it's probably also a carry-over from a childhood tainted by the necessity of self-protection. The tough, wee dander is the first line of defense, the silent message to the bullies of the world that you are not to be messed with. As a Belfast child ages, this dander becomes softened, even elegant, more personality than protection, but it is as good of a hint of one's place of birth as their brogue is. The verve for life that gives rise to the dander is also assuaged by art of any kind, particularly singing and storytelling, two of the most effective pressure release valves.

I said to my wife, "See that guy over there? He's from Belfast."

She looked at him and replied, "How do you know? Is he a friend of your dad's?"

"No, I've never seen him before, but I can tell by the way he walks."

"That's ridiculous," she said dismissively.

"Oh, really?" I said. "Watch this."

I aimed my voice at him and yelled, "Ach, away 'o that, ya bloody eejit!"

It registered with no one except the man himself. He stopped in the crowd and looked over, searching for the source of this familiar voice. I didn't let on right away that it was me. I could also surmise by his impish grin that he was a man of good humor so I continued the game and yelled, "Catch yerself on, ya silly bugger!"

This helped him lock on to the source, my smiling gub. He came over and asked, "Was that you?"

I answered yes. He asked if I was from Belfast. I told him, "No, but my parents are."

"Well," he said, "you've certainly got the accent down, lad."

I stood up and introduced myself and my family. He replied, "A pleasure to meet ya! My name is Tommy the Street Singer!"

I asked jokingly if all of that was on his birth certificate. He said "yes, it is!" then handed me a business card. It said nothing but *Tommy the Street Singer* on it with a phone number at the bottom.

"Wow," I said, "you really are a street singer."

"Aye!" he said, smiling. "Here, I'll show you."

With that, he burst into song right there on the sidewalk, startling me and a few other people who were passing by closely. He sang *Fairy Tales Can Come True* with disarming joy and total commitment in the slightly melodramatic, quivery voice of a 1930's crooner. The people waiting in line for a movie at the multiplex next door turned around and started smiling, quickly falling to his charm. I listened for a moment, my wife and kids chuckling at this wild character and myself standing there next to him silently. I decided to help him show my children the proper way to live and joined him in his song. I love the standards so I knew all the words. I even took off my baseball cap, put it on the ground, and collected a few dollars and some applause for him before we were done.

 Four Green Fields

When we finished, Tommy joined us at our table. I would learn that he was ninety years old, though I had figured about seventy. He told me some stories of old Belfast and his life in the states. A lady returned from shopping and said to him, "There you are! I've been looking all over." She then turned to us and said, "I'm sorry. He's always getting lost. Sometimes I think he's trying to get rid of me!"

Tommy said, "I'd like ya to meet my girlfriend." He whispered, "She's a younger woman. Only eighty-three. I know – I'm a cradle-robber."

We all laughed and she rolled her eyes good-naturedly, that look both unique and common to the wives of Belfast men, though she was American. (My wife has perfected this look, too. It's as inevitable as Irish rain.)

Tommy stood and thanked me for taking him on a mental trip back to Belfast. I shook his hand and thanked him for taking me back to Belfast with his song. It gave me a wee taste of what it must have been like to perform for the queue in front of the Park Picturehouse. My father used to tell stories about all the singers that would entertain the crowds there in the 1940's. When *The Jolson Story* starring Larry Parks came out in 1946, the street was lined with kids down on one knee singing *Mammy* and *Swanee*, all trying to drown out the other Jolson's on either side of them.

Part of me believes that, for the sake of world peace and the common good, human beings need to stop categorizing each other by race, nationality, religion and all the other ways we separate ourselves. But another part of me celebrates our differences. For instance, when I go to Europe, I want to see Germans wearing lederhosen, Spaniards flamenco dancing, Africans jumping up and down in bones and skins, St. Bernard's in Switzerland with little barrels on their necks, etc. I don't like the idea of everyone wearing khaki's and polo shirts. I would miss what makes us all interesting and unique. And I would miss tough, wee danders in a lockstep world. Even though I was born in California, I recognized my other tribe the day I saw Tommy the Street Singer, and what a grand tribe it is.

ÐUBLÍN CREAM BUN

"The only way to get rid of temptation is to yield to it."

- **Oscar Wilde.**

The first thing to cross your mind when you see the title above might be the capital of Ireland, and our bakeries, which are famous for producing gorgeous goods and tasty treats. Well, that's not correct whatsoever. You see, this story was born in a delightful, fabulous and welcoming community located within the City of Dublin, Ohio, USA – and a country that is home to my fellow author, Mark Rickerby, invaded by my fellow author, J.P. Sexton, and has provided several warm welcomes to this Irish author, poet, and storyteller, Greg McVicker. Well, that is except for one excruciatingly pain in the arse day when my friend of misery, Murphy and his Law, decided to join me on my trip.

You might be wondering what sort of a buck eejit would take the time and make the effort to write a story about a cream bun, and how it relates to Dublin? If you're sitting comfortably, then I'll begin.

A year ago, a wonderful lady and now a dear friend by the name of Barbara Cody-Burkholder reached out to this ruggedly handsome young lad in response to an enquiry I had made. The year prior, I was invited to attend and participate in the Milwaukee Irish Festival and had the incredible honour of being stationed alongside my fellow Belfast author, the one and only Tony Macaulay. Tony has written several brilliant books including *Paperboy, Breadboy, All Growed Up,* and *Little House on the Peace Line.* (Tony, if you're in need of an agent, you have my mobile number!)

It was at this same festival that I met a lovely couple who do an awful lot of baking, including breads and biscuits based on recipes from home. They bring their wares to events across America. It was they who suggested

I get in contact with the good folks at the Dublin, Ohio Irish Festival. Fate occurred that night.

At the Milwaukee Irish Festival, Tony and I met Cliff Carlson, a gentleman who has also become a dear friend and colleague. Cliff was in the author's tent showcasing the Irish Books, Arts, and Music (IBAM) Festival in Chicago, Illinois. As mentioned in **_Murphy's Law: My Friend of Misery!_** this glorious event and gala celebrates and highlights the contributions of Irish artists throughout the various genres intricately woven within the title – IBAM. He invited us to attend. Again, fate was made that night. It must have been the luck of the Irish.

When Tony and I went to Chicago that October and made our debut appearance at the Irish American Heritage Center, a truly outstanding building that houses an abundance of history, books, music, a theatre, as well as yearly celebration of all things Irish and the artists behind them, we were stationed on the lower level side-by-side. Another fellow came in and introduced himself, none other than J.P. Sexton, who like myself with **_Through the Eyes of a Belfast Child: Life. Personal Reflections. Poems.,_** was there to also launch his first book, **_The Big Yank: Memoir of a Boy Growing Up Irish._**

Tony and I had attended the dinner and awards presentation the night before as guests of Cliff and his beautiful wife, Cathy, but we did not know J.P. I must say there is truly something magical when a group of Irish men who hail from differing backgrounds and parts of our country all converge on one location and come together as a group. The stories as told by Tony, J.P., and myself, along with others who filtered through the crowd, were incredibly special and filled with lots of laughter and personal reflection.

Although we only had two days together, in meeting punters coming to our tables to purchase and have us sign copies of our books, which is always an honour and pleasure to do, we created incredibly special friendships. I kept in regular touch with Tony and J.P. after IBAM had ended and we all went our separate ways. Tony afforded me the opportunity of being interviewed on his Northern Visions NvTv program called **Novel Ideas** when I flew home later that year for the homecoming debut launch of my book in Belfast. Unfortunately, he already had plans sorted for around the same time that the Dublin, Ohio Irish Festival was happening and was unable to attend.

After filing my application, the interview telephone call finally came in for Dublin. I spoke to Barbara for forty-five minutes, telling her all about myself, my books, and what my presentations would be based on. Barbara extended a warm welcome and informed me that I would be joining her and many other amazing authors in August. Being the cheeky wee article that I am, however, I took an opportunity to also put forth the name of J.P. and part of his story. Barbara agreed to have him there and would just need to connect with him. I immediately called J.P. in Florida and let him know the fantastic news.

When the day finally arrived, I flew into the Columbus airport and was met by a phenomenal fellow named Mike. He is part of the amazing group of employees and hundreds of volunteers who make up the Dublin, Ohio Irish Festival, and fully extended a warm Irish greeting of Céad Míle Fáilte! One hundred thousand welcomes and then some awaited every artist and performer who arrived to be a part of this prestigious event! Mike is a true ambassador for and with the City of Dublin, as he answered every question posed to him, provided transportation services, and gave a full overview, tour, and history of the city and its yearly festival.

Arriving at our hotel, as I was checking in, I was met with another full Irish welcome by an amazing and inspirational author, a lady by the name of Sinéad Tyrone, who has also since become a dear friend. She has yet to figure out and understand the mad craic and banter that her fellow authors from Ireland bring with them, and is often left in stitches since neither she nor anyone else for that matter knows what us lot are going to get up to or what might fly out of our bakes. Like our fathers before us who taught us this strange language, comments spoken by an Irish gub often come without thought or filter.

Four Green Fields

Sinéad has written four books including *Walking through the Mist, Fragility, Crossing the Lough Between,* and *A Song Of Ireland.* Since she had been to the festival previously and was doing a return tour, she took the time to share as much of her insight and knowledge as to what I would need to know for the weekend ahead. She paused to let me know that Barbara would be joining us later that evening for a walk around the grounds and to help us get our bearings, since 140,000 other people would also be in attendance over the next few days.

A short while later, in walked a fellow who is not only a dear friend and fellow author who hails from the Inishowen Peninsula of County Donegal, he stands about the same size as our legendary Irish giant, Fionn Mac Cumhaill. The one and only J.P. Sexton! Immediately, the banter and craic from Chicago sprung to life between the two of us. Poor Sinéad was trying to figure out our rapidly-increasing-in-speed brogues as we told stories of our adventures and journeys. The festival hadn't even begun, yet the slagging by way of friendly craic and banter, as can always be found in Irish circles, was already in full swing.

That evening, as more people arrived, we finally had a chance to gather as a group. This included a fellow author from County Tyrone, Northern Ireland by the name of Colin Broderick who wrote his first memoir, *Orangutan,* along with his second book, *That's That.* Colin also wrote and produced two independent films based on his own experiences called *Emerald City* and *A Bend in the River.* Personally, it was interesting to be among so many amazing authors and the stories they brought with them.

Barbara came by the hotel with her husband, John, as well as our driver, Mike, and brought us over to the grounds to begin our tour and learn where we'd be stationed over the weekend and where our presentations would take place. It was exciting, as we learned the NHL Columbus Blue Jackets would be in attendance along with the Stanley Cup. J.P., Colin, and I all reflected that a festival like this never happened in Ireland, which is sad, as there is such a rich community of talent back home. To do something like this in celebration of the Irish culture and all that our wee country has produced and has to offer, would truly be out of this world.

The following morning, after we had all gotten ourselves settled, we joined a group of fellow authors for breakfast. While everyone went through their introductions, the banter started, which lead to many gaining a small glimpse as to what the craic was going to be like throughout this weekend. Just like our fathers, we too started gnawing at the fabric of one another, seeking to up our statements with light-hearted jabs and leaving others crippled with laughter.

Making our way to the festival grounds, I managed to convince Barbara to let me share a table with J.P. and Colin to his immediate left. The Irish were here in full force, along with another fellow author from Belfast who writes children's books, Jim McVeigh. After chatting with Jim for a bit, I discovered I had attended school in Northern Ireland with his younger brother, while Jim had gone to school with my cousin! Talk about a small world! We compared our experiences of growing up, the similarities, and the differences.

One of the things I had noticed while walking onto the grounds is that the Dublin, Ohio Irish Festival has the largest cream buns one could ever wish for! They are a meal in themselves and could easily require a knife and fork to eat them. We had these back home and they are one of the true delights I crave and miss. They are a fluffy, mouthwatering delicacy of the highest order, so to see a tray of them sitting, waiting, wanting to be consumed, made my stomach growl even though I was full to the brim from that morning's breakfast. Oh, the torture.

There were enough times throughout the day I made mention of those cream buns since they were freely calling my name over and over again. It was as if they were a poet whisperer, distracting my attention, pulling my thoughts toward their delicate texture, creamy filling, and delightful taste. It was a love affair at first sight. The temptation was far too much to resist. But my belly was full. Sadly, there was no room at the inn.

Four Green Fields

Setting up my book display, I busied myself by emptying my boxes onto the table when the flaps of the large, vinyl tent suddenly closed in rapid succession. An intense thunderstorm was barreling down on the area and would bring dangerous winds and lightning with it. Announcements came over the loudspeakers informing us to take shelter immediately and to evacuate the tents.

Making our way to a secure area, we waited out the storm while raindrops the size of marbles fell from the heavens. The storm did not dampen the spirits of the punters, however, as when it came time for the festival gates to open, it did not take long for the grounds to swell to capacity. J.P. had joined me by this time and put a Celtic design tablecloth down for the two of us and to make us both look the part of being Irish authors. It's not like we didn't have our accents and displays to give us away or anything. The fact I was wearing a blue golf shirt which had the words 'Belfast Child' embroidered with brilliant white thread onto it was not a dead giveaway either. Would anyone know where we came from?

Throughout the day, as people came into the tent to learn about our books and asked us questions about Ireland, as well as sharing their own families' histories, knowledge, and experiences of travelling home, my thoughts often became loud spoken word in that I wished I could go to get a Dublin cream bun, but I had to stay by my table. A fair maiden by the name of Danica Richardson came to my rescue. She had gone to get cups of tea for J.P., Colin and I throughout the day before heading off to check out other festival activities. As an avid reader, she was checking out all sorts of books. Actually, if my memory serves me correctly, I believe she was one of the punters who bought a small library in the process.

I guess Danica's inquisitive mind went to explore many of the other vendors and sights around the festival, as it was an eternity before she decided to pick up another one of those glorious, beautiful, mouthwatering delicacies. The one problem, in my opinion, was that a suave, attractive young fellow (yours truly) had gone off himself to set up an author signing banner outside of the tent as things were quiet and allowed for this opportunity. This helped to draw a lot of much-needed foot traffic to the author's tent.

Unbeknownst to me, many of my fellow authors had their eyes on that stunning creation when she arrived back at the author tent. She was gorgeous, a gift from the Gods. Never had anyone seen anything so perfect, so pure, and so special. Was it true the mold had been shattered after she was created? There was no other like her. She stood among the masses, alone, not paying attention to those who cast eyes in her direction, drooling, wishing, wanting. As time stood still and hearts skipped beats, glorious fails to come close to describing what occurred in the next moment. It seemed the herald angels sang choruses of Hallelujah within the tent. The dark, grey skies parted ways to streams of light which glistened down upon her. Low and behold, in that very moment, a lifelong dream came true. The Dublin cream bun finally arrived!

Cradled in Danica's hands, being careful not to disturb this gift from the heavens, especially the delicate filling which had been so carefully added between the outer layers of puffed pastry, Danica placed the Dublin cream bun down at the table where two authors sat. However, at this moment, only one author was there. His name was J.P. Sexton. With a ravenous look in his eyes, his stomach let out a large growl I could hear from over five feet way, and his eyes filled with a look of pure intent.

Seeing the breathtaking delight before him, unable to hold back his hunger any longer, J.P. made his move. Standing up from his seated position, adjusting his books, checking his forms, and licking his chops, he suddenly announced his fullest intention - he was going to the festival offices to have a bite to eat and a drink. But who would promote his books while he was gone?

In that instant, another dashing hero came to the rescue. It was the Irish lad, the poet, the storyteller, and the author known simply as Greg. Yes, folks. Me! Since I had previously read his book and could provide a very healthy case synopsis on J.P.'s story, I offered to look after his books, let

 Four Green Fields

the punters know when he would be back to sign them, and that they could purchase them in advance. This would also allow them more time to wander around to speak to other authors in the process. But the greatest outcome of this is that it ensured the Dublin cream bun did not find itself in a place it had not originally been intended for.

As J.P. exited the tent, I set about to adjust my books as well. My efforts of placing the sign did its job, as it caught the attention of many more people who came in and spoke to me about my memoir and life story. This also afforded me the opportunity of promoting J.P.'s and Colin's book as well, since Colin had gone for a break, too. Actually, all of my fellow authors were truly fantastic, supporting and providing coverage for one another. I managed to sell a couple of J.P.'s books for him, filled the sheets out, and let people know that he was out getting some food.

In fact, I was so busy that the glorious, mouthwatering creation which had been so prudently selected went completely untouched. Seconds turned to minutes. Minutes turned to quarter segments of time. 15. 30. 45. 1 hour. The Dublin cream bun which had been carefully sourced and eventually brought to the tent to meet its chosen fate along with moans of enjoyment while being consumed did not happen. Not during that first hour anyway.

J.P. arrived back from his feast and was updated on the events that had occurred over the hour he was gone. He noticed that the delicate delight still sat where it had been so carefully placed sixty minutes before and shared his thoughts out loud:

> **"How the hell does that mad hoor allow that to sit for an hour without taking a nibble out of it? Jesus, at our house in Donegal, that would never have stood a chance. It would have been inhaled and devoured in one bite and washed down with a mug of hot tea."**

What J.P. did not realize is since I had done so much talking (which is not uncommon for me), I didn't have time to eat. In true and tested fashion, I've been told I could talk the leg of a stool. A pure measurement in having the Irish gift of the gab! Since I am a very slow eater because of spending so much time talking, the poor Dublin cream bun sat for another full hour, so it did.

Needless to say, I too was growing hungry and decided that a wee break was needed away from books and chatting. J.P. kindly offered to take on the role of promoting my story along with his own, and even sold a few books for me, too. That is, until I came back to the tent after my own feast and saw that he had signed my name, to *his* book! Greg McVicker: author of The Big Yank! He must have been so consumed by the mouthwatering delicacy that sat in front of him that he forgot who he was, or who I was, or simply put, he assumed my identity. J.P. Sexton: The near Belfast Child from Newtownabbey. And here he thought that I was a mad hoor?

Upon discovering J.P.'s newly crowned identity, this would lead to absolute pandemonium in the authors tent. Seeing and hearing that a full-out slagging was unfolding, our intrepid leader, Barbara, came over to see what all the chaos was about. From this, a superb photo op was granted in which J.P. declared, "Well, if I'm going to be mistaken as Greg McVicker, the near Belfast Child from Newtownabbey and Irish author of The Big Yank, I may as well get stuck into his food" and set about to take a mouthful. The picture was priceless and has since made several rounds on social media. Funny enough, J.P. was asking me the other day how it keeps popping up, since he thought he had the global rights and wanted to sell the image to Rolling Stone Magazine. I told him I already sold the rights to the National Enquirer and am waiting for it to make front page news. He responded with sincere kindness by telling me that it sat for such a long time, the cream filling almost turned back into butter!

The tears that flowed from the extreme howls of laughter occurring because of that cream bun lasted all weekend. The testament, as is now reflected within the subtitle of this book, Wild Irish Banter & Stories along with Shenanigans & Poetry, were not only fully established; continued at every opportunity thereafter. Laughing at ourselves makes up a huge part

　　　Four Green Fields

of the thread and sense of an Irish identity. Not only does it help to keep us sane during all of the madness that we grew up in and have lived through, it keeps us grounded as to who we are as a race of people with such a truly beautiful culture. As we often say, there are those who are Irish, and those who wish they were.

Anyways, enough of me getting all squishy and mushy for a moment. If you are wondering how this story ended, that tasty morsel sat untouched for over four hours. The only time I managed to enjoy it was after we had closed our authors tent for the night and started walking back through the festival grounds to take in some of the other late-night entertainment that was already underway. It was at the Wake House when I stopped to ask if this was where the dead man lives, Dublin cream bun in hand, and began engaging in what else but another full-fledged conversation while having a few bites to celebrate the life of the stuffed mannequin lying there with coins over his eyes. As I stood looking into the coffin, as we do back home, I thought I would share a moment of respect and muttered words heard at many Irish wakes: "Sure. He looks just like himself, doesn't he?"

In thinking back to my story titled ***Chuckie Our Da***, I certainly have no place in calling him out for rationing his two cups of extra-large coffee from which he gets six servings over two days. The apple certainly didn't fall far from the tree in the McVicker gene pool. Guilty, as charged.

The beauty of all this is that J.P. and I were invited back to the Dublin, Ohio Irish Festival this year. Moreover, I asked and have confirmed our fellow author, Mark Rickerby, will be in attendance with us, which coincides with the debut launch of this book. More importantly, it will be a chance to have another opportunity to sink our collective teeth into what else but the puff pastry with the tasty interior. Perhaps in the sequel to this book, one of us will have written a poem for it. I can picture this being another Irish language lesson:

Baile átha Cliath borróg uachtar, a grá mo chroí.

Loosely translated: Dublin Cream Bun, love of my heart.

Food for Thought

Dee: "Why do you need such long ass names for your books? Through the Eyes of a Belfast Child. Life. Personal Reflections. Poems. Now this one. Four Green Fields: Irish Banter & Stories, Shenanigans & Poetry!"

Greg: "What's wrong with that? Others have long subtitles."

Dee: Why can't you just call it something much simpler: "This is Greg."

Greg: "Do you know any Irish men who make stories short?

Dee: "Hmm. Come to think of it, no."

Greg: "I rest my case. Say, any chance of a Dublin Cream Bun?"

PS. After this was written, J.P. came up with yet another word to add to the title. **Wild**. It's a wee description of his 3D tour.

CRAIC! BANTER!
hobby horses shite!

BLESS ME, FATHER...

"There is an Irish way of paying compliments as though they were irresistible truths which makes what would otherwise be an impertinence delightful."

- **Katherine Tynan Hinkson.**

While making the Sign of the Cross, this wee lad utters one of his first teachings in Gaeilge:

In ainm an Athar, agus a Mhic, agus an Spioraid Naomh, Amen.

Bless me, Father, for I have sinned. It has been, ummm, it has been, Jesus Murphy, it's, frig me, it's been a bloody eternity since I have last been to confession! Oh, pardon my language, Father. I shouldn't have said bloody. Oh, Jesus Christ of Almighty, I just swore again and took the Lord's name in vain. Sorry about that, Father. But, since I'm here in your confessional, I must confess my sins and ask for your forgiveness and absolution. Are ya ready?

Right. I went to an Irish Festival in America; it was in a wee city called Dublin, Ohio. It's amazing there, so it is! One of the best places I've ever been! I was brought there by the festival organizers and they were dead brilliant, so they were. They took excellent care of me and made me incredibly welcome throughout my weekend with them.

You see, I am a very proud Irish author, poet, and storyteller and was launching my first book there, so I was. Aye. You may have heard of it, Father. It's my personal memoir, *Through the Eyes of a Belfast Child – Life. Personal Reflections. Poems.* It's a bit of an emotional roller coaster to read, so it is. But, sure, when you're not gurnin' your lamps out or laughing your arse off, you'll love it, so you will.

Anyways, Father, in Dublin, I met a bunch of other lovely Irish and American authors. They were all dead on. But, this one bloke, J.P. Sexton, he stands the same height as Fionn Mac Cumhaill, so he does. He is a dear friend of mine now. J.P. that is, not Fionn although he would be handy to have around.

The craic and banter between us was out of this world. We kept winding each other up all weekend as well as punters who came to visit us and get copies of our books. That J.P. fella even took to signing his name to my book, so he did. I think he's one of them body snatcher's that I read about. Aye. I'm dead serious, Father. Here, let me ask you this. Did you ever get reading the story called *Murphy's Law: My Friend of Misery!?* It is in a wee book called *Four Green Fields: Wild Irish Banter & Stories, Shenanigans & Poetry: Welcome Home to the Emerald Isle!* The book is dead brilliant and is all about Ireland. The wee Murphy's Law story talks about body snatcher's who take on people's identities, eats their souls, and causes all sorts of chaos. I think they're politicians.

But, here, listen to this, Father. C'mere 'til ya hear this. After we wrapped up the festival, we all went back to the hotel for a night's sleep before going our separate ways the following morning. But do ya see me? My ma used to tell me that I'm full of the badness. Before I put my head down for the night, I was on that Facebook thing and put up a wee video I found on YouTube. I thought it was totally class. I was laughing that hard I couldn't breathe and sounded just like that character Muttley from the Dick Dastardly cartoons I used to watch on a Saturday morning. Unless my da was home from sea, that is, as he would drag our weary arses out of bed and make us clean the house and our lockers. Aye, I swear my father is none other than Darth Vader. He has dark, Jedi mind powers. Lucky for us, he doesn't have a light saber, so he doesn't.

But, do ya see yer man, J.P.? When he came to breakfast the next morning, he was raging mad, so he was. His bake was all red, and he called me a feckin' prick. A feckin' prick, Father! In front of everyone! Oh, sorry, I just swore in your confessional again. Here, but do ya see me? I thought there was going to be World War Eire that morning, so I did. Aye! I was planning for my own wake.

In the video, there was a man on the side of the road in County Donegal. Beside him was a field packed with a huge herd of sheep. Every time the man spoke or said a word, the sheep responded and would bleat at him. It was dead funny. At least I thought so.

I posted the video online and said it was my fellow Irish author, J.P. Sexton, reading his personal memoir, *The Big Yank – Memoir of a Boy Growing Up Irish* to his first full audience in Ireland. He was furious, so he was. It was a few hours before he cooled down, and even though I offered to take the video down, J.P. said, "Ack, sure, it's just a bit of craic." Thank goodness for Divine Intervention, for I am sure that's what saved my very pale Irish arse! What's that, Father? Why's my arse so pale? Ack, sure. It's actually quite simple; the sun doesn't shine there, so it doesn't.

Right. That's me all done with my confession. Do you want me to say an Our Father and three Hail Mary's for my penance and to be cleansed of my sins? You don't, Father? You wish for me to say a decade of the rosary instead? Frig me, that's an awful lot, so it is. Oh, it's because I was winding J.P. up and I've used bad words? Aye. I understand. I've the mouth of a sailor. At least I come by it honestly, so I do, as my da was one for thirty years, so he was. I don't even want to share half of the things he comes off with. Aye, it's shocking, so it is. It's completely unfiltered what jumps out of his gub. I'd be stuck in here for all eternity!

Before I leave the wee confessional box here, I honestly would do the same thing, Father, if I was sitting in your place. Right next the Big Guy in the Sky! What's that? You want me to also say the Apostles Creed as well as a Glory Be to the Father? You think this penance will only hold for a few hours? Then why you're tacking all these extras on? Aye, I suppose you're right. It makes pure sense why I haven't been to confession in years, so it does. I spend the day stuck at the pew begging for forgiveness and absolution. I'd better frig off here before you tack on an Act of Contrition!

ⲥhe pen & paper pυꝺ

"If there were only three Irishmen in the world you'd find two of them in a corner talking about the other."

- **María Brandán Aráoz.**

With that quote, and as the three of us are sitting in different parts of the world having a virtual pint to celebrate the completion of this book, Mark suggested we ask you to join us as we conduct our own interview. Sure, it's not like we have said much already. What's a few more words?

So here we are at The Pen & Paper Pub, a secret name for a watering hole specifically for Irish authors, poets, and storytellers. I guess that is no longer a secret since I have just told everyone about it. But, do you see that J.P. fellow? Jesus Murphy. I swear he could drink for all of Ireland, so he could. He has a fine palette for Guinness and Irish Whiskey. I have a fine palette for Harp and an Ulster Fry. As for Mark, he has a fine pallet that he stacks his several volumes of books on which he has graced the pages of over the years. Wait and see!

Anyways, while I have been putting this book together for all of you, there has been a tremendous collection of dialogue going back and forth by way of emails, calls, and text messages. We are Irish – would you expect anything less? With this, we would like to give you, the readers who have tempted fate and chanced a read of this book, a bloopers section regarding the madness which Mark has been exposed to by way of his two fellow authors. Heaven help him! And every time he edits this book, I keep writing more!

As a social worker by day, I offered Mark counselling to help him through the trauma of taking me up on the offer of co-authoring this book in the first place, originally suggested by the one and only, J.P. Sexton. ($180 plus tax per hour, Mark. A bargain!)

Speaking of one and only, would you believe our Donegal lad fancies himself as the next world renown Irish crooner? Names like J.P. Morrison or Sinéad O'Sexton (please note the not so coincidental reference to the initials of S.O.S. here) come to mind although to be honest, Sinéad, Nothing Compares 2 U.

Ya wanna see him. It's shocking. I swear to God. A few hours ago, I was speaking with J.P. via videoconferencing. Here's me working my wee arse off, putting this book together with every available second that I can scrounge. As I also noted, Mark has been working well into the morning hours as our editor, combing through our words and ensuring everything is spelt properly along with true punctuation and tightening things up. Meanwhile, John is in Ireland on a **3D highway tour**. When he first told me about it, excitement poured over me as he was getting into the digital world and was sourcing new forms of technology to bring this book to you. I later found out that he meant **D**ublin, **D**erry, and **D**onegal by way of the bus on the A5 and N2 motorways. So much for my dreams. That was my bubble burst. He is having the time of his life as he is visiting family in Inishowen, downing several dozen pints, revisiting his childhood, and doing his homecoming book launch.

But do you see when I saw him on the video screen? I almost fell over, so I did! With that wild lookin' hairdo of his, he looks like a modern-day Fabio, but without the muscles! And I know my music. If his singing career takes off as the next Irish crooner, J.P. could fill in as Robert Plant on the Led Zeppelin farewell tour with those locks he's sporting, so he could! I swear to God, the Life of Riley doesn't describe it! If he stands on the North Antrim coastline of Northern Ireland and points towards Scotland, people will be thinking Fionn Mac Cumhaill came back from the dead!

Sure, anyways. I am getting off track here. As I was saying, J.P. put his fingers to keyboard and using his exact words seen below, he composed a song in honour of a "beautiful wee delicacy which goes to his hips and makes his clothes tighter instead of his liquid diet, Tequila, which makes his clothes fall off."

 Four Green Fields

Here it is – you be the judge!

"When the day is done,
And the race is runnnnn (drawn out),
And McVicker ignores,
His lovely cream bun.

A hungry lad,
With no Donegal fish to be had,
Might just wander along,
And eat the damn thing for fun."

-   Composed by J.P. Sexton.
    Irish author, delirious musician, and mad hoor.

Moving on, I was speaking with Mark about the struggles that we have both faced in writing this book, as it has brought up a lot of painful memories when writing about his beloved father and my beautiful mum. Although it may seem easy to put such words to paper in that we are authors, I wrote the following to him:

> "I'm glad that you had a fun and restful and invigorating, rejuvenating weekend. I can certainly appreciate the struggles of bringing up the memories of those that we love the most and how much we miss them. As I say more often than not, I'm sure and certain that those who chance a reading of this book are also going to find themselves lost in reflective memory of their loved ones as well. People have said words on their minds that they are not able to speak… it is people like us, who are authors, that bring those words to life and speak on their behalf."

As much as the three of us have had a lot of hilarious moments poking fun at and not taking ourselves too seriously while writing, there is also that difficult component all of us were forced to face and tackle head on, even though J.P.'s experiences of growing up with his parents were drastically different. Mark came back with a heartfelt response which is a true reflection of our own struggles while putting stories together of those we love and miss the most:

> "We are definitely connected, my friend. Maybe someday many decades from now when you and I are sitting in heaven with my dad and your beloved mum, we will truly discover the deeper meanings and influences behind this book. We are being helped by hidden hands!"

Mark could not have been truer with his statement. As I was spending another late night putting together more of this book, I sent an email to him and J.P. which at first caught me off guard only for me to embrace the messaging that was attached to it:

> "In pure reflection, as is seen in Mum's Lament, today, which is the final day of production of writing minus what is missing and needed, is my mum's 13th anniversary since she passed away. It is also the day that one of our beloved authors, John Sidney Rickerby, was born."

Here we were, now celebrating the loving memory of two very wonderful and special people who share the same date. My mum, Catherine McVicker, and Mark's dad, John Sidney Rickerby. They are forever cherished, we miss them like there is no tomorrow, and would give anything for them to be there when we launch this book. However, deep down inside, we know they will be there in spirit with us!

In pausing for a moment, and for myself, I guess this book has exposed what some may feel is a gift of writing. For me, it is an attempt to constantly improve myself. If you get a chance to read my personal memoir, or my true-life, childhood adventures called, *The Adventures of Silly Billy: Sillogy – Volume 1* containing three stories with the next book already being partially written, one memory I included is that of a childhood trauma in which I was constantly being told by an abusive teacher that I "wouldn't amount to anything in life." This was coupled with her pleasure of strapping us to within an inch of our lives, as well as targeting me and saying I would not complete a swimming goal which was set out for us: one full mile of the pool by way of several laps (which included me being a full-blown asthmatic). The older I got, it seemed to me she relished in taking her frustration and aggression out on us since we were easy targets. She took pleasure in wanting to see us fail so it was our job to prove her wrong. A lifelong curse!

A while back, I almost choked on my own spit when that same teacher was trolling and posted a comment to our primary school online group saying we were all such good children. If so, why did she knock the shite clean out of us every given opportunity with her strap? To cement my statement, and within the introduction of his brilliantly written and very sobering memoir, J.P. states,

> ***"Brutal beatings would knock you down and leave physical marks, but the verbal degradation which dragged your inner being down, was soul destroying and left mental scars."***

Sound familiar? He was constantly told he would never amount to anything although this was at the hands of his parents. In saying this, I encourage you to pick up ***The Big Yank: Memoirs of a Boy Growing Up Irish*** as well as ***The Other Belfast – An Irish Youth***. I sincerely believe you will be blown away when you see the works of us as authors on individual levels, as well as to how we bring our experiences to life!

Going back to my teacher, those same crushing words which were muttered repeatedly have become the bane of my existence. I constantly try yet fail to prove to myself that I am successful in my writings as an author; my full-time job as a supervisor and social worker, and a proud father of my two children while wanting to see their successes in life. It is a critical self-analysis. Let me show you a prime example by way of an email in part to J.P. and Mark:

"I removed 79 pages, or 15,648 of my own words and writing and have put those over to a sequel or the sequel to the sequel. I know we were thinking about some of our world experiences and engagements with other cultures and having those as the first sequel. Time will tell."

It is obvious I am a man of very few words. Beware the strong, silent (and extremely attractive) type! In all seriousness, though, it was quite hard removing so much material, but it forced me to make sure you are getting a great read from what has been put forth. As I have written elsewhere in this book as a lesson from the Irish language under the heading, *Chuckie Our Da*, and to that teacher with her brutal mouth and lack of any filter, I offer her this: Póg mo thóin! Jesus, it feels good getting that off my mind.

Moving on, and as you have seen, I find it great to poke fun at myself and laugh constantly with the banter and humour shared with these two brilliant lads and fellow authors. As much as I slag J.P., he instills the trueness of being Irish with his Donegal charm and sense of hilarious and menacing ways, much like my da:

"You've done a bloody smashing job here...I honestly don't know what drives you (is it the Canadian snow?....as much as I want to be like you when I grow up, I could never go back to the snow). Don't be vexed with me...I don't know how to sugar coat things (it's the main reason, I drive women mad...that and they are pure knackered after too much sex and want their sleep!)"

What can I say? J.P. Sexton, you are one seriously, deliriously mad hoor! And you shouldn't change for the world, for we need this laughter in our lives and to remind ourselves of being true to ourselves, remaining grounded, and remembering where our roots came from. Although, in saying that and by reading the previous comment, it sounds like J.P. had populated half of Ireland. Either I'm in good standing, or perhaps I need to have a DNA test done:

Four Green Fields

"Greg… Search your feelings… I'm yer father. It's wile difficult to imagine, but you're my wain from Malin Head! Now, pass me a lock of that cream bun, my wee Padawan."

Que the frightening squeaky violin horror movie noises!

On another note, in case you were wondering, the lad on the front right of this book who is being chased by Mark Rickerby (left) and myself (center) for stealing my Dublin Cream Bun is quite possibly related to me as well. Perhaps I need to get back in to the confessional and beg for forgiveness and absolution! To further my point, here is part of an email from J.P. which may just confirm my fears as have been written here and his hopes of engaging our readership:

> "Hopefully, we will engage them sufficiently so they will want to go along and read my other 2 books and your other 5 books and Mark's 372 books (Mark; I also want to be like you when I grow up… I think I will change my name to Mark McVicker….and when I get famous, shorten it to; "Marky Mc Vick!!)

Mark, what can I say? If I search my feelings and use my non- Jedi mind powers, my fears have come true. I now believe that J.P. Sexton is indeed the near Belfast Child from Newtownabbey. This most likely occurred after he was claimed by Murphy the body snatcher.

I have rambled on enough and should bring this to a close. This, however, is J.P.'s last correspondence from his **3D highway tour:**

> "My own health is hanging in there, despite this being my 7th day in Ireland. I now hook myself up to the dialysis machine overnight…well, the night is shot by the time we get it cranked up, since I've forgotten what it feels like to be in bed before 4am. My main concern is for the machine itself. My brother-in-law's alcohol consumption has been increasing daily since my arrival

and he has jerry-rigged a second line to the machine by splicing something or other (much the same as a cheap bastard would do with the neighbour's cable t.v. wires/box). I'm happy for his liver, but I'm now concerned that my liver's rejuvenation is getting cut back with the back-street splicing job. It also means that I have to now sleep with my brother-in-law, which is an unexpected outcome. God be with the days when all a man had to worry about was his neighbour eating a chunk out of his cream bun."

- J.P. Sexton.

Honestly, words fail me at this very moment. As such, it's very much safe to say Mark and I are giving J.P. the last word. For our own sanity, that is. Quite possibly, for each and every one of you readers too! Nevertheless, the three of us leave you with this:

"It's the laughter that saves them from madness."

just about the end

GReG: The near Belfast Child

Through the Eyes of a Belfast Child:
Life. Personal Reflections. Poems.

ISBN: 978-1-7751622-8-5 (Hardcover)
                          978-1-7751622-6-1 (Softcover)
                          978-1-7751622-7-8 (eBook)

An Irish Heart:
Poetic Memoirs of a Belfast Child

ISBN: 978-1-7751622-1-6 (eBook)
                          978-1-7751622-0-9 (Softcover)

One Cross to Bear:
Humanity Through Narrative Prose

ISBN: 978-1-7751622-3-0 (eBook)
                          978-1-7751622-2-3 (Softcover)

The Adventures of Silly Billy:
Sillogy: Volume 1.

ISBN: 978-1-7751622-5-4 (eBook)
                          978-1-7751622-4-7 (Softcover)

John & Mark: A Paddy and a Half

Mark's stories can be found in the following books:

The Other Belfast – An Irish Youth – by John Sidney Rickerby and Mark Rickerby

Chicken Soup for the Soul titles:

Step Outside Your Comfort Zone

The Power of Forgiveness

The Spirit of America

The Joy of Less

Dreams and Premonitions

My Kind (of) America

Miracles and More

Chicken Soup to Inspire the Body and Soul

My Amazing Mom

Older and Wiser

My Very Good / Very Bad Dog

A Book of Miracles

Random Acts of Kindness

The Dog Really Did That?

The Dating Game

Touched by an Angel

My Crazy Family

Angels and Miracles

The Power of Positive

How to Know if You're a Musician – with Rick Balentine and Meri Doloevsky-Lewis

Mark Rickerby Poetry – Book One – Inspiration

Mark Rickerby Poetry – Book Two – Love

J.P.: Irish Crooner: Head the Ball

The Big Yank:
Memoir of a Boy Growing Up Irish

ISBN: 978-0-9979007-0-9 (eBook)
              978-0-9979007-0-5 (Softcover)

FORTHCOMING SEQUEL: (Working title)

"Living on the Edge" – sequel to The Big Yank, by J.P. Sexton.

ISBN: 978-0-0000000-0-0 (eBook)
              978-0-0000000-0-0 (Softcover)

Chicago's Premier Movie Theater
SAIC
a public program of the
School of the Art Institute of Chicago
GENE SISKEL
FILM CENTER
Chicago's Premier Movie Theater
2GINGERS
IRISH WHISKEY
James Cagney
Colin Broderick

Connect with the Authors

Greg:

facebook:	ThroughtheEyesofaBelfastChild
email:	gmcvicker70@gmail.com
twitter:	@BelfastChild70
website:	Coming Soon!

Mark:

facebook:	www.facebook.com/mark.rickerby
email:	markrickerbyauthor@gmail.com
twitter:	www.twitter.com/MarkRickerby
blog:	www.markrickerby.blog

J.P.:

facebook:	www.facebook.com/irishauthor.us
facebook:	www.facebook.com/johnsexton.169
email:	jp@irishauthor.us
twitter:	www.twitter.com/john_sexton
website:	www.irishauthor.us

Living the
Christian Life
IS THIS
THE
END?
DR. DAVID JEREMIAH
Christian Life   Heaven
Christian Life
Chicken Soup
Random
Acts of
Kindness
Chicken Soup
Random
Acts of
Kindness
THE GREAT
SPIRITUAL
MIGRATION
BRIAN D. McLAREN
Chicken Soup
for the Soul
A BOOK OF
MIRACLES
Jack Canfield,
Mark Victor Hansen
& LeAnn Thieman
Chicken Soup
for the Soul
My Very Good,
Very Bad Dog
Amy Newmark
A RADICAL FAITH
A RADICAL FAITH
JESUS
Chicken Soup
for the Soul
Tough Times,
Tough People
Jack Canfield,
Mark Victor Hansen
& Amy Newmark
Chicken Soup
for the Soul
Thanks
Dad
Jack Canfield,
Mark Victor Hansen & Wendy Walker
Foreword by Scott Hamilton
WORD

JDROLI
JDROLINIJA

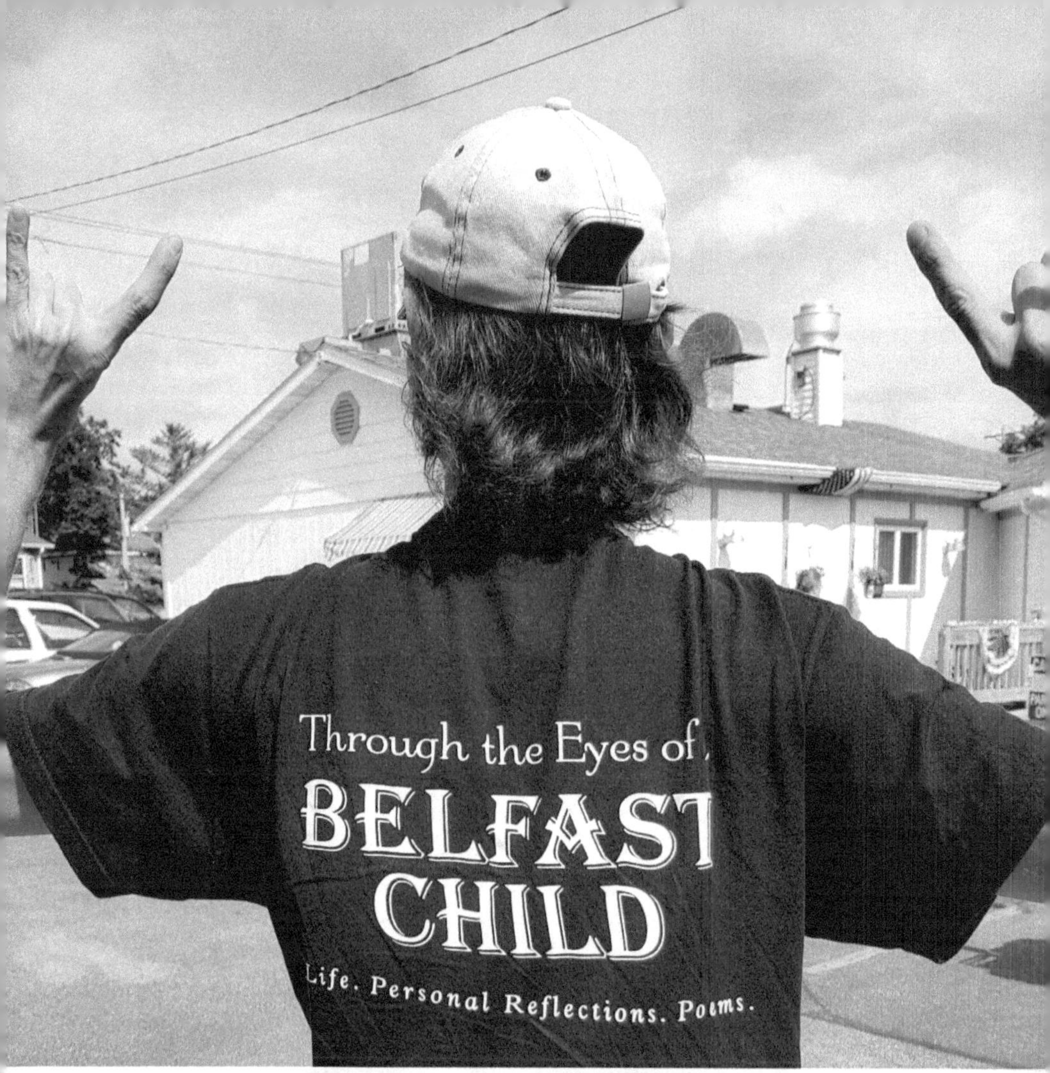
Through the Eyes of
BELFAST
CHILD
Life. Personal Reflections. Poems.

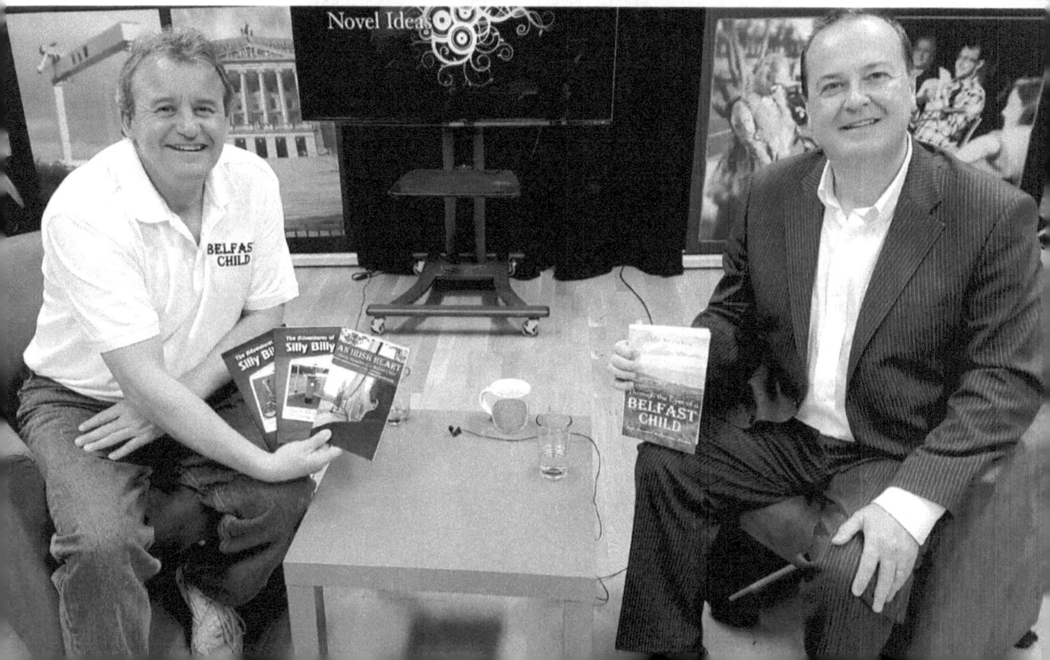
Novel Ideas
BELFAST
CHILD
Silly Billy
AN IRISH HEART
BELFAST
CHILD

rish Traditions

Donegal
Creameries

BELFAST
CHILD

BELFAST
CHILD
THE UNIVERSITY OF
WINNIPEG

BELFAST
CHILD

POWER
WATER REFILL ON
Licensed to Sell Beer
Wines and Spirits for
Consumption on the premises
Also to Deal in Tobacco
7 Days
MADIG
GUINNESS

Novosco
BELFAST CHILD
BELFAST CHILD

FOUR GREEN FIELDS

 Four Green Fields

HARP LAGER
BELFAST
GIANTS

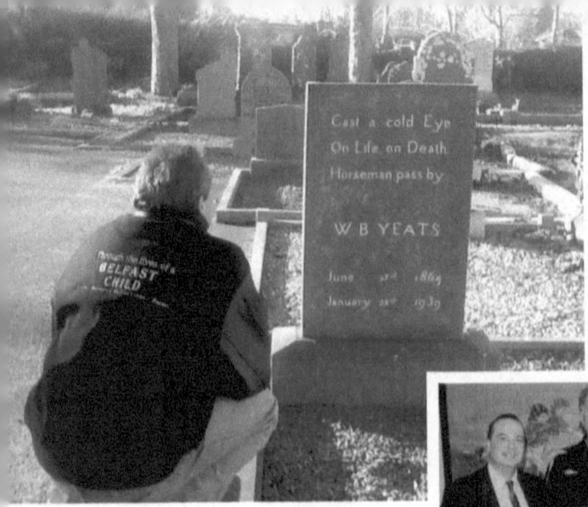
Cast a cold Eye
On Life, on Death.
Horseman pass by.
W B YEATS
BELFAST
CHILD

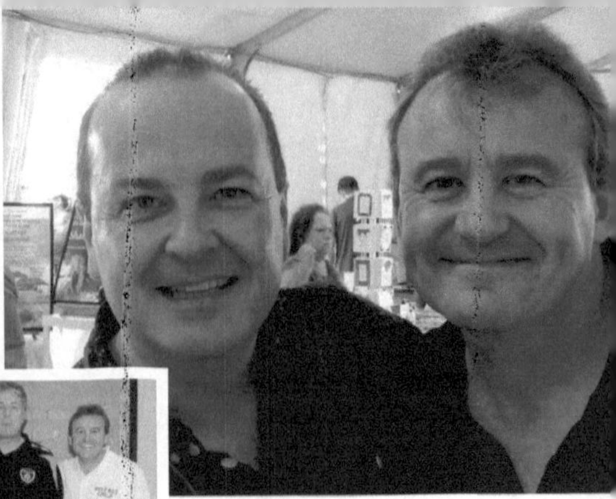

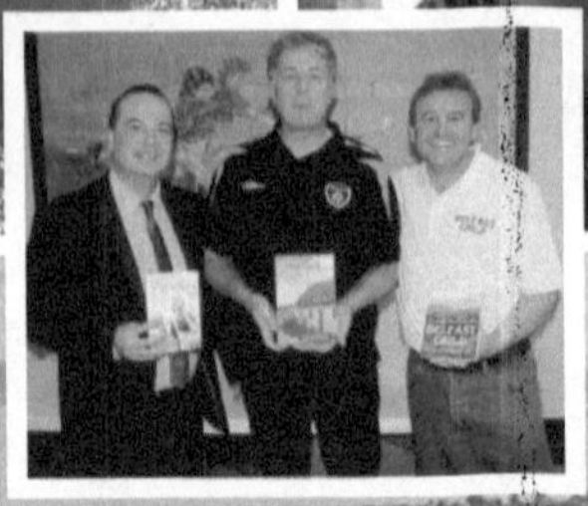

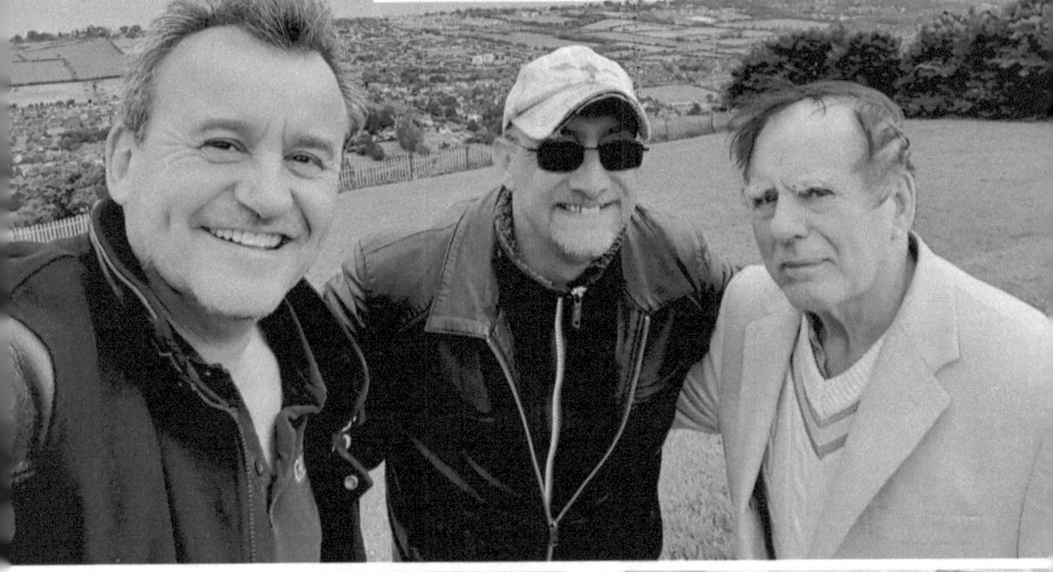

BLUE
Channel

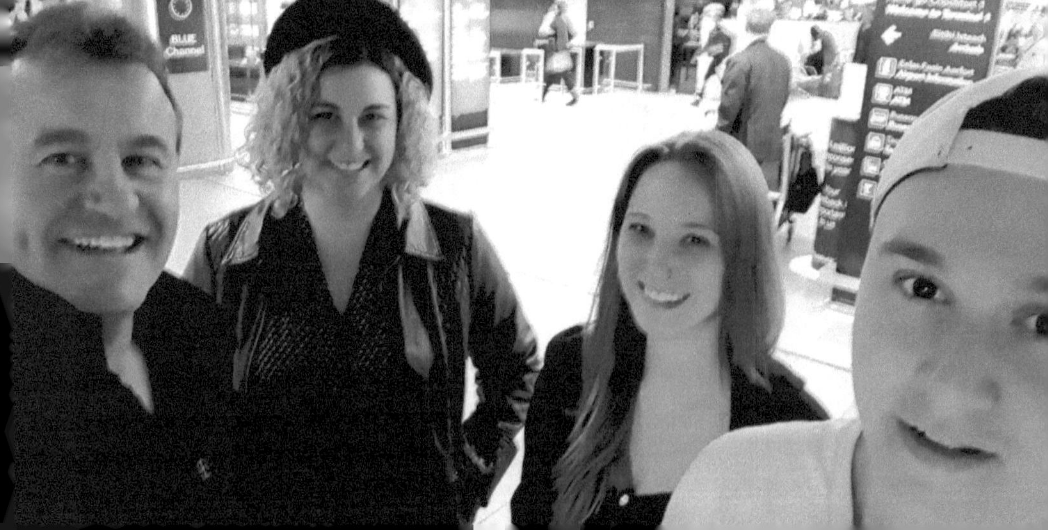

That's All, Folks!

There isn't much back here except for some numbers and a bar code on the next page. By book publishing standards, we must do this otherwise we each get a kick in the arse. Or, as my ma informed me several times daily, "I'll put my toe up your hole."

Sigh. As you have read, Irish parents exhibit loving ways when sharing their thoughts. You will have a chance to see this in more detail in our forthcoming sequel. Until then, we hope you enjoyed this wee book as much as we have in putting it all together for you.

In saying that, we sincerely hope you will come out and meet these three lads at Irish Festivals and book signings wherever they may be (including Dublin, Ohio!) If you know of one, please be sure to let us know and we will do our best to be there. We look forward to saying a wee hello!

One thing you could do for us, if you happen to know Ellen, Oprah, Barbara Walters, Brendan O'Carroll, Jamie Dornan, Liam Neeson, Bono, Gerard Butler, Colin Farrell, Daniel Day Lewis, Graham Norton, The Edge, Conan O'Brien, Roddy Doyle, or the Irish Taoiseach, would you mind passing along a copy of this book to them? We would be eternally thankful, so we would! The same is said if you are attached to a book club!

Sláinte mhaith, agus go mbeannaí dia Duit!

To your health, and God Bless!

Mark　　　　**Greg**　　　　**J.P.**

By way of Mark's Uncle Alfie and the enchanted skull,

he asks you to keep an eye out for our forthcoming sequel:

FOUR GREEN FIELDS

The pen & paper pub: untold stories of shenanigans, sweethearts & shitehawks!

www.ingramcontent.com/pod-product-compliance
Lightning Source LLC
Chambersburg PA
CBHW061305190726

48288CB00002B/354